CONTENTS

List of Figures	3
Dedication	4
Forward	5
An Introduction to Working with Older Persons	11
Learning about OPMH Recovery	24
Daley et al	32
A Focus Group Research Project	33
Views from my Recovery Exit Surveys	36
Recovery in Policy Development	38
The New Aged Care Quality Standards	41
The Covid-19 pandemic and CHIME	43
Recovery in Action – don't wait	54
Recovery, Petworth, and a system for Aged Care	57
A Five Foundation Service Structure	60
Attitudinal Learning in Recovery-based Clinical Practice	76
Connectedness	78
Hope and Optimism about the future	100
Hope and the Impact of Illness	111

Identity	122
Identity: Recovery of self	125
Identity: Perspectives on Ageing	135
Meaning	155
Meaning: Making Sense of the Experience	165
Empowerment	168
Empowerment: Understanding Illness	179
Empowerment: Dealing with Illness	184
Leadership in Recovery	190
Skills in Assessment: One Clinician's perspetive	197
Sleep	199
Diet and self care	201
Gathering Medical and Psychiatric History	202
Medication History	205
Risk Assessment	214
Legal issues	217
Care of children and pets	220
Drug and Alcohol use	222
The Mental State Examination	225
Appearance	232
Behaviour during Interview	234
Mood and affect	244
Speech	247
Thought Form	249
Thought Content	252
Perception	255

Cognition & Intellectual Functioning	258
Insight and Judgment	272
Falls Risk	275
Knowledge to Practice: One clinician's perspective	280
First, a quick quiz…	282
Psychotropic Medications	285
Side-effect Issues in OPMH	287
Depression	291
Grief and Loss	297
Erik Erikson's Developmental Stages	301
Delirium	311
Dementia	313
Lewy Body Dementia	318
Parkinson's	324
Anxiety	326
Post-Traumatic Stress Disorder	330
Personality Disorders	334
Schizophrenia	338
Appendix 1: Focus Group – Evidence for Recovery-based OPMH Assessment	339
Appendix 2: Thoughts about Setting up a Supervision Group	357
Appendix 3: Some Suggested Reading	373
Appendix 4: The 4A Delirium Screening Tool	375
Appendix 5: Glossary & Jargon	378
Appendix 6: My Recovery/ Satisfaction Surveys	397

References	403
About the Author	415

Recovery, Mental Health and the Older Person
Providing Care in the era of CHIME, Royal Commissions and the Coronavirus

Published by Michael McSweeney 2020

Copyright © 2020 Michael McSweeney

All rights reserved. No part of this publication may be reproduced, stored in a retrieval system, or transmitted in any form or by any means, electronic, mechanical, photocopying, recording or otherwise, without the prior written permission from both the copyright owner and publisher.

ISBN: 978-0-6487774-0-3

> All rights reserved. Unauthorised reproduction of any part of this work is illegal and punishable by law. No part of this book may be reproduced, stored, or transmitted by any means without the prior written permission of both publisher and author, except for brief excerpts used in critical reviews.

Disclaimer

All the information, techniques, skills and concepts contained within this publication are of the nature of general comment only and are not in any way recommended as individual advice. The intent is to offer a variety of information to provide a wider range of choices now and in the future, recognising that we all have widely diverse circumstances and viewpoints. Should any reader choose to make use of the information contained herein, this is their decision and the author and publishers do not assume any responsibilities whatsoever under any condition or circumstances.

LIST OF FIGURES

Figure 1: A Threefold model of Learning
Figure 2: A comparison of Covid impacts between older and younger people
Figure 3: Building a Five Foundation Recovery-based model in nursing care
Figure 4: Recognising Chronic Health Impacts in OPMH Recovery
Figure 5: Recommended work up prior to Psychogeriatrician Consultation
Figure 6: Increased risk concept during early period of a new antidepressant prescription
Figure 7: Undiagnosed Bipolar Risk with Antidepressants
Figure 8: Sample MSE profiles 1
Figure 9: Sample MSE profiles 2
Figure 10: Intersecting pentagrams
Figure 11: Clock face examples
Figure 12: Perseveration test
Figure 13: Possible Major Adverse Drug Effects (OPMH)
Figure 14: Focus Group project timeline
Figure 15: Themes, grouped with question numbers
Figure 16: Strengths Sandwich - an Iterative Process of Trauma Informed Supervision
Figure 17: Expanded Group Supervision roles by Stages and Functions of Supervision
Figure 18: Reading List suggestions
Figure 19: 4AT Delirium Screening Tool

DEDICATION

This book is dedicated to our elders, and to those who undertake to care for them.

Acknowledgments

I would like to thank Albury-Wodonga Health and the Wangaratta Older Persons Mental Health management and team for their support and participation. Thanks also to: Elizabeth Stanford for reviewing the book. Lisa Wong, Older Persons Psychiatry specialist at HETI Higher Learning who gave initial moral support to the project; Irene Jones and Peter Allen for their wonderful Social Work supervision; Dr Sid Williams for years of mentoring at Tumut SMHSOP; and Linda McSweeney for her recording, administrative support and transcription of research and for her loving long-suffering and putting up with me all these years.

FORWARD

It said that we should 'imagine that it is *our* relative in Aged Care' when exploring what care should look like. I feel that we could take that thinking further and imagine that it is *us* entering or living under care, and consider the importance of the values this book explores.

It is primarily a training resource aimed at helping the new worker gain a critical understand many aspects of older person's mental health care.

Within this book, the CHIME Recovery model from Mental Health is used to examine Recovery values in Older Persons Mental Health. It is further presented as an approach to the general care of older persons. This book also connects these Recovery values in OPMH to the urgent need for reform in Aged Care.

It discusses how Recovery can be understood and employed on the level of the individual service provider.

While discussing Recovery values in this book, I also advocate for a community-based business model of residential care, and a voluntary system of self-rating by service providers which fosters the implementation of these values. This proposal gets away from simply throwing extra money at problems, but campaigns for a values-focussed approach to care provision that overcomes the current policy and market conditions that have triggered abuse, neglect and precipitated the Royal Commission.

The Royal Commission into Aged Care demonstrated comprehensively that the system is broken, and I believe that in many ways it had gotten worse not better over time, prior to Covid-19. The "Royal Commission into Aged Care Quality and Safety's Interim Report found that the aged care system fails to meet the needs of its older, vulnerable, citizens. It does not deliver uniformly safe and quality care, is often unkind and uncaring towards older people and, in too many instances, it neglects them." (Royal Commission into Aged Care Quality and Safety, October 2019).

This book was largely finished prior to Covid-19, and it is not about pointing the finger about what has happened in the official response to Covid-19 although the international and national, state and local responses left me stunned, because the responses of planners generally failed to address the mental health of those most vulnerable to the disease, the older sector.

I found that the crisis in care provision during Covid-19 magnified the weaknesses of care of the older person in Australia, and is worthy of critique.

I believe the way forward involves local, well informed community-based ownership of care responsibilities combined with dedication to the practical, compassionate wisdom of open accountability under a Recovery-based framework.

To clarify some terms...

'Clients', 'Consumers', people

In this book, I have endeavoured to use the term 'person' when offering examples. However sometimes further classification is required. In mental health the people we serve are variously called clunky collective nouns such as 'service users', 'clients' etc. Although the term 'client' is not an appealing descriptor, at time of writing, locally it is the preferred label. Within the Recovery movement, 'consumers' is often preferred.

Recovery vs recovery

Capital 'R' refers to the Recovery movement in mental health and associated values. Lower-case 'r' refers to recovery in terms of the goals of treatment – control of symptoms of illness.

Personal recovery is about the goal of living a fulfilling and enriching life. It's a very personal perspective, because it means completely different things to different people. It's very distinct from the medical model, because within personal recovery people are not defined by illness and its constraints.

Clinical recovery is a natural goal of the mental health sector: It's about treating and protecting the person who is not well and who is not safe because they are unwell (i.e. control and safety), and minimising disruption to their life. It is also about protecting society from the person who is unwell. Additionally, as with any medical intervention, the reality of clinical recovery is not perfectly predictable, despite the application of the best available expertise and care.

'MSE or MMSE, that is the question...'

(Shakespeare is turning in his grave). The Mental State Exam ('MSE') is different to the Mini-Mental State Exam ('MMSE' cognitive test), although cognitive testing can sit within the MSE. In turn, the MSE is one part of the wider comprehensive and holistic mental health assessment. Hang in there...

SMHSOP/ OPMH

Used generically for Older Persons Mental Health, OPMH usually implies an organisational level of service, while SMHSOP stands for Special Mental Health Service for Older People, our version of Older Persons Community Mental Health in NSW Health.

Privacy, Quotes and Vignettes

Any reference to things said by consumers is given anonymously and generalised, and any vignettes are fictitious. Resemblance to former clients is unintended, and wherever there are unavoidable similarities, they have been edited.

Integrated Learning Domains

The NSW Government defined a set of Core Competencies with which new clinicians can self-rate. It does not set out to impart the *learning content* of competencies, but invites new clinicians to self-assess under three domains: Attitude, Skill and Knowledge. In the process of writing this book it was realised that it is at the crossover of these domains where the really interesting learning applies: Reflective Learning, Deeper applied knowledge and Values in Practice. For example, this book suggests you look beyond diagnostic criteria of depression and consider the development of depression in the psychosocial context of people's lives for a truer picture in assessment. Also, much more is needed than the self-assessment, in my view.

MICHAEL MCSWEENEY

Introduction to Recovery and the Older Person

AN INTRODUCTION TO WORKING WITH OLDER PERSONS

Imagine you have just won *(post-Covid)* a nursing job working with older people in care, coming into the sector for the first time. As you begin to work, you find there are many unmet needs among older people in your care. You may find yourself working very hard, almost running from resident to resident, and not having enough resources (such as pads and cleaning supplies), minimal breaks and low staffing levels. But there is one thing you realise is in very short supply – the time to simply have a conversation with the residents, including the ones who get few visitors and seem sad and lonely. It begins to seem like a harsh, neglectful working world.

Or perhaps, imagine you have been a general mental health clinician, moving into SMHSOP (OPMH) for the first time, you may have found there are vital differences in working in mental health for older people as compared to the general adult population. You gradually become aware that treating older people the same way as other consumers is risky and problematic, and could make their treatment ineffective or even make their situation worse. Older people's *particular* needs and vulnerabilities are often overlooked entirely in some clinical environments, leaving them at increased risk.

Or perhaps, imagine that you are tasked with designing an aged care facility. You have studied the Royal Commission into Aged Care closely, and it's clear that after 12 years of ongoing enquiries and hearings, that the sector is in a rolling crisis throughout Australia. Obviously we as a country are not getting it right. But what can be done, and where are the *values* to guide reform?

In any of these scenarios, what principles would you enlist to guide you in service design?

For example: Consider the impact of Covid-19 on service provision. Many consumers suffered greatly in an environment characterised by fear and isolation. Some became depressed, and the effects of the depression can impact the health of the older person most significantly.

How does your training prepare you for a eventuality such as this? To make matters worse, often clinicians felt their hands were tied - there was limited access to residents in care, or great trouble arranging appointments with people living in Aged Care. And very often there was simply not enough staff available to help.

> A consumer tells you that they would "rather face the disease than live like a prisoner" (*direct quote by permission, source withheld by request*).

> It would be reasonable to wonder if we couldn't do better for our elders - but how, and on what basis?

Value-based Models of Care

No doubt you bring much passion, life experience and knowledge with you into your role in the care of older people. As a care worker or nurse you may see the need for a recognised wholistic form of care that includes the need for support for mental health. Or, as an OPMH Clinician, perhaps you reflect on the values that underpin the development of well-informed, specialised, holistic assessment skills to aid in your work. Or, if planning a nursing home, your experience tells you that it is vital to build a service based on clear values of service.

Whatever your role, your values should be clear and consistent, and discussion of these values should be available for learning by new workers. Reflection upon this knowledge base will in many instances lead you to improving and providing good care. But unfortunately ad-hoc learning can take years, and you may find qualified, expert teachers thin on the ground, especially in rural and remote areas of Australia. And in the current highly pressurised environment of care provision, this need of learning is often left unanswered.

Mental Health Recovery as a Value Base

You may previously learned about the global Mental Health Recovery movement, and now, working in Aged Care or Older Persons Mental Health (OPMH, or SMH-SOP in NSW) you might wonder – how does Recovery values fit with the care of the older person?

Within this book I have attempted to capture what I have picked up over 6 years of service – my 'on the job' learning – and correlate it with what I have learned about the Recovery model to provide a *value*-informed perspective on the care of older people. The values explored within this book inspired me to outline a Recovery-informed set of practice principles and an information base for developing a skilled understanding of older person's mental health practice

This book promotes a Recovery-based, reflective, informed, and cohesive model to help development of workers and services that will make residents and consumers the primary focus. It could be used as a starting point for many communities to create their own solution following the failure of corporatised care created motivated by profit, but sustained by successive Government policy failures.

The Relevance of the Recovery Movement

This book attempts to examine and imagine where Recovery might influence service design, clinical and residential support. It needs to be recognised that these areas of work deeply influence each other, and should be aligned in terms of values, knowledge and approach.

It is clear to many that there are significant pitfalls under the current policy/funding arrangements in Australia, and that the whole sector faces major problems in the way services are currently delivered – hence the Royal Commission... and hence this book!

This book is a personal response to the learning curve as I experienced it – i.e. experience-based, tied to *my* learning experiences as an OPMH clinician, and also as a worker in Aged Care. The outcome of my study is that a Recovery framework brings together all the best ideals of service provision.

Realistically, what we need goes beyond supplying the knowledge required to practise. (OPMH is both broad and specialised and can't be covered comprehensively in any one book anyway.) It is also essential that, as we study skills, we can explore values that can enable us to make a difference (for example, to advocate for structural reform).

If, for example, the day-to-day care environment is lacking in simple physical resources to the point of ignoring or indeed contributing to mental health problems in older people, the Recovery framework and the new service standards fall short if advocates fail to promote specific reform in the wider care environment.

There are many relevant conceptual frameworks. You may seek understanding of culturally sensitive work with older Aboriginal and Torres Strait Islanders and Elders. Perhaps you have come across an issue where the rights of an older person in decision-making present a dilemma against duty of care issues, and you need to learn more about rights and duty of care. You may like to know more about what theoretical models of mental health can be useful in Older Persons Mental

Health. All of these remain important discussions, and all are linked to Recovery.

I present this book as a resource to encourage reflection upon our work, particularly if you are working in an isolated area with minimal clinical support. It's a beginning point to further learning, research, discussion and advocacy. At this point in time it should also critique the Covid-19 service response from a Mental Health perspective.

This book starts from the limited perspective of just one clinician's understanding and experience, so please continue the conversation and talk further about issues in your work with your own mentors, clinical leaders, and psychogeriatricians, if you have access to these. Also, if you spot flaws in the book or see a need for deeper analysis and conversation, I would love to hear from you!

My intention in writing this book is that the compassion and the respect you feel for our elders is fortified by good learning, the building of awareness and assessment skills and the strengthening of clinical knowledge, to help support and improve the lives of older people. I hope you find joy in serving this most special group of people, our Elders, to the best of your ability.

BACKGROUND: MY GROWING AWARENESS OF RECOVERY

Today, the global Recovery Movement is current, timely, and a widespread reform movement in Mental Health, both here and overseas. It includes consumer consultation backed by research, discussion, and developing Health policy.

Earlier, in my work as a solo OPMH clinician I became curious about how Recovery fitted into OPMH, having had little *OPMH-specific* clinical supervision at the time (with the exception of the visits of a psychogeriatrician one day every month or two). Thankfully my local manager supported heuristic (self-guided) learning. So I phoned around to other SMHSOP services in Sydney looking for written guides to work that might help, but without success. Local management had no input into how to relate Recovery to OPMH, nor was there appreciation of approaches or theoretical models such as Erikson's Theory of Psychosocial Development or any other models that might be used in OPMH.

The visiting psychogeriatricians modelled beautiful narrative approaches in assessment which I have realised were consistent with Recovery values. Also, our (non-OPMH) clinical leader promoted Recovery and the immense value of narrative "social history".

I came to understand Recovery as being about the deeply personal journey, a *social* definition of Recovery (beyond the medical perspective with its emphasis on the *clinical* absence of symptoms of mental illness), where the individual attempts to regain or retain a **foothold on their life**. It requires balancing the medical model of psychiatric care with the consumer's experience and insight gained from living through the medical model. This perspective has given rise to certain values in care - an attitudinal approach - through the consumer consultation and acknowledgement of the consumer's experience.

Mental health cannot be understood without thinking about the effect of the context and environment of a person's life and its interaction with their mental health. Aged care, as a case-in-point, demonstrates this comprehensively, as the residents of care facilities are vulnerable and often completely powerless to challenge the way their care is administered to them.

(Note: the Royal Commission used language in 2019 such as "kindness" to describe what is lacking in the current Aged Care system – advocating for a re-linking of the personal experience to professional outcomes.)

I have seen *worst-case scenarios* of disempowerment, especially under the Covid-19 policy response, but in contrast I have also seen how beautifully values-driven care can uplift and empower vulnerable people.

One nursing home I worked at in a care assistant role provided such a high standard of care that I will hold them up within this book as a shining example of high value care (See the section below – Petworth Cottage).

Applied Recovery in the working environment

In retrospect, my study has found that Recovery principles of connection, identity and meaning are often present, if not overtly identified, in OPMH work. Concepts of practice that could be termed Recovery-focussed were developing over six years, by researching well-informed patient-centred values and principles of practice.

As a solo SMHSOP worker without a team, I enjoyed some flexibility, as guidelines allowed that SMHSOP could take two or more sessions if needed to build therapeutic relationships and undertake a *more* narrative-style assessment. Working within time constraints, I noticed a tension between **narrative assessment**, compared to the use of the proscribed **Comprehensive Assessment tools**. I was not the only one to notice this tension.

(For example, I have heard more than one psychogeriatrician strongly critique an over-reliance on assessment forms at the expense of connection, while another only wanted me to provide a brief written summary of my assessment –summarising the 30 pages of forms from a SMHSOP Comprehensive Assessment. He was asking for me to think primarily in terms of a consumer-friendly plain-language impression of the consumer's needs, history

and situation.)

Other correlations with Recovery values were present in OPMH. For example:
- the most consistent contributors to local consumer consultation were SMHSOP clients
- My role involved a liaison role to promote better communication between consumers, inpatient units, GPs, and hospital staff toward transparent, shared, holistic, person-centred care.
- The value of lived experience

Lived experience - the clinician

Lived experience, an important value of the Recovery movement, meant acknowledging how my own life experiences affected my professional development in OPMH. Lived experience affects the way a clinician:
- includes and empowers consumers to be heard in the design of care and treatment;
- challenges stigma around mental health; and
- understands triggers to illness (a principle of trauma-informed care)

In the spirit of this I would like to share a little about my family's own mental health journey.

When my own father had Alzheimer's, his mind sometimes took him back to World War II. He experienced frightening delusions about Nazis in a neighbouring apartment, and medical help was sought to help ease his suffering. In contrast, his actual WWII experiences were in the jungles of New Guinea against Japanese soldiers. I imagine that his delusions involved a combination of his own past experiences, current brain function problems and the influence of post-war books and films. I ultimately can't know exactly why his Alzheimer's delusions differed from his ral-world experiences, but I do know that for him they were very frightening and I felt appreciative of the help the psychogeriatrician was able to give. I have often reflected on this and I have come to feel that my experiences as a family member have informed my understanding of the consumer and also of their family's perspective.

Petworth Cottage

Another part of my personal experience I would like to relate is about my time at Petworth Cottage. After some years of working as an OPMH clinician I decided on a break and headed with my family for an extended working holiday based in the UK, my wife's country of birth.

Once there I discovered that the process of registering in the UK to practice as a Social Worker was very complicated and drawn out. During that period I got work in various aged care facilities as a care assistant. This became an extremely valuable experience for me personally and professionally, as it provided a basis for comparison of various care facilities.

Some of the *least ideal* facilities I worked at in the UK were run by big companies with an aggressive business agenda of expansion. They would often buy large country manors, retrofit them to fit as many beds as possible, and then run with as few staff and supplies as could be managed. Similar to the big business model of aged care in Australia, it appears to be an extractive business model of care where profits for the company are the first concern. Staff would literally be running throughout the whole shift, and the effect upon resident's care consequent to this, was abysmal. There was no time for connection, no capacity for reflection, and no scope for empowerment.

However there were other nursing homes that I worked at that ran much better than that, and I was lucky enough to experience a truly inspiring example of a care facility - **Petworth Cottage**. Petworth Cottage enhanced my conception of Recovery values in Aged Care, based on my observation as a care assistant.

Petworth is a small country town and the connection to the community and pride in ownership was tangible. Petworth Cottage is wholly owned by the Trustees of Petworth Cottage – i.e. its own community trust, clearly with one single focus – to properly run their small 32 bed care facility.

I remember one friendly visitor asking me for assistance. I later learned he was a trustee, and it then made sense that I had the distinct impression that I was being silently evaluated the whole time I spoke with him.

It seemed to me, as an experienced OPMH clinician working in direct care, that Petworth Cottage experienced few of the problems of the bigger nursing homes. Each resident had their own room. Pets were allowed. Each of the three sections had their own supply cupboards, always full of supplies (No need for stealing pads from other resident's private supply, as was the practice in more than one place I have worked). Remarkably, staffing levels were amazing – providing almost the same raw numbers of staff that much larger care facilities seemed to get by on. The meals were great. Staff were happy – there were plenty of breaks and most importantly there was plenty of time for staff to hold proper conversations with the residents – which they often did.

At the start of each shift, all the staff – right down to me (an agency casual) would gather in the Matron/Managers' office and they would as a group discuss every resident and their current needs, and work together as a team on solutions for the resident's needs. I was tasked, as a casual care assistant, with answering any bed calls that arose during the meeting, but for the most part even I was part of the meeting at the start of each shift.

It appears that funding costs to residents per bed are unremarkable at Petworth Cottage – perhaps on the low side – and possibly less than what nursing homes seem to charge in the UK, Australia or the USA in general. However, Petworth Cottage reinvests all the money it gets directly for care, not business expansion or profits. The investment is not measured by profit taking – it is in the care of the residents. It was amazing to see what the allocated money could achieve, when implemented with appropriate standards and values.

I think it is accurate to say that the residents were more emotionally connected and secure at Petworth Cottage than anywhere else I have worked in residential care – they were treated better and the effect on their mental health was obvious. In fact I learned a new appreciation for the marriage of living context and mental health.

LEARNING ABOUT OPMH RECOVERY

Figure 1: A Threefold model of Learning

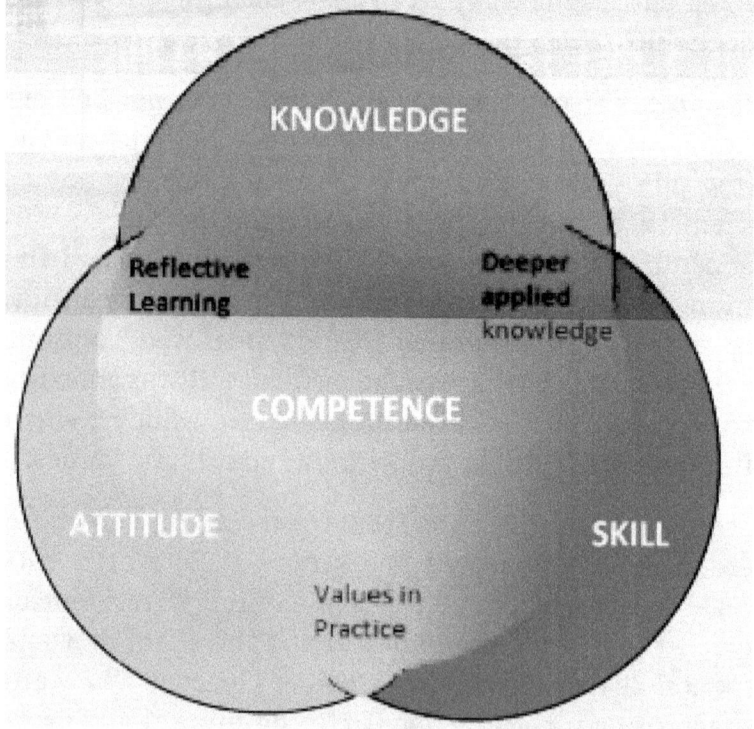

In this period of reform involving Recovery values within Mental Health, how do Recovery-based reforms mesh with OPMH? And how do we provide skills, attitudinal learning and knowledge to help the new clinician deliver Recovery-based services?

The Mental Health Commission of NSW has produced "Living Well: A Strategic Plan for Mental Health in NSW 2014 – 2024" which has been adopted by the NSW Government, and maps an agenda for change that "puts people, not processes, at the heart of its thinking in the care and support of people who experience mental illness" (p.4).

Recent publications, such as that by the Mental Health Commission (2017) called *Living Well in Later Life* observe the slow uptake in adapting to Recovery principles in OPMH. It briefly refers to the particular nuances of Recovery in OPMH and expressions of Recovery in Nursing Care. While professionals must strive to promote clinical recovery, people's Recovery moves beyond this, to acknowledging how the person's *whole life* is bound up in their Recovery. It is early days - conflict and inertia occur within any system experiencing a process of reform. This book explores how professionals might support Recovery while assessing the person toward clinical recovery.

> A useful definition of Recovery is "'being

> able to create and live a meaningful and contributing life in a community of choice with or without the presence of mental health issues" (Australian Health Ministers Advisory Council, 2013). There is no reason to suggest that the definition is somehow different to a person older that 65.

Power Relationships, Reactions and Reforms

Statutory care can easily slip into a defensive psycho/bureaucratic mode which is connected to both a seductive pull toward risk avoidance, and control of the consumer's safety to try to prevent inevitable blowouts of accountability.

Grieving families of people who lose loved ones often naturally want answers and accountability when failures in care occur, often precipitating a blame/avoidance reaction in institutional culture.

Adding to this pervasive tension is political, social and media-based pressure to 'get it right'. This fear-laden culture can easily, but perversely lead to institutional disempowerment and compromises of consumers' rights.

Thankfully, within these tensions the views of the consumer have gradually been recognised by compassionate health and legal professionals, academics, political leaders, consumer movements, family, and carers who argue for more person-centred principles.

Recovery principles challenge the hegemony of (i.e. *persuasive influence or unmitigated assumed control over*)

Mental Health care by balancing it with principles that consumers identify with such as empowerment, positive risk taking, transparency, and consumer consultation.

These principles are correlated and hopefully balanced with other progressive (and legislated) reforms such as least restrictive practice, the right to choice in medical care, time-limited schedules for transport and assessment, and current models such as community-based care, primary health care and health promotion.

What has happened to the balancing of mental health and physical health concerns?

> a) What follow-on effects do you think experiencing involuntarily care would usually have upon a person's sense of well-being? Disempowerment? What else?
> b) How might it affect physical health in frail individuals?
>
> c) What might this mean to older people facing aged care, experiencing depression-like symptoms of grief from loss of home, partner or independence, if a nursing home offers minimal mental health support during the transition?
>
> d) In what way might these situations be similar?

The Australian Government has reinforced national support in its National Standards for Mental Health Services (2010) for the following core Recovery principles:

- Uniqueness of the individual;
- Real choices;
- Attitudes and rights;
- Dignity and respect;
- Partnership and communication;
- Evaluating recovery.

Aligned to these values, from Scotland comes 'CHIME' – a wonderful acronym: It stands for Connectedness; Hope and Optimism; Identity; Meaning and Empowerment (Scottish Recovery Network, Accessed 19/02/2018). For a more detailed study of CHIME principles as applied to OPMH, please refer to the "Attitudinal Learning" section of this book.

Deferring Recovery-based reform in OPMH

Deferring of responsibility for Recovery is contrary to National and State policy (Australian Health Ministers Advisory Council, 2013). Some who work within clinical care actually *avoid* Recovery thinking and defer responsibility for supporting Recovery to outside agencies, seeing personal recovery as the domain of special Recovery-based services, and prefer to focus on a medical view of recovery.

This is simultaneously a missed opportunity and a failed responsibility. In my experience, the principle of connection that Recovery promotes, for example, often leads to much better clinical outcomes, and genuinely listening to a person in a narrative style assessment and with sensitivity to Recovery values can build the trust and openness that leads to 'compliance' with treatment, and therefore better efficiency of clinician's time and resources.

This issue extends beyond Personal Recovery into discussing how recovery-oriented services must act within legislative and budgetary constraints toward recovery orientation and values (Australian Health Ministers Advisory Council, 2013, p.17). Even during an acute phase of care with clinical priorities including risk management (p.11), Recovery values remain a priority, requiring nuanced approaches within each step of the person's Recovery journey. "Viewing recovery as a normal human process 'demystifies' the process of recovery from mental health problems and puts people in a better position to support someone in their recovery journey" (p. 14).

I have visited inpatient units where nobody actually talks to the inpatient through most of the day. Post discharge, people have told of feeling disconnected and powerless in these environments, and often display genuine fear of the experience of care. Older people in particular can feel very vulnerable and isolated, especially in general inpatient environments.

As a health employee I was taught to frankly apologise when a complaint is disclosed, and so I often have done: I have apologised that, when the person was unwell, their rights were temporarily overshadowed (in a tribunal-supported decision) even if necessarily. I have also apologised that their care left them feeling disempowered. Since then, I have come to the point of wondering why it is not standard approach to always acknowledge these impacts on dignity, autonomy and rights that occur - even when these actions are seen as a necessary part of clinical care. This would be consistent with Recovery and CHIME values. Are we exercising enough compassion and awareness of the impact of our management of Covid-19 on the rights and therefore mental health of older people?

Although it isn't you or me who brought about the policy failures during Covid-19, I have apologised to consumers on behalf of the health system I am part of, especially older consumers who have seen their personal happiness and lifestyle decimated. It isn't hard to say sorry, e.g. "I am sorry this has happened to you". I have offered support, recognition of the impact, and understanding while I have provided therapy. And *I am troubled* that it has cost them so much. Conversely, I have heard little evidence of understanding of mental health impacts, as yet, from any official or organisation that really recognises personal impacts to so many.

Recovery goals are usually defined through consumer consultation at a grass-roots level. I have not heard of any aged care facility, health department or government policy maker actively consult with the most vulnerable consumers during the pandemic.

Most published research on Recovery at this time focuses on younger age groups (McKay et al, 2012). Within OPMH the issues may sound different but the overall effects share similarities. Older Persons Mental Health clinicians should certainly familiarise themselves with the Recovery movement and how to think about consumers in terms of Recovery.

During assessment for example, impacts and meaning of events in the lives of older people can be overlooked, in favour of gathering data about signs and symptoms of illness. To date, too little has been written about recovery in Older Persons Mental Health although identified within a recovery framework, but there is some evidence to draw from.

DALEY ET AL

Daley et al (2013) is an (*increasingly*) influential English study that identified mental health recovery principles in interviews with 31 older people, with or without dementia. In their local context they identified Recovery issues under the following themes:
   (i)   the impact of illness;
   (ii) the significance of personal responsibility;
   (iii) specific coping strategies;
   (iv) an established and enduring sense of identity;
   (v) coping strategies, which provide continuity and reinforce identity; and
   (vi) the associated impact of physical illness.

Additional components of Recovery identified for people with dementia were:
   (i)   the changing experience over time and
   (ii) support from others

Later in this book I attempt to integrate these ideas into Recovery practice principles.

A FOCUS GROUP RESEARCH PROJECT

During the preparation of this book I had the opportunity through my Masters degree studies to research views of a focus group within a rural/regionally-based OPMH service (See Appendix 1). I was delighted to find an extremely well-conceived and delivered service with its own premises, regular support by a full-time specialist, and a solid team with a strong service philosophy underpinning their work. Their model included such working principles as:

- A very strong emphasis on narrative-based assessment
- A psycho-social developmental perspective coupled with the medical model
- Erik Erikson's Life Stage Model (which provided a alternative theoretical approach to depression)
- Person-centred and Holistic practice
- A mentoring framework for new staff, and an open and supported approach to learning and supervision
- The sharing of care and knowledge across the community

There are different approaches to care, from service to service. The focus group participants had worked in other services which contrasted with their current practice principles and that did not share reformed values. The participants criticised disempowering "*silos*" of expert care, endless tick-boxes in assessment, failure to connect with the person in their care, a medical model emphasis, and strongly hierarchical leadership models. They seemed to be critiquing over-officious and over-busy practices that found little time for real connection.

Within the Focus Group much was said (with great passion) about their overall philosophy that aligned to Recovery values. However, little comment was made in response to my direct prompts about Recovery-awareness within their organisation. That these clinicians (and others elsewhere) have astute values is not in question. It's just that the group of values known as Recovery-aware was not really clear conceptually.

This may indicate that Recovery has not been conceptually integrated very deeply in OPMH, although many values and practices easily translate to a Recovery model. I think it is only a matter of time until Recovery in OPMH is integrated in the focus group's service philosophy.

The focus group precipitated within me a view that many services and practitioners currently strive to work in ways that correlate with Recovery, but without a clear idea that they are doing so. I began to realise that conversations about Recovery in OPMH need to appreciate the strengths that services are already practising in line with Recovery. This enables an understanding of how they might continue to develop in line with these principles.

VIEWS FROM MY RECOVERY EXIT SURVEYS

I can only speak of general impressions about my marginal survey responses (See Appendix 6). However some insights are worth thinking about (and possibly suggest themes of future research). As Recovery is personally defined, with no exact formula, promoting a set of values to train new workers in Recovery requires a kind of adaptive 'fuzzy logic' that must remain open to the very personal views of the individual consumer.

The overall impression I received is that:
- Older people certainly *do* relate to CHIME values, with nuances;
- It is possibly the impact of chronic illness that accounts for some of the differences in Recovery values seen between older and younger consumers;
- The life stage, and adaptation to the life stage, seems to indicate that Identity is a more settled concept to older people. It may be approached differently, but is still important to them; and
- Coping mechanisms, including counselling, can mean a lot to Recovery in the eyes of older con-

sumers.

RECOVERY IN POLICY DEVELOPMENT

It has been identified that a shared paradigm is needed. Both the Person-Centred Care (with its narrative emphasis) (Brijnath, 2015) and Recovery models (McKay et al 2012) are essential. *The Specialist Mental Health Services for Older People (SMHSOP) Community Model of Care Guideline* (NSW Health, 2017) promotes a model of care that: "… places the consumer, their carer(s) and GP at the centre of recovery-oriented, person-centred, biopsychosocial care." This model of care covers the entire service design of SMHSOP, and it also promotes good practice called "Philosophy and principles of care" that:

"SMHSOP community services adopt a recovery-oriented, person-centred, biopsychosocial philosophy of care. This may be demonstrated as follows:
    a. Respecting a consumer's autonomy and incorporating substitute consent only when absolutely necessary;
    b. The use of open, transparent, honest and clear communication with consumers, with clinicians actively listening to, learning from and acting upon

communications from the consumer and carer(s);
c. This philosophy is evident in all policies and procedures;
d. Key features of the philosophy and principles of care are included in orientation material for staff, consumers and carers;
e. All clinical staff have completed training in the application of recovery oriented practice to the mental health care of older people, including the interface between this practice and the principles of person-centred and biopsychosocial care;
f. The Consumer Wellness Plan is completed prior to the care plan and informs the development of the care plan." (NSW Health, 2017)

The need for recovery is recognised throughout this new *Model of Care* (MoC), including being the first term in its Key Principles section. However, more detail about Recovery is needed and Recovery is mainly discussed in terms of future directions. On page 77 it states:

"There are a number of areas of practice, particularly recovery-oriented practice in an OPMH context, peer work in OPMH, and the recovery / trauma-informed care and practice (TICP) interface, which will continue to evolve as more evidence becomes available, and will need to be considered in future revisions of the SMHSOP community MoC" (NSW Health, 2017).

Actual discussions about recovery *are* mentioned (e.g. about the relationship of CHIME to OPMH and the study by Daley et al (2013), but risk management approaches, the emphasis on a Comprehensive Mental

Health assessment style, and redirection of personal recovery toward themes of clinical recovery seem to get much more analysis and support.

If a service does not also promote Recovery-aware assessment it cannot be said to satisfy NSW Health policy reform. You may feel the weight of inertia against reform: from systems, colleagues, management and from your own lack of experience. However, the goals of Recovery can not be delivered within OPMH without acknowledging the tension between the medical model and Recovery approaches to assessment and then finding a way forward.

The two approaches may seem to conflict in the purest sense, but they are not mutually exclusive. Even during the most structured assessment, while applying whatever documentary standards are required, the clinician delivers most of the assessment through the interpersonal connection of their narrative style.

THE NEW AGED CARE QUALITY STANDARDS

The New Aged Care Quality Standards are contained in the Quality of Care Amendment (Single Quality Framework) Principles 2018 as applicable from 1 July 2019. These standards are applied to various service environments as appropriate.

Standard 1 - Consumer dignity and choice
Standard 2 - Ongoing assessment and planning with consumers
Standard 3 - Personal care and clinical care
Standard 4 - Services and supports for daily living
Standard 5 - Organisation's service environment
Standard 6 - Feedback and complaints
Standard 7 - Human resources
Standard 8 - Organisational governance

These standards each require that services have a statement of outcome for the consumer, a statement of expectation for the organisation, and organisational requirements that demonstrate that each standard has been met. These standards demonstrate overlap with Recovery-based care frameworks. However, experience has shown that identifying minimal standards of care can be problematic, a kind of race to the bottom with the goal of saving dollars as the main driver of reform.

This book argues that residential aged care facilities are certainly mental health services providers and therefore should fit firmly under the government's Mental Health strategy. However, no mention of Recovery, is made in the Aged Care Quality standards, that I yet have been able to find

THE COVID-19 PANDEMIC AND CHIME

<u>The Effects of the Pandemic on Consumer rights</u>
During the current Covid-19 crisis, these reformed values appear to have quickly slipped far from the mind of planners and policy makers. Protection from infection, suffering and untimely death is obviously the prime consideration of the government. However, why did they preclude other considerations such as Mental Health and autonomy? Especially considering that these factors lead to poorer quality of life and life expectancy?

Preventing connection is usually used as a punishment for prisoners, and this will affect their lifespan even if that is the sole measure applied to measure wellness. Stripping away access to loved ones without providing innovative solutions was a harsh, careless and reckless compromise of wellbeing. Keeping someone breathing is not the usual measure of quality of life.

The nexus between mental and physical health needs to be addressed in this crisis. Open discussion of the issues between residents, families, staff, management and policy makers / funders needs to be enabled, rather than sacrificed. The response has provided a very lonely death for many nursing home residents.

There has always been significant risk that people in care are susceptible to illnesses brought in from family, staff, and visitors. It is a real risk that I am sure has cost many lives, inadvertently, over the years. And yet many older people who have family visits would rather run the risk than live without family contact. Up until this time, the service providers would have agreed that this definite but balanced risk was worthwhile.

To put it bluntly, would you rather live out your last days on earth in near-total isolation, in a frantic, understaffed nursing home, or with you family visiting? Answer for yourself, but also consider the autonomy of the elder who might decide one way or the other.

With the Pre-covid average life expectancy of those entering care being less than a year, and the predictions of a vaccine being longer than that away, there are many that will never see a "cure" no matter what, even if some vaccine proves 100% effective.

Other casualties of the Covid policy reaction.
Frontline care workers are then left absorbing the grief experienced at the coalface, where unmet emotional needs have been most pronounced. Many of them are in crisis - emotionally spent and physically exhausted. Staff have, in some cases not been replaced through hiring as they have been quarantined, they burn out and

leave, or leave in fear of contracting the virus.

At the same time, nursing staff have not received extra training in infection control (even though the government has shown in funds that were not explicitly tied by accountabilities to improved training or increased staffing). Staff have been allowed to work in multiple nursing homes potentially spreading the virus among the most vulnerable, also inadvertently increasing the likelihood of their own positive Covid-19 diagnosis.

Meanwhile, families that might have been able to advocate for their loved ones care have faced a sense of panic as they have witnessed these waves of infection, and as the media has focussed on hotspots, without even being allowed to communicate with their loved one.

Aged Care funding in Australia is currently a responsibility of the Federal level of government, while the state health departments run the hospitals. This division of care is untenable. This has meant that the established pressure to avoid cost by shuffling elderly residents back and forth between hospitals and the care home may have led to an increase in transmission.

> The Covid-19 pandemic, an era of increased

> risk to older people, has meant an inundation of media with bad news about its risks. What might increased fear mean to the mental health of the older person? What about the isolation? How are nursing, community health, home care and health providers responding to enforced isolation?

Positive Mental Health values during Covid-19

A practice nurse at a location I work at explained that for many older people, visiting the doctor and going to the shops constitute their entire social connection with the outside world. Fortunately at this small practice, she supports connection in the following ways:

1. Many older people have lost the chance to play bowls, their main exercise activity. She encourages them to walk.
2. Many used to get together to shop, an important social activity. The loss of this has had an impact on wellbeing. She monitors if they are getting adequate food and talks it over with them, has intervened directly in extreme cases by delivering food, and discussed issues with the doctor and other stakeholders including the manager of the local IGA supermarket who was very supportive.
3. When the GP was mainly consulting via telephone, this nurse supported the process, recognising that the concept of a telephone consult

was foreign to many consumers, and supporting the process by talking the experience through with the patients.

While all of the above protect physical wellbeing, and as the nurse pointed out that they relate to **connection** for older patients, and as we have learned, connection is crucial for maintaining social and emotional health, and is a value of Mental Health Recovery.

While the evidence for Recovery-based reform has been growing for some time, the advent of Covid-19 and the international, national, state and local responses left me stunned, due to:

- Reactive policy decisions that comprehensively blanketed older people's lives without consultation or evident consideration of policy on older people's mental health.

- The vulnerability of older people to Covid while the response, ironically, led to increased risk of infection, their near-total isolation, disempowerment and some really awful mental suffering.

- The lack of acknowledgement about older person's mental health needs in services, government and even the WHO international response, despite the concurrence with the Royal Commission in Australia and recognition internationally of the need for better standards of care.

- Carers, staff and aged care nurses who have experienced significant extra stress while caring for older people, which has affected attrition, staffing levels, and the healthy mindset required for provision of care.

- The grief of families of older people in care, being devastated by learning their loved ones were dying without the normal dignity of being with them in their final hours.
- The passing of Covid positive elders back and forward between state and federally funded levels of care, which has taken the focus away from holistic care.

Currently, the Royal Commission is hearing that the separation of funding arrangements has resulted in state and federal services failing in liason of appropriately shared care.

They have heard that the Federal Government has provided Covid-19 money to nursing homes for staff infection training without demonstrated accountability, and nursing homes have taken the money but failed to spend it on extra staff or Covid-19 infection control training. There was also a significant gap in planning around the issues of carers who work in multiple nursing homes becoming vectors of transmission. Staffing levels at nursing homes, already at crisis point before the pandemic, became a critical need for extra nursing staff (resulting in talk of calling in the Army to help). In this highly-stressed environment, what happens to the care recipient?

Further, social and other media is replete with distrust - including claims that families of the deceased have been offered money by care providers while being asked not to discuss the nature or conditions of the death of their loved ones. Some are saying that Government statistics are unreliable, and the "Dying from Covid/Dying with Covid" has recently been borne out as an issue internationally as within Australia. It is a mess.

However, I feel the point is that the problems above, exacerbated by Covid-19, were already problems existing in the system. However there will be much learned from the Covid-19 response in the future.

This will require that the issues of older people will need to be examined and understood seperately.

The table below identifies some differences between older people and younger people following Covid-19 and policy responses. It demonstrates the need for nuanced and specialized policy responses that have received little to no attention during this crisis.

This comparison is made using the CHIME framework as a reflection tool to break down common issues I have heard about during 2020.

	Older people	People 55 and under
Mortality risk	Very High	Very much lower
Impact on...		
Connection	Near complete isolation, particularly in Aged Care settings. E.g., family not being allowed to visit, not being able to play bowls etc. Fear of health-based transmission prevents older patients attending doctors. Older people often dependant on services much more than younger age groups Loneliness a massive problem among older people prior to Covid, made much worse.	Problems of forced isolation eg in domestic violence, worsened by lockdowns. High for isolated people. Lower for people in family settings, however reports of increased domestic violence touches on the risk of use of isolation as a suite of strategies in DV. People's work, income, etc have experienced major losses through lack of connection under lockdowns However, younger and fitter age groups may have greater resources / resilience.
Hope	"I hope to see my grandchildren again. They live interstate" Hopelessness as fatigue sets in - leading to depression. Hope of survival impacted, however not necessarily to the same degree by everyone. Worries about the young stated as "I wonder about the world we are leaving to them."	A mixed impact - lower risks to health => better hope in the future, encouraging resilience. E.g. Some young people speculate whether housing might be more affordable after the crisis Sadness about risk of seeing sick older relatives again. Negative health repetition a factor in increase in suicide.
Identity	"Is this it? The rest of my life, in isolation, disconnected from my family.	Online courses, Facebook, home schooling, fears

		about the future of work, desires to travel, and the effect of total control are engaging people's sense of who they are. These are widespread issues affecting identity.
	"Who am I now?"	
Meaning	If living in nursing care, with no visits allowed, situationally similar to feeling like a prisoner. One man recalled fighting the communists as a soldier and said "look what is happening here"	Covid has represented a challenging time for many people. Many will have a lot of adjustment to process including loss of work, businesses social life, connection. The meanings can be very negative for freedoms as well as for older people.
	Worry about the future - especially about whether new measures to protect society will ever be lifted. A sense of forced changes and agendas.	Talk of the "new normal" precludes recovery of personal liberties previously enjoyed. Many in our community discovering new ways to express positive meanings.
Loss of autonomy	Understood under Recovery principles as a major impact, Covid policy runs counter to current reforms. For those in Aged Care settings an increased impact has occurred around Covid-19.	Moderate to high, depending on social role.

Figure 2: A comparison of Covid impacts between older and younger people

These various factors of the pandemic and it's response upon the mental health of older people can show a magnified, perverse relationship in comparison to what younger persons might experience. As the table above shows, that although (and certainly, because) older persons are at increased risk the management of their care has been more severe and restrictive in practice. So as age increases, the threat to health increases, yet so too do potential negative impacts of care which can of themselves shorten the lifespan. For example, depression can have very serious detrimental impacts upon self care, help seeking and medication compliance etc.

My local area is not representative of the higher risk areas for Covid-19. Little or no cases have been found as yet, and no deaths have been attributed to it. Many consumers have expressed concern about infection, and many others have downplayed or denied concern.

While I cannot assert that the views of people in my local area are representative of the whole Australian community, I can say that there was no consumer-consultative process apparent at any stage about compromises in service provision due to Covid-19.

The above table demonstrates that the mental health considerations are massive on older people, but not well understood, and that the policy approaches cost lives, health and dignity to older people even more significantly than the rest of the community. This has been a very backward, even Agist policy response.

If self-regulation remains the status quo after the Royal Commission and Covid-19 are over, let's at least attempt to self-regulate adequately. I personally will be deeply troubled if the pandemic response is not examined deeply and critically to ascertain the impact of current aged care policy and business models on older person's mental and overall health in the future.

I believe the way forward involves local, community-based ownership of care responsibilities combined with dedication to the improvement and wisdom of open accountability under a Recovery-based framework.

RECOVERY IN ACTION – DON'T WAIT

Australia has been through over a decade of enquiries, reports, legislation attempts and the current Royal Commission into Aged Care, and the situation on the ground is becoming worse. The feeling is that the 'market' based 'industry' is too profit centred and that during Covid-19 the profit motive relentlessly drove staffing decisions.

(Note: see Royal Commission into Aged Care Quality and Safety, Interim Report: Neglect, p9, and Eagar et al., 2019, a research report developed for the Royal Commission that directly discusses staffing levels and subsequent care. Friends of mine who work for corporate-based nursing organisations are not feeling optimistic and I think for good reason. The 'industry' seems to have inordinate influence over policy makers.)

Covid-19 is essentially a crisis. The crisis hopefully will one day be over. It is true that a crisis requires a crisis response. However, whether or not the crisis is precipitated by a virus or by a business model that is profit-extractive rather than primarily values-driven, there is clearly a need to think through the values that drive policy and come up with a values-based response to any crisis. In other words, a crisis response is a very poor justification for discontinuing movement toward a values-based stance.

Although it is doubtful that the Royal Commission can create a desire within profit-based businesses to want to improve their care through spending more on care, I believe that more communities should stop waiting for government and big business to provide the answers. Surely, as the baby-boomers age, they and the communities that love and support them, can take their considerable experience and economic power and set up their own small trusts for their own truly not-for-profit smaller care centres.

It is our responsibility – not someone else's. And, likewise, as we try to respond to Covid-19, and have seen caring nurses, doctors and other health and care providers recognise and respond to issues of connection among older people, these principles must be supported. At least, at a national level, a media release from the Ministers for the Australian Department of Health (22 April) announced "free COVID-19 support line for Senior Australians".

We must follow suit and think about the social and emotional needs of older people and plan for their wellbeing during this crisis.

For example, I saw a news story in October about an

Italian innovation - a plastic barrier with two sets of arms to allow relatives to hug one another. Although this may seem a late arrival, it shows an awareness of the responsibility care providers have to manage the mental health needs of their residents while attending to the crisis response.

The massive uptake of Zoom as a platform for connection has been facilitated in some nursing homes as well, creating contact where being in the same room was forbidden. Where this has not happened, imagine how the resident in care might feel about their last days on earth, forbidden from seeing family.

RECOVERY, PETWORTH, AND A SYSTEM FOR AGED CARE

Although existing businesses may find it onerous to meet statistical and reporting requirements, I would like to introduce a model for Aged Care design, a Five Foundation rating system that proposes minimum standards can be creatively *exceeded* using a more principle-based, voluntary approach to care provision.

When I returned to Australia and continued my studies, the experience at Petworth Cottage created a frame of reference for appropriate best care and I wrote a paper around a voluntary five star self-rating system for nursing homes (I was unaware at that time of the highly effective USA-based "five star" system around staffing numbers – a mnemonic coincidence). My paper had a strong emphasis that one of the 'Stars' would be based in Recovery principles. So I have had to change it to being called a "Five Foundation" system - for theoretically, foundations underpin a safe, comfortable home where family often meets.

I strongly doubt the government will want to wean itself of it's ideologically-driven privatisation and GDP-based model of aged care. I don't think we should wait for them. I propose a Five Foundation accreditation system and add discussion about Covid-19 response principles. It fills a gap, because the 'industry's' emphasis is on self regulation, and this system would be a tool to guide development of nursing care along Recovery values and other principles of best practice.

Five Foundation will not work for everyone. Facilities that are huge, profit or expansion driven, not interested in allied health, not interested in mental health, or human geography, or embracing research and passionate care through evidence base and accountability to consumers, probably won't consider signing up. They probably would not score very well.

This Five Foundation system works on positive bias, values and assumptions and is there to help the community-based care facility refine continual improvement. Of course, Five Foundation services will absolutely *shine* when they are audited or going for accreditation, because the agendas of Five Foundation principles represent a demonstrable structure of accountability toward consumers, and reflective practice. This would help the facility to set and achieve consumer outcomes, organisation statements and reportable requirements which they are answerable under the new Aged Care Quality Standards.

The next section is based upon that Five Foundation idea. I include it in this book because a Recovery-based framework of mental health care in Older Person's Mental Health has to provide a positive critique of the chaotic landscape in which it operates.

We have to advocate and put responsibility for poor mental health care of older people where it sits, even if it means challenging the hegemony of the 'market'.

As communities age, and arguments over funding and accountability models swirl endlessly before our eyes, lulling us into inaction, perhaps some well-informed communities will band together, form their own small trust, and create truly Recovery-consistent aged care facilities. It can be done, I have seen it at Petworth Cottage.

Following that the book will return to the discussion about Recovery values in OPMH care.

A FIVE FOUNDATION SERVICE STRUCTURE

We cannot separate mental health care from all other care where care extends to all aspects of life including the residential setting. It is useless to try to patch up older people using antidepressants while neglecting the overall situation and their holistic needs.

Current funding arrangements in aged care non-specifically cover mental health care, which is therefore generally overlooked and has been described by a leading professional as "a blatantly discriminatory ... disgrace" (Magarey, J., 2017). Evidence shows that 52% of people in aged care have symptoms of depression (Mental Health Commission of New South Wales, last accessed 2017). A web-based training instrument has been funded by the government to provide skills in recognition of depression in Nursing homes (Beyond Blue (2016), but under the current funding arrangements, nursing care, already under pressure, has experienced further downward pressure, particularly in the private sector (Russell, 2016). Training staff is not enough – the workplace needs to support implementation.

So, before this book delves into Recovery-based mental health care in older people, it is necessary to consider the broader context of care and explore a conceptual framework for overall service design of aged-care businesses to support Recovery-based mental health care.

Building Up to Five Foundation Rating, Not Down to a Price

This Recovery-based Five Foundation rating structure could become an adaptive, *aspiration*-based evaluation process which could take a care business well beyond the current and predominating funding/accreditation and risk-oriented model, which currently has the unintentional side effect of constraining quality in profit taking care businesses.

Note: This Five Foundation approach shares commonality with a business model which has been discussed globally in recent times, which promotes the idea of "Stakeholder" capitalism (Search World Economic Forum). I am not sure why *capitalism* has to be specified in this instance. While I have no objection to a variety of business models per se, it is ironic that many leaders of the World Economic Forum themselves run the chaotic global mess and perpetuate the problems. So I select their term 'Stakeholder' as a way forward under advisement, but believe that grass-roots Trusts, dedicated to their first love (I.e. providing care for their elders) will always do a better job than those dedicated to expansionism and the 'growth' model. My view is that stakeholders can be the foundation of an appropriate community-owned service.

Ownership and pride in delivery of care is damaged by minimum standards being linked to funding. Perhaps accreditation will remain linked to minimum standards, but the industry has to believe we can do better, and structure their whole approach around that goal.

Service planners and funding bodies should not expect current reporting models to go far enough to resolve nursing home quality problems (Clement, Bazzoli & Zhao 2012). While the for-profit sector has been leading a charge for *less* regulatory oversight and increased funding, it is problematic that nursing staff levels and nursing quality in many instances suffer without some guiding principles of care provision (Keast, 2015). This would lead to less time for staff to provide even basic level mental health-informed care.

Large profit oriented business, with profit agendas, expansionism and marketing strategies diverting funds away from care, are not helped by funding models inadvertently focussing on minimal standards. In contrast, a Recovery-based, voluntary rating system could positively guide the development of services. Innovation is not a direct function of budgetary constraints, and such a system could channel and direct the creativity and talent of people within the industry.

Figure 3: Building a Five Foundation Recovery-based model in nursing care

A "Five Foundation" rating system, rated by an external

entity (similar to Michelin stars in the restaurant industry) could guide services to aspire to develop a better, higher standard of care than the mandated system. It could also benefit consumers by allowing them to locate and influence services who aspire to delivering the best care. It could also promote pride in qualified, informed service provision by the businesses and staff who care.

Five Foundations

Each of the following suggested five domains could be rated individually and then aggregated to show a number of stars. Five Foundations would not be easy to achieve. The domains cover:

1. Recovery Principles
2. Links to Learning: Teaching and Research
3. Business Model: Accountability and Service Funding
4. Working in Care: Employment Principles
5. Human Geography of Aged Care

Foundation One: Recovery principles in Aged Care

Recovery-influenced care implies that mental health, chronic care and physical health care are managed in such a way that older people are treated as indivduals, and their needs and voices are taken into account throughout the process of care.

In terms of the new Aged Care Quality Standards, this Foundation is used to rate performance under five of the eight new standards:

Standard 1 - Consumer dignity and choice
Standard 2 - Ongoing assessment and planning with consumers
Standard 3 - Personal care and clinical care
Standard 4 - Services and supports for daily living
Standard 6 - Feedback and complaints

An Australian government definition of Recovery is: 'Being able to create and live a meaningful and contributing life in a community of choice with or without the presence of mental health issues'. It is right then that so many of the standards come under the Recovery Foundation rating, and that it should not be very easy to achieve a full score.

Little has been written about recovery in older person's mental health although an English study identified a recovery framework that was developed with 31 older people (Daley et al, 2013), discussed above.

If 45% of people develop depression entering aged care, then staff who view it as a 'normal' part of decline will not recognise and support Recovery (Mental Health Commission of NSW, 2017). Consequently, residents receive 0.00 to 0.04 hours/day/bed of therapist care of all kinds, *including* mental health therapy (Department of Health and Ageing, 2010). Aged care facilities need to accept their role as providers of mental health services. This includes:
- Providing Recovery-oriented activities to people in care
- Educating nursing staff with training in mental health care
- Access to trauma-informed, strength-based specific therapeutic support

- Maintaining connection to the community in support for maintaining identity
- Support of family members who provide links to identity
- Fostering choice over residents own lives

As you will see below, a great deal of this book is spent getting into the details of recovery-based skills and practice, particularly in OPMH, but also generally applied to the care of older people. An OPMH Recovery model is discussed below, featuring an adaptation of the Scottish CHIME model.

Despite the new standards, the problem remains that clinical care around mental health is poorly implemented in the nursing home environment, despite representing so much of the needs of aged care residents. The person in the OPMH role is more likely to understand the importance of addressing mental health.

Foundation Two: Links to Learning: Teaching and Research

Can the care facility better train staff? Can a relationship be developed with a learning institution whereby the experiences of care provision can support academic study? Can staff engage in study to assist in the development of their career?

This has no direct correlation under the eight standards, although Standard 7 – Human Resources briefly mentions staff training. This Foundation would deliver services far superior to the deliverables from the eight standards. Working for a 'cutting-edge' organisation can be invigorating. Why not in Aged Care? Aged care nursing needs to be re-conceptualised involving excellence in older person's mental health care education.

A Five Foundation service will be concerned with not only achieving 'best practice' but will be part of a network of learning and reform, with links to the Five Foundation organisation, advocacy and to educational facilities. It will be proactive in staff training, supervision and career development. Staff can be continually developing their knowledge base and have access to learning usually considered above their grade, so that they have capacity to provide appropriate mental health support to residents and eventually, achieve qualification in Recovery-based care qualifications.

Staff should also be encouraged to:
- Know how to identify illness
- Develop older person's recovery-specific skills
- Study and disseminate knowledge within the team
- Understand processes of grief, adjustment, illness, brain changes
- Participate in research projects
- Understand culturally appropriate care
- Develop a sense of competence in Mental Health care
- Know how to communicate with Mental Health organisations and professionals
- Eventually provide supervision, coaching and mentoring of junior staff

Aging In Place (Olsberg, Accessed 2017) represents a

current shift in policy wherein people have continuity in their accommodation as their care needs change. Unfortunately it can be misapplied where *what previously were* low-care facilities keep people in place without being set up for higher care needs. This Foundation interprets that risk as an opportunity for development. The Five Foundation facility is eventually fully equipt to cope with all the levels of care, including management of mental health related needs. The knowledge and ability to cope with issues of safety, distress and challenging behaviours should be seamlessly integrated, reducing the need for psychogeriatric or hospital admissions, and supporting older people going through major life challenges.

Foundation Three: Business Model: Accountability and Service Funding

While it is not impossible, it is unlikely that a business that extracts profit or diverts funds away from care will ever achieve best practice in terms of care. It is also unlikely that a service that is not able to demonstrate how, where and why it exceeds minimum care standards for funding approval will ever achieve much more than the minimum basic care standards.

Although government funding does not require a nursing home to use bed funding for all care including mental health care, a Five Foundation service would do so. This considers how the service spends income on care, including Mental Health care.

This consideration covers Standard 8 - Organisational governance of the new Aged Care Quality Standards. Internationally, For-Profit nursing homes provide lower quality care than Not-For-Profit ones (Geraedts et al, 2016), possibly because For-Profit follow an expansionist agenda intrinsic to corporate culture, which distracts from care. (In contrast, Petworth Cottage was a clear example how a truly not-for-profit organisation plans and delivers superior care.)

In a climate where doubt exists about how consistently extra staff are added in some nursing homes, where high care need was identified in funding applications (Department of Health and Ageing, 2010), a Five Foundation service would be able to demonstrate appropriate use of every available cent (or penny) of bed funding for the consumer. (Interestingly, in some states of the US, alternative models are being tried, such as funding being tied to the number of nursing staff employed, rather than beds filled (Foster & Lee, 2015), so this connects with the "Working in Care" Foundation).

This principle needs to be enshrined in the ownership model. For example, a nursing home owned by a community trust, who are wholly interested in the care of their elders, and who regularly receive consultation from residents and families, (ie no expansionist/profit agenda) might score highly due to clarity of resource use. This is counter-culture to the current economic philosophy, which has created the problem of extractive profits before care. Research has found that in many aspects of care, "the quality difference between for-profit and non-profit nursing homes existed independent of the price charged" (Geraedts et al, 2016). It must not be assumed that the beds need to be privately funded beds to provide high quality care.

While the eight new standards may be useful in that they can be equally applied to all types of facilities, they do not document how the self-monitoring aspect may provide a comparable, critical level of service. This Five Foundation system, linked to business model, consumer consultation and research, can provide the evidence of and structure of governance principles. The current industry is not ready to be bound by such high standards, but individual services certainly could start to work in a more highly developed way.

Foundation Four: Working in Care: Employment principles

Employees are the front line of care. How does a care facility maximise ownership of the processes of care? Are employees encouraged or discouraged from the work they perform and the management of the facility?

This Foundation correlates to Standard 7 - Human resources, of the new Aged Care Quality Standards. However, Standard 7 fails to outline appropriate levels of care staff. There is a nurse to patient ratio but most of the work is actually done by the care staff. So much of the implementation of other standards – particularly those that come under our Recovery Foundation – swings on the liberal staffing levels through successful basic planning of the roster, that this issue deserves to be carefully evaluated on it's own.

The first issue is around the supply of staff, which is

at risk from management focussing on as a cost-cutting opportunity. It is currently too easy for a facility to fudge and manipulate staffing levels. They may use techniques such as over-rostering someone or poorly communicating shift changes and then not replacing them when they eventually fail to show, or putting care staff in the kitchen after sacking kitchen staff. It is harder to replace statistics of staff actually on the floor for each shift when the positive rating system pays close attention to these issues.

It has been argued that 6-8 residents per staff member is a 'Golden Ratio' – a good level of care, with waiting times of less than 10 minutes maximum for the answering of patient calls (Rickard, 2019). At Petworth Cottage there was one care staff per wing plus a floater, which was within the 'Golden Ratio'. This did not include nursing staff. And the care was the best I have ever witnessed.

In contrast, I have seen multinational-owned nursing homes who redefine the care role by making them also responsible for cooking, cleaning and maintenance jobs which enabled them to deceptively over-report their level of care staff.

This links quality of care to available, happy, compassionate, well-supported staff. The less time-pressure that well selected, trained, led and supported staff experience, the more they have to give to the residents (Van Hoof, *et al.* 2016). Downward pressure on staffing reduces resident contact and increases stress on staff which will impact on residents and the quality of care (Schwendimann *et al.*, 2016). Mental Health care, which depends on relationships, is the first casualty of staffing pressure.

Petworth Cottage always had plenty of staff available, in comparison to any care facility I have visited in the UK or in Australia. Breaks were regarded as important. At the start of each shift, *all* staff were included in daily conference about each resident's needs. Staff could (and would) buy a meal from the kitchen for a nominal cost.

Staff happiness transferred to the residents because a positive mood is infectious. All the staff being present for shift handover, with time for discussion of each resident's needs, felt empowering because each worker's view is able to be shared – it encourages care.

Factors contributing the to creation of a positive work environment for Nursing Home (Schwendimann *et al.*, 2016) staff include: conflict management over client care, being consulted in resident care planning; adequate staffing on the roster; recognition, leadership mentoring and supervision, the level of pay; opportunities to develop professional interests that they can identify.

Also, in practical terms, issues like the amount of breaks and the availability of equipment and supples are going to have significant effects on the stress and health of workers, and residents in their care (Van Hoof, *et al.* 2016). Is a profiteer ever likely to commit themself to the above findings with their implications for improving care?

Foundation Five: Human Geography of Aged Care

Geography of human space is about the person's journey through their physical environment. In the design of nursing homes, geography can refer to the location of the care home relative to where the person's home community is, through to recreational space, privacy, autonomy and ownership, and the sensory experience of the care facility - the sights, smells, touch and feel aspects of the care home.

This incorporates Standard 5 - Organisation's service environment, of the new Aged Care Quality Standards. For a residential care facility, or indeed any service, to put itself up for a perfect score would mean that it could show a ratings agency how it deeply it has considered the size of the facility, the use of space, and the feelings that that space generates within consumers.

Contemporary ideas of human geography are advancing concepts of the use and meaning of human space in health-related facilities (Dummer 2008). Rethinking the use and meaning of human space has led to movements such as the GreenHouse set of principles for Nursing Home design (Zimmerman et al. 2016) which has been used in 174 facilities internationally by 2015.

The GreenHouse principles include *'real home'* (e.g., no more than 12 residents, whereas in contrast Petworth Cottage housed up to 32 people – both a huge improvement to any of the 120 to 150 bed nursing homes I have worked at. The principle is that smaller equates to more, and better care.

Petworth Cottage overlooked the town of Petworth, and residents could maintain their feeling of connection through this physical co-location with their town.

In GreenHouse, meals cooked in a central open kitchen, elder-directed living); *'meaningful life'* (e.g., elder control over time to wake, eat, and sleep, and access to activities in the broader community); and *'empowered staff'* (Zimmerman et al. 2016). Although these low numbers can be seen to have correlation with certain recovery principles, GreenHouse is quite prescriptive and not as responsive to Consumer defined Recovery-based planning. However they present an excellent starting point for thinking about human geography in a Five Foundation facility.

This physical design/ geographical Foundation can conceptualise the ideal location and relationship of the facility within it's environment and community. Residents would experience better mental health in aged care if the home is:

- connected to the community the residents identify with
- aesthetically and functionally conducive to good mental health
- adaptive to supportive relationships (especially life partners)
- comfortable
- designed for social, physical and occupational activity (eg gardens)
- favourable to indoor/outdoor options

Board members and staff's connectedness will also be influenced by the building. Staff administrative areas, rest areas, education and support areas, all have impact on the quality of care. A man who had worked as maintenance manager for a multinational company-owned care facility once told me that he had been disciplined by the manager because he had gone out into the rose garden and cut a few roses and put them in a vase where residents could enjoy them. No discussion of why it was disallowed was entered into by the manager, just a warning not to take liberties. For him, this was the beginning of the end of his work there, because he had come to view the depersonalisation of the physical environment seemed to be very much reinforced by both policy and management.

The market may indeed face many dilemmas introducing Recovery values in the workplace. To implement recovery we must first understand the principles of Recovery, and use it wherever we work, whether in the residential setting or through the OPMH team. Only you can make the difference in a consumer's experience of care.

The next section dives deeper into the principles of Recovery as applied to OPMH, and addresses the question of attitudinal learning, based on all the background sources described above. This book advocates for narrative-based, holistic bio-psychosocial assessment skills, strongly linked to Recovery values.

Section 1: Attitudinal Learning

ATTITUDINAL LEARNING IN RECOVERY-BASED CLINICAL PRACTICE

"Attitudes are important... Positive individual and community views of ageing, that promote dignity, support and respect for what older people offer in our society, can go a long way towards helping people to live well in later life." (Mental Health Commission of NSW, 2017)

"It needs to be one of the criteria learned to have respect for older people and in fact respect for elders, almost in that traditional sense of acknowledging all the older people that have come before us and that's why we're here now" (psychiatrist, see Appendix 1).

OPMH CHIME: An OPMH Adapted Model for Recovery-based Assessment

You may hear how proponents of Recovery often seem to critique 'the medical model', though the hope of clinical recovery remains of primary concern in OPMH. For many consumers the diagnostic and medication-based elements of the medical model underpin hope and their best chance of improvement in their symptoms.

However reliance on the 'medical model' alone never did go far enough – Recovery values that support our conduct as health providers can indeed complement and, at times, even outshine the priorities of clinical recovery. For example, a rushed assessment can not only miss important aspects but alienate the consumer, preventing engagement between the consumer and services. However, connection and empowerment achieve the opposite.

This section reflects attitudinal aspects of practice that support consumer-informed Recovery values. The headings of the attitudinal section of this book reflect things consumers have said they value, correlated with Scottish CHIME Recovery concepts and other related values such as those from the Focus Group and from psychogeriatricians who I have worked with.

CONNECTEDNESS

Connectedness is about how a consumer feels connected in positive ways to other people, their own lives and the world. It is about relationships. One lady told me, in response to my asking her what underpins her sense of recovery:

> *"It's about watching my grandkids grow up, and helping my kids."*

A therapeutic relationship can be impacted by connectedness at various stages. As with all health services, building the caring relationship in mental health is key to good outcomes for the client because engagement is a two-way street. Whether or not the clinician is conscious of their influence on the client's engagement, they contribute a massive amount to outcomes. It is the responsibility of a skilled clinician to provide a physically and psychologically safe environment for the client and, in doing so, create an environment where rapport can be developed, trust can be built and assistance rendered. Showing people your regard for their rights, comfort and dignity is an excellent starting point.

Connectedness throughout OPMH services

"Who is this person and why are they asking me all these questions!?"

(This question was asked by a new client.)

Referrals come from a variety of sources including nursing home staff, concerned friends and family, crisis lines and GPs – i.e., through someone *other than* the client.

> Consider how you might react if someone referred you to Mental Health? Would you naturally feel a sense of 'psychological safety'?
>
> Try to imagine you lived 40 years earlier. How do you think historical awareness of mental health care might add to or detract from the feeling of safety in care?

Often, especially in older generations, significant stigma around mental health services and fear of inpatient admissions play on the mind of the person, becoming a barrier to cooperation and sometimes directly affecting their wellbeing.

OPMH often supports home-based assessment where possible. It is the consumer's own turf, and can be more reassuring than starting at a clinic or hospital. Speak with the primary consumer where possible. Allow the consumer to speak, and listen to them. When arranging appointments over the telephone, conversations should convey interest and respect.

Connectedness may also involve telephone calls to educate GPs, work collaboratively with supports, and interface with shared care across the community, particularly in the rural context where distance is a factor. Including the consumer in these discussions will help maintain a connection to their world. It is quietly respectful of consumers' rights to engage with their chosen services. If they have a strong relationship and trust in their GP or a family member, include them in the process.

Initial contacts lay the foundation of Connectedness. First impressions make a great deal of difference and consumers may decide very quickly whether you are someone they can trust. Have you, in the initial part of the clinical relationship, shown respect for the rights, privacy and dignity of the consumer? Have you shown compassion and humanity toward them in the way you have made initial arrangements? If so you have set the scene for Recovery-oriented practice.

The Impact of the Assessor on Assessment

Some basic starters: After you walk in the door, smile, introduce yourself and politely greet the consumer and then any other people who are there in support of them. Wait to be invited to sit or ask if it's ok to sit with them. Be honest and transparent about your role, and give them opportunity to speak and ask questions. At that stage you may inform them about the reason they were referred: e.g. "I understand you have been going through some difficult times".

The consumer will be assessing you at the same time. There are things about you that you can't change, things that can be improved with experience, and factors which you are blind to. At times all these can put a strain on the relationship, even at the outset.

This can be a challenging issue that you may reflect on many times in your career and it is worth thinking about. What is it that you do that inspires trust in the consumer? Are you transparent, responsive, respectful? How does it influence your assessment? For example, some action/reaction relationships to illustrate the point:

1   Clinician avoids eye contact, asks mostly closed-ended questions -> Consumer remains closed and retains significant, unasked information -> Clinician completes an assessment which is lacking in depth and clarity

2   Clinician is tired and yawning -> Consumer (with depression) perceives a lack of interest -> Consumer responds sarcastically -> Clinician notes engagement: "Disinterest", "Sarcastic"

3   Clinician is young -> Consumer feels awkward, makes inappropriate joke -> Clinician records "Inappropriate humour"

They say that your body language conveys 75% of your true meaning. Your tone of voice, use of jargon and pace with which you conduct the session also speak volumes. All of these examples affect the consumer's sense of connection or disconnection. The first example in particular demonstrates the absence of both good communication skills and a good narrative assessment style, discussed later in this book.

The motto "Do no harm" could be a starting point to managing a new client, i.e. kindness. It could also be linked with the Law of the Harvest/ Karma principle, because showing compassion, interest and intelligence often elicits a positive response where people will try to help you understand. If your presence creates tension within the person for some reason, remember they have *rights to choose* in health care and it is, after all, about them. If they will not engage with you at all, are there alternative ways to complete the assessment? Perhaps there is a health worker they know and trust, who they might like to have with them for the assessment.

Boundaries and Sharing

I always watched with interest the way psychogeriatricians would structure interviews. They always gave the consumer the opportunity to speak for themselves about what the issues were, and connected with them on an interpersonal therapeutic level. The psychogeriatrician visits I attended were often superior to assessments by general psychiatrists.

One psychogeriatrician I worked with connected well with consumers. He would initially take time to get to know something about a person's life. For example, if a person started their life around places that he had known as a child in Sydney, he would reminisce with them.

If they had a craft, hobby or interest, he would appreciate their handiwork. I thought he was a very kind man, and I often tried to emulate his style. It's not only an issue of measuring the consumers engagement or their social history, but also of connectedness in assessment.

This approach potentially raises a question of boundaries. The doctor provided education to me on the difference between boundary crossing and boundary violations very early in our working relationship.

However, through readings and supervision it is clear that good mental health workers know how to share a little of themselves without abusing the consumer-worker relationship by changing the focus to their own self. The approach engages the consumer with equity, without exploiting the relationship for their own agenda, and without doing harm. It adds warmth to the relationship.

On the other hand, when boundary violations occur consumers can often tell when their boundaries are violated, and it's not a comforting, safe experience for them.

Connectedness, as a consumer value, involves the way mental health professionals relate to them. There are many instances of 'old school' clinical approaches that rely on power relationships over consumers. Ironically, these approaches tend to be officious boundary violations, enforcing power imbalances, and showing poor awareness of the importance of connectedness to Recovery.

Narrative-based Assessment

> ."...stories are the form of language most often used to convey experiences" (Hall & Powell, 2011).

Narrative is the way the consumer talks about their life experiences and how it relates to current challenges. Eye contact, empathy, reflective listening skills – all these have a bearing on Narrative Assessment.

Narrative assessment is using the power of conversation to truly understand the thoughts and feelings of the person being assessed. It relies on connectedness, utilizes skills such as reflective listening and other spoken and unspoken communication styles, but has no exact formula to follow.

The assessor has key issues and questions to cover, but there are useful, open-ended key phrases that you may develop in your narrative style: "Asking *(with interest and sensitivity)* 'What is your story?' will provide more knowledge about persons than asking *(a closed ended question such as)* 'How are you?'" (Hall & Powell, 2011, *italics added*). It tells the consumer you are interested in their perspective.

During the Narrative assessment listen for evidence of positive future-focus, which helps with engagement and contributes to MSE data such as mood, thought content, insight etc. Again, narrative assessment is an issue of approach as much as anything.

A key skill in narrative assessment is knowing how and when to 'shut up' and really listen. If a person has trouble focussing, keeping on track, or remaining lucid, it will show in the way they tell their story. Where people's mental health issue is impacted by unresolved, unstated feelings or a sense of being isolated, listening is the beginning of building a bridge between the health worker and the consumer.

A pause in the consumer's speech can be a moment where the person decides whether or not you are listening and worth disclosing their memories to. If the person appears to stop and consider, you might ask them to tell you more about the thing they have been explaining. Appropriate silence, reflective listening, and summarising for the consumer are powerful tools. Obviously if you are focussed on a tick sheet you probably won't be considered by them as worth the effort.

Understanding of wider themes, cultural and social contexts, and the way the person feels about their experience in the light of these contexts can be achieved through listening for the story behind the story.

In issues of thought form, narrative assessment reveals what is happening. For example, when talking to someone with a strong history of alcohol dependence you may notice confabulation - a tendency to fill in gaps in their memory with small fictions.

Asking reflective questions can help. For example, in listening to an older consumer recall hallucinations with catastrophic themes featuring earthquakes in distant cities, I asked what this said about the world. The consumer hesitated. I reflected that the city is a frightening place and he then disclosed significant crimes that had been done to him while living in Melbourne. He later expressed satisfaction that he had been listened to, and I felt this connection had helped him derive meaning from his situation, helping in his recovery.

Tick Sheets

Consumers have shared with me complaints about clinicians doing a "Comprehensive Mental Health Assessment" with their eyes and attention concentrated on their forms – an issue of connection.

During the focus group (Appendix 1), tick-boxes were seen as a barrier to a therapeutic relationship. The group was strongly oriented toward a narrative-based assessment - building working relationships through understanding of the person and the systems around them, coupled with a psychosocial / medical approach. As the psychogeriatrician declared:

"I'm anti-scales, anti-tick boxes, I'm about talking to people."

He emphasised that 'endless' rating scales alienate the consumer and generally are rarely if ever read once written down. For the Focus Group participants, this view was linked to:
- sensitivity
- awareness of the consumer's rights
- valuing personal meanings
- valuing the narrative of the family and GP

As far as cognitive examination goes, the feedback from the Focus Group was to do a basic observation of cognition via narrative assessment, then only use instruments such as the MMSE or Rudas when indicated. As with collecting MSE information during assessment, you might jot brief notes as you go. The forms may be filled out in greater detail as required. More about this later.

One psychogeriatrician described how, when speaking at a Health District-level conference, he explained how just filling out standard measures does not really provide a true assessment. After his speech the Health Service Manager told the audience to disregard what had just been said! It is NSW health policy to complete the Comprehensive Assessment. It should not be done, however, *at the expense of* connection. You may find that once you are familiar with the assessment forms, you will be able to complete them after the face-to-face session. You are then more able to watch, listen and really connect.

If a narrative assessment style is preferred by a specialist, is it not equally important for allied mental health clinicians to understand this process? It supports the consumer's sense of connection at every stage.

Clarify your organisation's policies with your clinical leader. Comprehensive forms can be like training wheels for the new clinician, and essential information could be missed without use of the forms. They can be used to reinforce awareness of key details such as 'Is the GP notified?'. They cover diverse, essential issues including legal issues and risk assessment, which might get neglected in a given situation.

For example: You might meet a consumer who is referred for a medication review, is otherwise healthy, asymptomatic, well supported, and future-focussed in their narrative, and engages with you in good humour. You might just forget to assess risk and ask about legal issues including whether there is a guardian appointed.

The issues may be complex: Some consumers come away from mental health assessments with a definite impression that you have to be suicidal to get listened to. One consumer told me that she had never thought of a suicide plan until her doctor asked her if she had any plans of suicide. There is also a risk of 'lumping' all consumers together either as high risk or low risk, thus de-prioritising the low risk and diminishing the sense of person-centred care.

Clinicians may feel a lack of control over their assessment style due to organisational policy. You may even feel certain questions lack relevance. Do you still read through the questions? How does this leave the person feeling? However, your duty of care dictates that they must be asked. You may say something like "Most people will agree that at some times in their life they have had suicidal thoughts. Have you experienced these?" This gentle approach can lead to further investigation if needed.

Regardless of how you and your management handle this type of issue, narrative assessment is not a replacement for a thorough, quality assessment. It simply moves away from the extreme of a Q/A format at one end of the spectrum towards providing a therapeutic connection.

> Starting with an open-ended narrative question such as:
>
> "How do you feel about your life at the moment?" may promote 'connectedness', introduce the risk assessment and prepare the person better than initially, bluntly asking "Do you have suicidal thoughts? Yes/No".

The Comprehensive assessment tries to capture everything pro-forma, while the Narrative assessment tries to engage the person and understand their point of view. It is more fluid because it is person-centred in style. The styles need not be considered mutually exclusive.

Two 'legs' of any assessment are the psychosocial history and the mental state exam - the 'then' and the 'now'. In SMHSOP I was permitted to take longer to complete assessments, and I was taught to start with the psychosocial history, a narrative mode of assessment. This is where Recovery attitudes will show, as a narrative style gathers more information than simply the history.

Narrative assessment has also been linked to culturally-aware practice. Hall & Powell, (2011) point out that narrative assessment is not only kinder, but is linked to other Recovery values like identity and meaning. Recovery values (e.g. CHIME) assist culturally sensitive practice through narrative engagement and the clinician can widely apply these to diverse cultural contexts. Connection is created and maintained through listening to and really hearing the person (Brijnath, 2015). More is said later about culturally aware practice.

Narrative, psychosocial assessment is an opportunity for the consumer to speak for themselves and be understood. As a clinician I enjoy connecting with older people, learning how they see the world, their memories of their development and what is important to them. Of course, they can tell if you are really interested.

One particular psychogeriatrician would ask me to prepare a one-page summary for him prior to his meeting with the client. It would include a summary of the assessment, working diagnosis and my impressions. We would then discuss it as a background for his assessment. He wanted a description, not 30 pages of assessment. This process required me to think through the consumer's situation which provided a deeper insight into the consumer's needs.

Reflective Listening

(Although this section might have been in the skills section of this book, it is also relevant to attitudinal learning.) Reflective listening is a powerful set of skills that shows the speaker that you are hearing what they say and are trying to understand what they feel about it. If communication is a doorway to understanding, asking the person for closed-ended 'yes'/'no' responses is more like a door that doesn't open. Reflective responses fed back to the speaker opens the door and invites the speaker to clarify their point, if needed, and continue on.

Reflective listening responses can be simple in construction. There are two parts to reflect back - content and feeling. The clinician simply restates the content of what the speaker has said, usually paraphrasing it. The clinician then also acknowledges the *feeling* attached to what was conveyed. This may be understood through the speaker's words, facial expressions, body language or emotion in the voice (E.g. "I'm *fed up* with...").

The speaker who disclosed the issue benefits from hearing back both their content and feelings. It gives them a fresh perspective as well as a sense that they are getting their message across and that the listener understands them. If the feedback reflected is not quite what the speaker was saying, it gives them a chance to correct the clinician. It the clinician got it right, the speaker can move on to the next point with added confidence in the clinician. This is a very powerful skill in assessment and will add to the consumer's sense of connectedness.

Biopsychosocial Background and History taking

The narrative assessment may start with gathering biopsychosocial information. Upon being asked a question about their early life, some clients will start at the beginning of their developmental history and lead the narrative sequentially right through to the present. Some will give high levels of detail which will require of the clinician to use sensitive communication skills in directing the flow.

Some will focus on major aspects and leave out important considerations. For example, if you ask a person about their childhood, and they focus on the strict discipline at home by their parents, your general awareness of development may prompt you to ask about what they were good at, how their relationships with their siblings were, and if they enjoyed learning, sports or the social aspect of schooling. A useful question can be to ask if they faced any major challenges.

I generally ask about personal and family history, in-

cluding:
- Family of Origin history including economic, physical and mental health history
- Developmental impacts and coping style with disruptions when needed
- Geographic and cultural background and social change
- Social confidence and happiness
- Education –> school –> employment? When did you stop? Were you happy about it?
- Relationships and grief and loss
- Their own family
- Spirituality and religion
- Hobbies and interests

As you work in a district you will probably develop insights into local history, and this can be extremely useful as part of your searching question style. For example, here in the Snowy Mountains, many older people were part of the original Snowy Mountains Hydroelectric Scheme. Some consumers I worked with gave interesting personal insights of being part of the Scheme, which developed the narrative of assessment by giving me clues and hints to unusual, subtle perspectives about their world view. (I coincidentally had previously written an amateur community theatre production about the Scheme, and was able to understand the background of how difficult it was in a historical sense.)

The goal of the biopsychosocial narrative assessment is to assess the person in a way that is understanding about their baseline personal and social functioning (i.e. Recovery focussed). Exploring this allows strength-based assessment, not just snapshots of pathology. It can lay the foundation for understanding the person's usual coping strategies, the application of developmental life-stage perspectives (E.g. Erikson/ Recovery/ Meaning/ Bereavement) and reveal much about the person's sense of empowerment, their grief and loss journey, and their approach to dilemmas.

The contrast between the biopsychosocial model and a diagnostic medical model is that person-centred, recovery-aware, culturally appropriate care is underpinned as the clinician attempts to understand the perspective of the consumer.

Assumptions (Example: Literacy & Ageism)

An example of the benefits of narrative assessment is seen in appreciating the impact of early-life education on the adult's baseline, through understanding the varying standards of education available to children of earlier generations, eras and cultures. In our region, many children had little education, or left education before they developed higher literacy and numeracy skills.

This is an issue particularly affecting MSE of older people, especially where a cognitive test is applied involving literacy and numeracy. If a cognitive test is blind to baseline literacy and numeracy factors, an incorrect result may follow, for the cognitive test is mostly applied in search of indications of declines in ability and function. When the person's baseline picture is affected by the fact that they simply never had the education, poor scores in literacy/numeracy tasks cannot be taken as evidence of recent cognitive decline.

Also, many people carry a deep sense of shame and inadequacy over literacy and try to hide their low literacy levels. This in turn can lead to a great deal of internal tension about being assessed, adding to a sense of powerlessness. A narrative assessment would have taken into account the person's lack of education and worked sensitively around those issues.

Without clarity, sensitivity, skill, knowledge and reflection, a long-term picture of poor literacy is a great example of how assumption bias could confound good assessment, and how a lack of critical thinking could effectively be ageism on the basis of a blinding assumption that cognitive decline is *the* cause of a poor score on literacy-based questions. The Recovery-aware clinician will have openness to critically deeper perspectives.

Assumptions (Example: Depression and Admission to Aged Care)

Without a Recovery focus, acute mental health wards might prioritise risk management over the establishment of connection. Aged care residential services may likewise cause a parallel result during admission – disconnection at a time of great need.

Older people enter residential nursing care often in periods of crisis and loss. Losses may include the loss of independence and autonomy, and deep changes to family relationships. Quite often this period is of course characterised by anxiety and depression, and a connection may be particularly helpful. Adjustments to grief and loss, otherwise known as bereavement, is a process

– adjustment doesn't happen instantly, and one of the key helps is to have someone to talk it over with.

Yet new residents often enter a system where the adjustment to care is overlooked on the basis of ageist assumptions about permanence of symptoms. Specifically, I have heard it said that a new resident is "just old and depressed". During this transitional, loss-laden period I have seen disinterest and even hostility in care staff and neglect of sufficient counselling and support by nursing home management. As a compromise, the majority of older people find themselves put on anti-depressants as an almost automatic response, and these medications are very often never reviewed, even if the crisis passes.

The reluctance to fund counselling services to nursing home residents while almost everyone else in the community can access counselling can be seen as a failure to support recovery oriented practice. Happily, the Medicare bulk-billing/claiming website appears to have removed a question asking if the person for whom the claim is being made is in nursing care - a systematic improvement. This is a massive opportunity to help people in their transition, perhaps without additional medication which can effect health adversely and in some instances be considered heavy-handed or even a *chemical restraint*.

Connectedness and Covid-19

Never before have I heard of "social distancing" expressed as a positive value - to me it is co-linear with agoraphobia (fear of the marketplace). All that mental health services usually do involves recognition of the healthiness of human community contact, and resilience in the face of a threat.

Naturally, when there is a disease there has long been the principle of quarantine but this is usually imposed on the ill, not the rest of the community. It feels unnatural to drive everyone apart, to have new boundaries where isolation is the goal, and where political leaders have used fear and shame to reinforce normal social intercourse.

Depending on your beliefs about the adequacy and the need that drive systemic Covid responses, no-one should deny that fear, shame and coercion runs counter to normal approaches to social cohesion and wellbeing in almost every sense.

Within two days I heard two seperate accounts from astute leaders (a Clinical Nurse Consultant - Aged Care, and a leader of a community organisation) whose stories were remarkably similar. Both have mothers who are leaders in their communities, holding up others, doing charitable work, reading and studying. Both conveyed that their respective mothers had finally met defeat due to isolation during Covid-19. Both remarked on the health impacts of the loss of freedom, and alluded to the depressive nature of their circumstances.

If government showed due care about the most vulnerable people they were trying to save, they would recognise the sense of defeat people are enduring and make much greater efforts to address this.

I believe that in years to come, we will attribute many issues to the mismanagement rendered in this era. It has been a backward step in terms of reform values in the care and mental health care of older people. Sadly many who die in isolation due to Covid restrictions will not be able to speak for themselves on the deprivation of family being allowed to be with them at the end, but many family members are speaking out against government policy and nursing home mismanagement of care during the final hours of their loved one's life.

In the competition for media airtime this has been reported mostly during the recognition of the issues at the Royal Commission, but it has largely gone unreported. Some family members have allegedly been silenced by a bereavement payment that effectively restricted the families from speaking with the media about the care their loved one received. However my feeling is that the issue is widely recognised but poorly reported in the media.

Promoting connectedness

> What can I as a clinician do to help protect or improve a consumer's sense of 'Connectedness'?

Connectedness is a reason why places like the "Men's Shed" can have a positive impact on people's mental health. Maintaining social engagement provides benefit in living long and living well, and clinicians can therefore promote health by encouraging social engagement.

Social disengagement is a risk factor of depression and in dementia, but often one that older people don't choose voluntarily. Life is hard to predict, and many older people find themselves facing these challenges on their own. Feelings of isolation may be triggered in many contexts: during bereavement; loss of physical independence; or starting retirement. Many older people endure a lack of connectedness in their life, particularly as they lose friends, loved ones or when they enter care.

There are many aspects of care by services that can prevent, diminish or destroy the consumer's sense of connectedness. Issues may include:
- lack of consumer input,
- poor accessibility to supports,
- *a sense of* lack of informed consent about e.g. medication in nursing care,
- the way people move through services, sometimes feeling propelled from one to another
- an absence of awareness about Advanced Care Directives and unaddressed fears about living on life support with no quality of life.

Although the clinician's engagement is often brief, the style of engagement can certainly reduce or magnify feelings of disconnection. For instance, a clinician who understands the historical stigma of mental health care and appears warm, genuine, receptive, respectful and transparent can better connect with the consumer. Further, how the clinician asks for the consumer's point of view, listens, and works to answer difficult questions all are aspects of connective practice. Like it or not, you are in a position of power when you serve someone as a professional. When that contact results in a feeling of shared trust, healing is enabled.

Ronnie the Magic Red Garden Gnome

One of the best responses to Covid isolation amongst the elderly I have ever heard of occurred in our small town's retirement village. The care manager, part of a theatre group, enrolled seniors in her care in a humorous film-making project. The short movies feature "Ronnie the Magic Red Garden Gnome" who goes about the village helping the residents address the problems they are having during isolation.

During the lockdown, and obeying social distancing, the care manager filmed the willing residents having conversations with Ronnie about their needs and experiences. Ronnies voice was dubbed in later. A lot of fun was had, with an emphasis on resilience and problem solving.

Eventually the residents had the chance to see the eight movies and much joy was added to their lives by this creative connection. It was beautiful to see.

HOPE AND OPTIMISM ABOUT THE FUTURE

The lady, sitting opposite looked downcast. By the end of the assessment it was clear the experience had been difficult for her. She had psychotic symptoms of depression that were happening all the time, especially when she was alone, but the acknowledgement of them during assessment seemed to make her feel even worse about herself.

Dr Williams tenderly said "Try not to worry too much. I think we can help."

She looked at him.

He continued: "I suppose it's difficult for you to see right now, but there is hope."
He often spoke about hope to consumers. Hope, in this case, was 100% accurate as the woman responded well to antidepressants and eventually returned home.

According to older people in my user surveys, hope is a Recovery value that many regard as important to their recovery. For example, they "hope to be around for their grandchildren", they "hope to get help" with illness, and "hope to be allowed to stay at home".

> How do *you* promote Hope in Older Persons Mental Health care? How do you promote Hope in an Aged Care facility? Do your own features display hope or a lack of it?

Optimism is a wonderful strength when facing adversity. Generations of people who have lived through so much, often understand much about the power of hope. Many older people cherish songs from WWII, such as "Pack up your troubles in your old kit bag and smile, smile, smile", and their values have been shaped by surviving difficult times. Sure, a lot of people died in the war, however the cultural value of hope was a well trusted foundation.

In depression, optimism or the lack thereof is part of the central issue. Optimism can be infectious, can be part of the solution, and can motivate someone to take steps to look after themselves and take responsibility for their own wellbeing.

If a clinician can see hope, this optimism can transfer to the consumer. Deeper depression including organic depression might prevent the consumer from being able to identify or accept hope. In these cases, it may not be fair to ask for too much hope when the consumer can't see it.

This is where the medical model comes into its own, as the allied clinician and the psychogeriatrician support the process of finding a medical response. That is – even when the consumer is bereft of hope and optimism, the hope of the health professional is essential in finding an answer. There are many occasions where the strongest of psychotic symptoms of depressive illness have been successfully treated and within a short time the person has regained their life and their independence.

Many older people have already processed and resolved what younger people often avoid thinking about (e.g. their mortality), and still manage to live with hope. It is important that the OPMH clinician tunes in to the personal ways hope works.

Be genuine, because they will know. Hope is *not* based on false hope. Belief in a possibility of recovery does not mean a stubborn unrealistic belief that the person will enjoy 100% clinical recovery. This is extremely important in OPMH due to the high incidence of factors such as chronic illness, heavy grief and loss, and dementia.

Sometimes hope is enabled in a person simply by giving them the opportunity to reflect upon the realities of their position. Once they have explained it to you and you have used your reflective skills to feed back what they have said, they can process and move on from what specifically was bothering them. This adjustment may allow whatever resilience and sense of hope they possess to resurface. Likewise, the broader process of clinical treatment can help them regain their intrinsic hope.

Hope in Context

Working in OPMH you will hopefully get used the way older people have processed their own mortality. At your own age and stage, you may still be quite unable to relate to death and dying. When the person adjusts to their situation; you may be surprised at how matter-of-fact they can be about these issues. I certainly have gained perspectives about these issues, including acceptance and a view about the 'circle of life'.

I remember discussing with a lady in a nursing home about how she felt. She was dying and she knew it. Without any particular religious beliefs, the beautiful lady remarked that she was "not long for this world." Over the conversation we reflected on the circle of life, as visible in a garden, and how a preceding generation of flowers must, under the natural order of things, fade, but that the next generation blooms in their place. We discussed how it has always been that way, and why it might be so. She looked out the window at nature, and a tear came to her eye, and she smiled.

While we talked, the processing she was able to do around that viewpoint also gave me perspective about her mood and mental state. The tiredness she felt and any physical discomfort could have also contributed to her depression, but she was able to discuss such concepts which helped me form a picture about her insight that I shared with the psychogeriatrician during handover.

Ageism assumes hopelessness.

An ageist assumption such as 'older people naturally

get depressed' leads to possible exclusion from treatment and care. In my experience, these are not people who, as a whole, have simply given up any hope. Having worked with older people moving through bereavement as they process loss and adjust to their new life, I have admired their bravery in the face of suddenly having, for example, to live alone.

There are many ways older people live in hope: They may focus on their grandchildren and their future; hope of better medication; hope for help with chronic illness, and relief from pain. Sometimes their spiritual perspectives contribute much to their resilience against loss.

> "Recovery may require assistance from individuals with specialised knowledge, but fundamentally it requires the maintenance of hope: by the person, their family and carers. And when that hope requires building up, an older person with mental illness requires support from professionals with knowledge and skills in working with older people, and an ability to 'come alongside' them." (NSW Health, 2017, p7)

It is possible to improve, adjust and regain hope in retirement, chronic illness, mental illness, and in grief and loss. The kind clinician is an important link to these processes of resolution and should portray hope. In entry into involuntary psychogeriatric care, transition to a nursing home, or asking about choices of late-life care, hope is key to Recovery, and the clinician can and must support hope.

Some older people may have quite an abrasive persona, but the experienced clinician may perceive that this is linked to their hope to handle their difficulties on their own. Many times older people come to be seen as annoyingly persistent in their quest for help (*their way*), sometimes seeming intransigent and inflexible. There can indeed be stubborn hope at the core of this, which should be recognised from a *strength-based perspective*. They haven't given up speaking for themselves.

Hope under a Life-Stage Developmental Model

In the discussion of Erikson's life stage model (later, below), a sense of despair may develop when the person moves from 'Generativity v. Stagnation' into a life review stage of 'Ego-Integrity v. Despair'. Erikson framed 'Ego-Integrity v. Despair' as a very different crisis than simply worrying about getting old and dying, or 'old-age depression'.

If the person does not have a sense that they have been productive in their life, or they focus on lost opportunities through guilt or grief etc, then their personal sense of integrity is compromised and they are left with despair. This is a developmental perspective with cumulative impacts.

Counselling can help the person reprocess their view of achievements. Self-critical assumptions can be drawn out and re-examined, comparative to how the person might critique a young person facing similar dilemmas. Empathy for the person's ignorance at a younger age, recognising the impact of life events on their development and choices, and a philosophical perspective can flesh-out reflective processes. A person may be enabled to revisit old 'failures' and reframe outcomes of previous crises with added value perspectives, reflective support and empathy. This can lead to increased self-respect, and a more complete sense of Ego-Integrity.

For example, a man who is embittered about having to retire, when his business partner (in the man's view) acted deceptively to edge him out of the business, may eventually adjust! Counselling may help him process his losses, explore values about his delight in more time with his grandchildren, and identify strategies for him to socially engage with the community. This is an example of Recovery-based support, integrating hope.

Communication and Hope at Work

> *"Narrative assessment creates hope that someone is actually listening…"*
> (OPMH nurse clinician, Wangaratta)

The narrative format strengthens not only connectedness, but hope, as consumers begin to see clinicians as open, transparent, responsive, interested and caring. However, communication is not just a skill you turn on for clients – a communicative person brings a positive attitude to their work.

When the clinician is fully engaged, hope is embedded with communication in many aspects of the role, and can involve the wider shared-care approach to its fullest potential, including:

- Being honest and transparent with consumers,
- Asking them about their views and feelings, and respecting the answers

- Networking and writing to doctors and other allied health professionals including dieticians, OT's etc, to help find solutions
- Having your assessments ready for the visiting psychogeriatrician
- Communicating with family and carers

You may be seen as positive, effective and supportive within your team, or alternately, sometimes you can feel very disconnected in remote and rural practice (as sometimes you are!) One can feel disconnected anywhere, even when sitting with your team at morning meetings. It can be unavoidable at times.

Often you may come across consumers, families, colleagues, doctors, management and systems whose views, style, interpersonal politics, or personalities cause you to struggle internally. At these times the clinician needs to look after their own 'bucket' of hope. Cynicism as well as hopefulness can cross-infect not only clients but also other team members.

There will of course be moments when the caring clinician feels the limits of their own hope being challenged, as is natural and unavoidable in our profession. These moments require careful consideration, and there is research and advice available about managing the sometimes overwhelming nature of our work. There are techniques we should employ, such as:

- Carefully attending to the self, how you feel, and knowing the warning signs of burnout – such as sleep problems, thinking about clients on the weekend, avoiding watching the news etc.
- Nurturing boundaries and the ability to switch off from work

- Get supervision
- Forward plan so that you are not feeling trapped, but growing within and sometimes out of your current position

The coordinated approach is the best hope of actually helping the consumer, and it is important to remain engaged, client focussed and positive toward your colleagues, the health system and most importantly the consumer and supportive networks. It is important, even when working in rural/ remote locations, to see yourself as part of a team. A commitment to team involves developing a positive, assertive style. Knowing how to communicate with respect – and knowing what is expected of you, is a big part of it.

In contrast, the clinician who is bogged down in feelings of inadequacy, frustration and negativity is possibly showing signs of burnout, and needs to attend to their own professional and personal progress so they can deliver appropriate, hopeful services to consumers.

Person-centred care can mean you occasionally push the boundaries of your normal area of work and open up communication channels with new players that can help. Many health services suffer from operating as '*silos*', but the more you integrate with those outside your team, such as GP's, nursing home staff etc, the better the chance of making a difference.

One communication skill that busy services rely on is the ISBAR model, that is designed to help an assessor give a timely and concise handover to the team. ISBAR was developed (as SBAR) for timely sharing of brief, of critical information on board submarines, and has become adapted to health. It is worth learning how to do ISBAR and practising it to know how to convey what is necessary, briefly and concisely. ISBAR stands for Introduction, Situation, Background, Assessment and Recommendation. It is not narrative in style, but depends on the clinician having made a proper and full assessment. Its structured approach can be useful in handover and circumvent a lot of conflict in the team. Brevity – concise communication – can be effective in getting the point across, without taking a defensive stance.

It is your role to be respectfully proactive when you see a need. It can take a lot of courage, but you can't ignore it and remain effective, as unaddressed structural frustrations lead to burnout. It is important you know your boundaries, but boundaries run both ways, and dilemmas, conflicts and varying perspectives will occur.

During the research phase of preparing this book, it was observed that some OPMH workplaces lean heavily on the views of the visiting psychogeriatrician with little autonomy of other supporting clinicians. As expressed by one clinician:

"In a way the overuse of the psychiatrists … disempowers the clinicians to actually make clinical observations…" (see Appendix 1)

Don't give up hope of changing things. If your views are guided by consumers, carers, research and by principles, the best way forward involves advocacy, finding common ground, and sometimes, surrender with dignity and humour.

That is not to say that in every instance the responsibility of good communication only lies with you. Maybe others – or you – are having a bad day. Or maybe the issues go deeper because people (and systems) suffer from inertia.

Supervision can help, but essentially the responsibility sits with you to respond well, for the sake of positive changes you bring about, and for your learning. Knowledge of your role (including theory, models, and reform processes in Mental Health) builds a foundation to work from. You also have to balance discretion with passion and integrity, which pivots on good communication. As discussed above, this involves hope, an essential part of Recovery.

HOPE AND THE IMPACT OF ILLNESS

The evidence from Daley et al and also from my own Recovery-based satisfaction surveys broadly links 'Impact of Illness' as important to Recovery ideas in older people.

Most people in my satisfaction survey seem to equate this question with physical illness – (probably related to the fact that the majority of my counselling clients experiencing mild-to-moderate issues in their mental, not meeting the "Illness" threshold in mental health.)

Some older persons with chronic pain and illness answered that their mental health issues would disappear if they could find an answer to their physical problems. This led me to wonder about the meaning of Chronic Illness in Recovery. The diagram below is a representation of the overlap of conceptual frameworks that might contribute to the development of an adequate OPMH Recovery model.

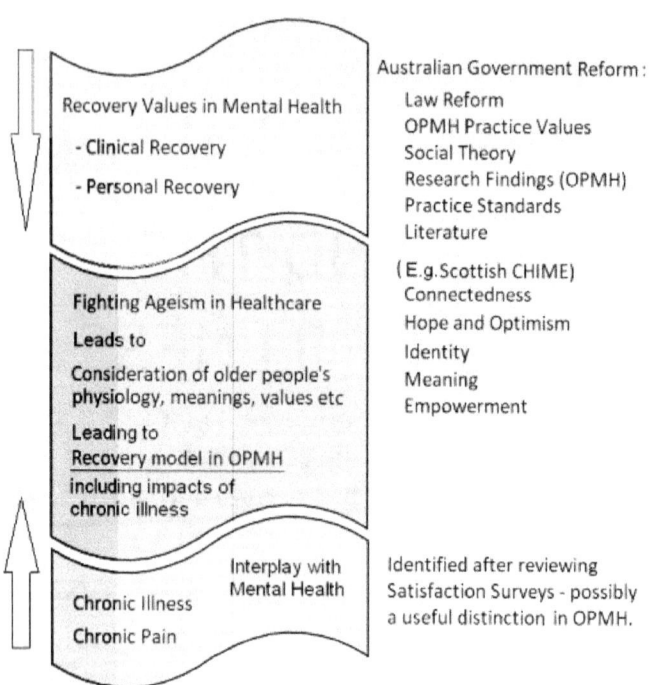

Figure 4: Recognising Chronic Health Impacts in OPMH Recovery

However not all older people were equally interested in Impact of Illness in my surveys – those who were relatively fit and well physically did not score this value particularly highly. I also noticed that younger adult age-groups were equally interested in this value where their situation involved chronic illness, meaning that chronic illness can impact on Recovery at any age.

This value is likely linked to the reason that most OPMH clinicians and specialists I have met talk about the importance of holistic practice. Health problems, old injuries and chronic pain impact the mental health of many older people. The assessment therefore needs to identify physical wellness issues as relevant to treatment, coordinated planning and care. Where there is an unfulfilled need that the clinician identifies, referrals to other health specialities need to be made if OPMH is truly integrated.

For example, I have often heard consumers remark that their basket of pills is like a "shopping trolley", or that they "rattle when they walk". Lack of review, longitudinal drug interactions and side effects, quality of life issues, and drug effectiveness are some of the issues that might impact on the consumer's mental and overall health. The Recovery-based assessment incorporating a broad awareness of holistic health factors will explore what the person with chronic issues is hoping for and if a medication review (in this example) might lead to improved outcomes for the consumer.

Hope during Covid-19

The main hope presented by the government seems to be measured in their hope of avoiding death. It is a whole of society view, but it is not complete. Many older people, already struggling with health problems, loss of autonomy and loneliness are going to need extra hope during this period, for quality of life to be strengthened through compassion, contact and hope. Instead, fear seems to have taken the place of hope.

Authorities hope to contain the spread of the disease, but fear of disease is an anxiety. Can the two coexist? This is a dilemma. To fulfil the hope of government for safety, the authorities have taken the approach of eliminating social and family contact. The one thing that many elders hope for - time with family before they die - is eliminated by the exclusion approach to the problem. Naturally, time for important moments is of the essence when you are in your senior years and your health problems are getting worse. With contact displaced, therefore time is stolen: What would people have left to hope for?

I am sure some carers, nursing homes and services have tried very hard to understand the issues and come up with better solutions, but in reality, conversations have been lacking around this issue. The WHO site, for example, had a pictorial info sheet about how to talk to children about Covid-19, and also one for the general population, but nothing to facilitate conversation on how to talk to the elderly, who were the ones locked away.

We know that there are many factors that could be considered in relation to this complex issue:
- Health and care workers who contracted the virus and passed infection to people in their care.
- Families, including young children are unlikely to spread the virus, being carte-blanc excluded from visiting.
- The risk of transmission is lower outdoors, and sunshine kills germs and strengthens the immune system.
- The importance of free choice in medical care, a time-honoured legal principle.

Failure to consider these kind of factors has had a disastrous effect on hope. It is not that quarantine is unnecessary, it is that hope is a primary consideration and even a duty of care that has been woefully neglected during the chaos of the pandemic.

On the other hand, I saw examples of person-centred

care that contributed to the hope experienced by the elderly. Applying actual care and thought to care management has made the pandemic more manageable on the part of care providers. Of course, the for-profit model of nursing care puts extra strain on the care workers making it unfeasible for them to assess and tap into the hope, an opportunity in many cases forever missed.

Hope in Dementia

When people become aware of early changes in their mental capacity, it can cause them great anxiety and upset. However, to a degree, these changes can be processed as a loss (bereavement) event which allows a hope of adaptation.

If people want to talk about what is happening to them they should be responded to. Unfortunately there are barriers to providing a detailed picture to them about their illness. Firstly, dementia is a complex thing and there is no definite timeline against which the person can prepare. Secondly, dementia is so complex that it requires expert knowledge to discuss these types of issues sensitively and accurately, knowledge usually beyond the level of a mental health clinician. However, where these questions exist, the clinician still has a role. Reflectively feeding back to the consumer about what their question is and how they feel about it, provides hope that someone is hearing them. Offer them a promise to follow up on their concern with (or through) the specialist.

When someone has questions in assessment, it is very important to note them down for discussion with the psychogeriatrician or clinical leader. It is ok to say,

"That's an (interesting/important/great) question.", or "I don't know but I can ask someone who has a much deeper understanding of these things." This may very much please the person and can be a good way of introducing the specialist to the client.

People with dementia can go on reasonably well for many years which helped me realise the importance of *hope* in these types of issues. Additionally, experience teaches that helping the person to focus on the *now* can in fact free the person to cope. This should not come across as paternalistically telling someone not to worry, ideally. I find being transparent is an honest way of connecting in these issues. Observing strengths that exist in the now and the simple reality of things the person can enjoy is part of this process.

Sometimes a person's distress is functionally set within their physical brain changes. It may require be some time before further brain changes alter their apparent symptoms of distress. Speaking to families and carers about the often transitory nature of these stages sometimes help them cope.

Holistic assessment

It is tempting sometimes to think of mental health and physical health as separate; however mental health is integrated with physical health on many levels. A holistic focus in mental health takes into account changes in the body, particularly in the physical and functional brain. In practical terms this can mean being aware of possible physical problems that trigger mental health issues.

As Dr Williams taught: "The brain *is* the body, the body

is the brain! There is no separation." That gave me a lot to think about. He emphasised that the systems are so completely integrated they are one unified system – the person. Many health professionals forget the value of holistic assessment, potentially to the detriment of the consumer.

I have observed that psychogeriatric assessment is leading the way for prioritising holistic assessment compared to other divisions of mental health. Psychogeriatricians always wanted as much medical history, recent blood screenings and if indicated, CT scans as could be accumulated prior to their visits. More so than in general psychiatry, people's health is seen as having a big impact on mental health. Holistic assessment should be promoted as a value, beyond Older Persons Mental Health.

In one instance a woman I assessed had some subtle signs of depression with psychotic features of a type that seems to be common in OPMH. She was calm and conversant, but had had some fixed ideas about the plumbing being broken and the water tainted, and that she was thereby poisoned with arsenic. The plumbing had been checked by the family and the water tested with no significant results. The issues of her delusional ideas seemed annoying to her family, but not further acknowledged as significant. However, after a time she became convinced that she couldn't eat. No medical basis could be identified for her lack of appetite. She appeared very thin and had been losing weight. My plan involved referral to a dietician, who arranged protein drinks and helped educate the client and family about the risks of losing any more weight. The aversion to eating appeared to be putting her close to serious risk to her health, as confirmed conversation between the dietician and the GP. Perhaps a less visible risk profile in general psychiatry, where younger patients are perhaps more physically robust, the risks caused by such nihilistic delusions are intensified the more frail the person.

Within this scenario, there were differences of opinion with the consumer and their family about whether the issue was one of mental health, stomach health, or plumbing. Nobody was talking about grief and loss.

The local GP in the small nearby town had been away a lot over this period, making medical support inconsistent. At various presentations to various hospital units, including the general inpatient unit 150km away, MHECS general triage personnel would hear the competing issues and struggle to understand if the patient was right about the plumbing or if the diet issue constituted threshold risk, with inconsistent treatment outcomes. The consumer was pleasant and persistent, and somewhat convincing. Eventually the SMHSOP role was most useful in the liaison of services.

My invitation to involve the dietician was seen as strange by both primary consumer and family, and the invitation to assessment with the psychogeriatrician were initially declined, but mental health as a theme became gradually accepted. There were consequences if the family didn't support the strong views of the consumer, and they themselves were very dubious about mental health services in general. To understand illness is to undertake holistic practice including mind, physical and emotional health – as well as the social constraints that can inform thinking about these issues.

The nihilistic delusions (See Williams, 2017, p. 474, ref. 33) had developed after the death of her spouse and the woman gradually revealed feelings of self-blame for his passing. My involvement only really went to assessment with some case management as suicidal thoughts subsequently developed and she went to general inpatient care – which may have included antidepressants and antipsychotics in combination or ECT to help manage depression, the psychotic delusions and also help preserve her overall health.

Evidence-based values

I came across strongly held alternative health ideas early in my SMHSOP experience. To sort out conflicting perspectives, loved-ones, and also the primary consumer's ideas of health management should be acknowledged and treated with due respect, however "Decisions are based on evidence; knowledge of the consumer, their social context and the consumer's own experience; *and* clinical judgement" (NSW Health, 2017). We will have differences of opinion from time to time about best practice.

In my experience, when a family seems entrenched or even stubborn about their ideas and that these perspectives may be negatively impacting the consumer, the opening up of honest, respectful communication over these issues can provide the best way forward. In the scenario above, the woman declined my services, but by then the family had accepted that her body-weight issue was critical. When she later declined even the protein shakes and lost more weight, they saw the risks I had detected and asked for an admission to inpatient care. In other words, her family were educated about the risks which she was unable to manage at that time, and they trusted me because I had shown enough respect for their various ideas. I had reviewed the complex issues with the psychogeriatrician.

(I must say the busy psychogeriatrician was placed in a tricky situation and only able to give limited support over the phone, as it wasn't his role to be my clinical leader, and he frankly hadn't met the consumer. I suppose this type of challenge is common to rural / remote work.)

Within Recovery it needs to be recognised that the consumer has rights, and that dilemmas about what care can be applied comes down to informed consent and the right to accept or decline medical care. Duty of care includes a question of whether the person is mentally ill to a degree that they can't be said to have the ability / capacity to consent to or refuse treatment. Where there are definite risks, rights need to be balanced with duty of care.

Assessment in Progress: Proceed with Caution

It is vital to avoid developing fixed ideas about signs and symptoms too early in the assessment process, which may blind the clinician to other very important factors. For example, the MSE stage of the assessment *is not* about rushing to a provisional diagnosis - so don't 'jump the gun'! Spend the necessary time observing.

It is the psychogeriatrician who will make the authorised, formal diagnosis, if necessary, or to support or refine the diagnosis already given (e.g. by a GP). Mental health clinicians are generally expected to form a provisional diagnosis as *a working premise* at the conclusion of their assessment. As your knowledge grows, you may see patterns of signs and symptoms that will trigger ideas for exploration and intervention during assessment. However it remains problematic to form opinions too early in the assessment process.

In particular, clinicians should be ever sensitive if attempting to convey to a primary consumer and their carers a diagnosis – speaking too early and without specialist support may cause undue confusion and suffering. Humility and professionalism dictate that the good clinician is always learning. While your studies and books like this one may be a *starting point* in learning, as the clinician progresses they will gain knowledge from research and articles on many issues, through discussions with psychogeriatricians and clinical leaders, or through reading journal articles.

The cumulative effect of supporting the 'Understanding Illness' value touches on Connectedness and Empowerment, however I see it as a key to the Recovery value of 'Hope'. Having a sense of what is happening to you may open the door to acceptance. It does not need to be an overly technical understanding, but I think it does need to be earnestly the best available information, authoritatively sourced and sensitively delivered. The psychogeriatrician is responsible for that process, but the OPMH clinician will have a role in answering questions, seeking out answers, and letting the consumer feel that their questions are important.

IDENTITY

"When I get better I'm going shopping. I will wear my red dress – because I can"

- A quote from a lady being assessed prior to an inpatient stay.

The older person's sense of self has been in development for a relatively long time – a life time. The agendas that drive younger people, such as worries and aspirations about working toward careers and families are often behind them. The older person remains after all life has thrown at them - failures and victories - with a sense of *their* belonging, identity and culture. The sum total of their lived experience, culture and their physicality contributes to their sense of identity.

> The man being assessed had been working in the Forestry all his life, since finishing high school early. He now lived among the plantations on

> a private block, surrounded by the pines. In the narrative of the assessment it was clear that he quietly enjoyed his working life.
>
> Dr Williams reflected this back to him and the man agreed. His life's work had been vital to him. Now that he was unable to work due to emphysema, it was a major impact on him. Did identity contribute to this assessment of his mental health? Most definitely.
>
> How does the mental health clinician respect, work with and help the person gain from their sense of identity? In older people, what value is there in helping someone in "Getting back to me"?

One of the greatest gifts older people can give to the younger generations is the very fact of their presence – that they have survived so much and have simply come through – often learning and developing much as a person in the process, even in the presence of hardship and trauma. While it is sometimes disregarded or overlooked, older people often seem to have the edge over the young in this aspect. In some ways older people may seem stubborn, but this can be linked to a lifetime of learning what works for them and what can be disregarded (right or wrong), including medical care.

> We were discussing an assessment in the car as we drove away. To me, the woman looked like she'd been exercising a uniquely high level of power and control over her husband all their life.

The man had allowed or enabled certain of these behaviours, as he seemed to live in fear of her. At this point though, the separation of the two that had occurred as one of them had entered nursing care precipitated some borderline trays in the wife. When I mentioned about the crisis possibly bringing about adaptation with support, Dr Williams said "I think that dice was rolled a long time ago."
This was not judgemental, in my view, but acceptance of who they became long ago.

IDENTITY: RECOVERY OF SELF

Possibly connected to this long-established sense of identity, common Recovery values may need to be nuanced for older people – which is ok because Recovery should be individually focussed anyway.

Whereas younger people, when talking about Recovery tend to talk about discovering more about themselves or redefining their identity according to the changes that they have experienced post illness, older people may tend to focus on restorative aspect of their identity to as it was before: "Getting back to me" seems to have more traction than "Discovering the new me". Within the CHIME model, Identity is defined as "Regaining a positive sense of self and identity, overcoming stigma and being recognised as a whole person – rather than being defined by illness or diagnosis..." This probably accounts to the way many older people *tolerate* health care.

To improve the user experience, services and clinicians need critical awareness of themselves and their practices. Some important areas of identity that clinicians need to become aware of include age-related thinking and culturally sensitive practice.

Ageing and Ageism

As mentioned earlier, Ageism is really a position of ignorance and an often silent rationale for compromises in the quality of care. It can be systematic, and it can have a huge impact on assessment.

I recall a case where an older patient had been transported by ambulance back and forth from a remote local hospital to an acute inpatient unit three times before he was offered treatment consistent with his mental health symptoms. There were no psychogeriatric beds at that stage in the district, and the patient was denied admission to the general inpatient unit, firstly on the suggestion of dementia, next on the basis of delirium, with the suggestion that local medical treatment was the priority.

The nursing staff at the local didn't understand how to negotiate the issues. However, once the right questions were pulled together in the right way, and the bloods came back clear, and yet another mental health assessment completed, an inpatient admission could not be denied. (This is an example of the liaison role and an advocacy role for the OPMH).

There are certainly nuances to assessing older people. Acute psychiatric illness in older people may look 'low risk' in the eyes of an acute intake team, when in fact the person is extremely unwell and at risk in ways that might not be immediately recognisable. The particular sensitivities of the older body and vulnerabilities facing older people can mean the rules have to change, because to offer an inferior level of care to an entire class of people equates to Ageism. Transporting them back and forth without treatment *can* itself trigger delirium in older people, and can add confusion to diagnosis.

Ageism and its effect on assessment

You may have heard the term 'Ageist' or 'Ageism', and these are particularly hazardous to the assessment process. We are not necessarily talking about blatant discrimination– it's also a subtle problem that can creep into work with older people.

I find I have an internal signal - I react internally when care, hospital or MH staff routinely use terms such as "just old", "going downhill" and "getting a bit doddery" as cover-all explanations of mental health issues. It becomes clear when doing the MSE that age-related generalisations gloss over a multitude of observable indicators of potentially treatable problems.

There are of course common problems associated with ageing, and the clinician must carefully assess the mental state and narrative history and do their best to come up with a working hypothesis. Narrative assessment helps us form an idea about whether the person's behaviour and mental state are perhaps an amplification of their long-term personality, or alternately a radical departure from anything they have ever done before. In either case, we need to try to see clearly what it is happening.

Conceptualising Aging

As a kid I watched a science fiction movie called Logan's Run, where people were ceremonially disintegrated in a pretty shower of sparkles on their 30th

birthday, for 'the greater good'. I suppose the question is: 'Whose greater good?' As a child, 30 seemed fairly ancient. Now, approaching 50, looking back to 30, I know I had barely even lived yet. It may shock some health providers to realise that, to a degree, rationalisation of mental health services in nursing homes, for example, is related to a 'Logan's Run' social mindset. The kind of rationality that associates age with redundancy seeks to be ignorant about the value and dignity of personhood and the desire of people of any age to live, and live well.

There are many aspects of the way we understand Ageing that inform what we feel and how we act, both personally and professionally. These are influenced by our broader world view and our life experiences. For example, (a value about older people I hold dear is that) the greatest gift an older person can give to someone of the rising generation is their stories. Stories of survival in the harshest of times bring a gift to the younger person who can then conceptualise that they can survive much worse and come through.

Another value I hold dear is that older people may have survived much and through the stages of their life adapted and came to terms with the setbacks of life – not just that they have survived, but how they have developed through the process, like a rough diamond getting their rough edges knocked off to reveal the beautiful perspective of years.

Personally, I also had training in Social Work, which contributed to my critical thinking skills and included sociology, psychology, anthropology, Australian history, law, philosophy and ethics, which all contributed to my take on the world. I was influenced by older family members and by other elders who had guided me. Some of my elders had deeply spiritual lives, while others had radical or political lifestyles, on the left and on the right.

My childhood was in the 1970's, a time of change. I had read The Gulag Archipelago by age 14, which taught me not to blindly trust big programs, and influenced me deeply. A rising awareness of the Stolen Generations also played a part in this perspective. Music, social inclusion, mental health, sexuality and economic hardship all also had their places in my chaotic formative years. Ideas of Ageing are woven into this tapestry.

As I grew I learned about my maternal grandfather's abuse of his family after his return from World War II. He had been a gentle and good father and husband before the war, but suffered from the trauma of war. When he passed away at age 82, he had by then settled down and overcame the worst of the PTSD. He had become a painter and had an incredible rose garden. On the last day of his life he got up from his deathbed and he played "Endearing Young Charms" on the violin for my mother in private. From this I learned some things about recovery, and that family love runs deeply despite the trauma.

My father also had a huge garden – a vegetable garden which helped to sustain the family during a period of unemployment, when I was young. Later in life I learned that he was a survivor of childhood sexual abuse by a Catholic priest; that his two friends were killed alongside him during the war; and that he had his successful business stolen from him by a Masonic brother prior to the above period of unemployment. He spent the later years of his quietly life working in a factory never quite getting ahead of my mother's spending habits. He was a quiet man with a sense of humour, who probably suffered the worse when he couldn't find work.

My mother was a gregarious music teacher and classical singer, who also wanted twelve children but had to settle for seven. The trauma of her early life, the health complications that crushed her dream of a *really* big family and the ensuing period of poor mental health never seemed to diminish her energy. She like my father, she was indeed a hard worker. Her impulsivity, religiosity and generosity (very often *to a fault*) caused a lot of problems for her children. But in the end, mum and dad were together. As dad's dementia set in, she was loathe to entrust his care to others, and fought to keep them together – trying to find diets to protect his brain, for example.

> What, and who have influenced your conceptualisation of ageing and older people?

All of these things can influence our conceptualisation of aging. I have noticed an optimistic bias within myself that couples can push through difficult times in their marriage that doesn't always match reality. I daresay this bias has possibly impacted negatively on a person in a marriage they were thinking of leaving. On the other hand I have understood more about people desperately and protectively seeking to maintain their loved one's health through my parent's experience.

From my grandfather, I gained perspective about the impact of the trauma of war and a man overcoming this to firmly re-establishing trust in his daughter's heart, into older age. Many ideas can help us to critically understand how we think about Ageing. Some major aspects include:

- Biological ageing, which refers to 'the' physical changes that may accompany the aging process
- Similarly, chronological ageing – the persons age in years and months, and ideas of what level of functioning 'should' be predictable on the basis this. (E.g. *'He's 95 – so he won't remember much!'*)
- Psychological aging - psychological changes that may develop. Can lead to ageism – (E.g. *assuming depression is normal and acceptable*)
- Social aging - changes to a person's roles and relationships with Ageing (E.g. *Some people may be regarded as Elders in their society*)
- Healthy aging - maintaining optimal mental, social and physical well-being and function in older adults.

These ideas of ageing interface with each other in ways that differ from person to person. It is within pre-judgement about the way these aspects interact that dangerous and unfair assumptions lay. Then there are contextual factors that influence how we think:

- Marketing messages that define ageing as negative – (E.g. the Olay ad)
- Modernist thinking, as exemplified in the nuclear family model (Dad, Mum and 2.6 kids, with Grandma in the nursing home!) This may be driven by political, ecological and economic nar-

rative that can define older people as redundant.
- Medical model thinking that defines people in terms of their ailments, life expectancy, and the availability and cost of cures for treating them. In this model, older people can be defined under such terms of 'burden of care'.
- Reformist, rights-based movements (Grey power, Recovery, Health promotion) - Valuing all people, through advocating for maximum autonomy, rights, safety, health and well-being. These drive reform of health services and community programs to prevent or minimize disease.
- Demographic and Statistical blaming and the "ageing demographic". An older person can be wrongly blamed for structural inequalities. E.g. a drop in home ownership amongst younger generations, ignoring other factors such as bank and government policies.
- Historical awareness of cultural themes around ageing – wisdom, leadership, trust, kinship, belonging and connection – particularly close to Indigenous societies, and culturally and spiritually diverse groups in society.
- Social Reform movements such as feminism and the LGBTQ movement that seek to challenge entrenched values of previous generations.
- Anti-abuse movements that seem to characterise older people as unsafe.

With all this at the back of our minds, are the elderly a burden, are they to be feared and shunned? Are they to be respected, revered and listened to? Do they consume more than they contribute, and what if they do? Do they matter as human beings?

> What if it were the first day of **your** retirement today: What might you be feeling?

Aging in Australia

We are in a period of significant growth in the number and proportion of people aged 65 years or older, with an increase from 3.7 million in 2016 to over 5.7 million by 2031. There are many people who are entering older age much fitter than before, and the majority of older people will experience good mental health (Mental Health Commission of NSW, 2017).

Older age brings with it many opportunities and challenges. There is time for interests and passions, and the unique delight, for some, of watching grandchildren grow and of spoiling them against the wishes of the children's parents. The accumulated wisdom of age can mean that life's experiences can be faced from a more philosophical perspective, and this perspective can be shared with those who one cares about, bringing a sense of role and purpose.

A positive approach to Ageing in Australia is working in health prevention/management. We know that regular exercise, good nutrition, stress reduction, involvement in personal networks, and religious involvement all enhance successful aging. "Now that we know that a substantial number of people can remain robust and healthy through their 90s, at least, that should change our attitude about old age. It is no longer a curse, but an opportunity"

(Hilts, 1999, as quoted in SOCIOLOGY: UNDERSTAND-

ING AND CHANGING THE SOCIAL WORLD (see reference)).

There are also increases of experiences of grief and loss, problems of purpose, identity and finances related to retirement, plus more free time, for better or for worse. Major problems in earlier years can lead to feelings of unfulfillment, and there are issues of ill health that can affect wellbeing. Then there are the challenges of chronic forms of mental illness, including impacts of long-term medication on the 'graduates', or survivors of long-term mental health problems and treatment. Over half of people entering Aged Care will experience depression

Evidence shows that 9.5 per cent of older Australians experience mental illness, and almost 11 per cent experience a high level of psychological distress. Overall, older people are at higher risk of "anxiety and depression, especially with a co-occurring physical illness, dementia, disability, or difficult life experiences such as bereavement, or social isolation" (Mental Health Commission of NSW, 2017), and that the highest age-specific suicide rate across all ages is observed in males 85 years or older. "Older people say that the loneliness, social isolation and stigma associated with ageing and mental illness can also impact negatively on their mental health and wellbeing."

IDENTITY: PERSPECTIVES ON AGEING

Here are some theoretical and other perspectives that can inform practice, with some interpretation according to things I have seen and felt (including pros and cons). The developmental theory of Erik Erikson is given it's own section in the chapter on Meaning.

Medical Model vs Psychosocial Theory

Under a medical model, ageing is viewed as a predictor of illness, mental impairment, poor psychological health, dependence and death. It is true that we change as we age and face challenges in these areas. Assumptions about cognitive, psychological and biological changes amount to a negative bias in medical care. There *will be changes*, but to provide services based on stereotypes is poor practice and is neither person-centred or evidence-based practice.

Under a psychosocial construct, ageing may relate to impairments, however the impairments should be addressed in an equitable society by overcoming structural bias against those with impairments. This is an opportunity to empower older people to live full and rich lives.

Disengagement

A functionalist analysis of ageing that induces older people to 'get out of the way' of younger and fitter people, and demands they be less of a burden. Retirement is an example of this, and is often a major crisis. (See 'Logan's Run').

Perhaps families who anticipate their inheritance of the family home, while their parents still live there, are thinking this way. This is a moment when the health worker should emphasise Recovery and justice principles in the care and protection of the older person. Those considered 'old-old' as opposed to 'young-old' may more likely attract discrimination along these lines, which encourages disengagement from previous roles and that they take on roles considered more appropriate to their physical and mental decline.

Activity theory

If people maintain positive perceptions of themselves and their value into old age and from this maintain activity and engagement, they will continue to be of benefit to themselves and society. This is an interactionist explanation of the aging process, a two-way responsibility where systems are needed that support engagement. I hear echoes of this when I have suggested to older men to engage in social activity such as the "Men's Shed" on the basis of data revealing participants live longer and live better.

It prompts a critical question about how a person in ill health might feel if they are expected to try to continue to live as they had when they were fit, or face further loss. We know for example that hospital care might emphasise trying to get people back on their feet to aid clinical recovery, however a man with severe depression might not receive equal encouragement.

Conflict theory

Prejudice and discrimination can occur on a person-to-person basis, but also on structural, and societal levels. That older people endure bigotry at all of these levels precipitates the conflict theory of society. It addresses power relationships and results in empowerment movements (eg 'Grey-power', and Recovery)

A common technique of discrimination is to 'otherise' people: This happens as we interpersonally and politically separate ourself from the vulnerable, to firm up our own sense of power and authority. It takes very little to turn this around if we first become aware, then listen with empathy and treat people as equals. One barrier to doing so is the threat to our own self-concept, which implies that at some level we are aware that our world view is fragile. Otherising may account for attitudes of hospital, nursing and care staff.

It can happen in any situation: I remember visiting a nursing home when a group of youth from a church were visiting. One very fashionable young lady found the whole concept of being around older people too challenging, and had to leave in discomfort. Ideas of beauty and youth are fine, as long as we can accept that, if we are lucky, we also will be old someday, and might still be beautiful. This might be a radical idea in some circles.

Life-cycle theory and life stages concepts

At different stages of life, people depend on others differently and also contribute at different levels. These stages can come full circle from birth to death, and all stages take on meaning when the entire circle of life is respected. For example, while it is unusual to resent the level of dependence of a newborn baby, many people fear becoming dependent on care toward the end of their life. However, in the circle of life, parents care for their little ones, so why should children feel different about caring for their elders in need?

I have heard people characterise the need for aged care as a signal for suicide, if they ever reach that stage (*"If I ever get like that, shoot me"*). I have asked why they feel that and have heard some say disparage the idea of becoming dependent. I asked them to consider how a newborn baby is fully dependent, but highly worthy of life and care. I was in effect asking them to challenge their thinking about the life cycle.

I feel that Life cycle theory provides a positive philosophical adaptation of ecological perspectives - that we come from nature and will return to nature, but in the mean time will provide a stewardship toward nature and society and also at times receive care from others fulfilling their stewardship.

Human ideas and behaviour change over the lifespan, with age-based and contextual expectations on individuals shifting at each stage. Also, the meaning of death and dying is individualised through personalised adaptation, choice, assertiveness and response to diversity within the life cycle. Talking about these things can become part of the therapeutic value of care. A person who dies having fulfilled their life's passion, work and mission as they define it will feel that their integrity is intact (See the section on Erikson). Certainly many older people I have known don't want to be left to die just because they have reached the latter stages of their life.

Family Systems Theory

Changes within the family unit that occur from time to time come into conflict with the 'gravitational' pull toward familiarity and sameness that gives meaning to our home and family life. This resistance to change (or, *homeostasis*) does not survive without the need for great adaptation of the unwritten rules, roles and mores of family life.

For example, when a father, who in the past was the controller of aggression between the children, suddenly dies, the unrestrained, pent-up antipathy between the children may finally escape into new family violence. This has far-reaching implications for the continuation of the family and in lives of members, as the aggression is linked to grief, possibly ignoring the great need for adaptation and healing within the family. However, bereavement is adaptation. If the family realise their ongoing need for each other, but without the conflict, the family system as a whole has adapted.

Spiritual Perspectives

Spiritual traditions may impart sensitivity concepts such as compassion, social justice, the worth of the individual, and the sanctity of life. Another major impact of spirituality is upon people's experiences of death and dying, which often defy rationalism – economic, scientific or otherwise.

None of these types of elements can be ignored without alienating actual people, and therefore decreasing the sense of connection needed in the care of older people. Societies have, in the past, tried to mandate care without respect to belief systems with terrible implications for individuals within – from intolerant theocracies to atheistic governments on the left and the right. For example; the Nazi's had an economically efficient approach to euthanasia that ran counter to the sanctity of life and the worth of the individual with disabilities.

The health worker who is able to accept and respect the diversity of human spirituality will more likely be in a position of respect and influence with the consumer. An appreciation for what a person is feeling interwoven with the consumer's beliefs, learned through a narrative approach, offers a sense of connection, and a pathway to internal processing. When it comes to grief and loss, so common among older people, this worker may link them to hope.

A client of mine who was suffering in palliative care was hanging on for months. After a conversation where this person revealed to me their fears of meeting their former spouse in the afterlife, I reflected with them on this, and gently and positively challenged their anxiety (within the context of *their* belief). The person experienced an emotional release, and quietly passed away later that afternoon. I believe this release of tension allowed the person to be at one with themself. Spirituality is highly relevant to Meaning in Recovery, including in palliative care.

Universal Human Rights Approaches

The concept of rights (E.g. a 'Bill of Rights'), is not enshrined in the legal framework of our country, however this doesn't mean that rights don't exist, even if it's simply as a personal construct tied to identity. There are a lot of ways of looking at rights – there are legal protections from discrimination on the basis of ageism (Age Discrimination Act 2004) and advice from the Australian Human Rights Commission that proposes Australia create a Human Rights Act. Although the Australian Government opposed a UN Convention on the Rights of Older People, support is growing internationally for international legislation and the process seems to be underway. At the moment Australia is of course signatory to the UN Convention on Human Rights. As such older persons have access to their rights such as control over their medical care, freedom to live where they choose etc, the same as everybody else.

We also have a Guardianship Tribunal system designed specifically to protect the rights of those who may be deemed to be vulnerable. As yet, Australia has not followed the UK in creating an oversight framework for protecting vulnerable adults in care by having any Deprivation of Liberty and Safeguarding systems, but this is a possibility in the future.

Concepts such as natural justice find support when cases are tested in courts, and precedent can therefore help to gradually codify rights. Any health worker that overlooks the rights of older persons may one day be accountable even if the violation of rights doesn't meet previous standards and definitions.

Rights can also be looked at in terms of not-legal, but as personal rights. This can be complex, contextual and may be more felt than read about. This is where sensitivity trumps the factuality of the medical model. For example, a nursing home had a husband and wife in adjoining rooms, and the husband developed paranoid delusions about the wife. He begins wandering into her room and accusing her in the middle of the night of being unfaithful. In this scenario, this causes the wife significant emotional pain, anxiety and depression. Once this situation is understood it is only reasonable to advocate with the nursing home and offer the vulnerable wife protection by suggesting she moves to a different room. After a few weeks, you review her symptoms and possibly book the appointment with the psychogeriatrician after the situation has settled down a bit. Perhaps the psychogeriatrician will find that she won't need antidepressants. (This scenario is an amalgam of three or four situations I have been involved in).

Culturally Sensitive Assessment

Connecting through narrative assessment with a consumer from a non-English speaking background can require the use of TIS – the Translating and Interpreter Service, who can be pre-booked via the booking links on the right side of the home page at https://www.tisnational.gov.au/ or via email at tis.prebook@homeaffairs.gov.au. At times using a family member or friend provides sufficient service however at times this may not be appropriate due to relationship dynamics.

Cultural sensitivity can impact much of the assessment, and it is the assessing clinician's role to identify cultural variables and have respect to their impact.

An excellent resource in cultural awareness featuring a whole section on mental health assessment in Aboriginal Health is called *Working Together: Aboriginal and Torres Strait Islander Mental Health and Wellbeing Principles and Practice* (Dudgeon, Milroy & Walker, 2014). This downloadable resource is an authoritative, thorough and reflective work that will enrich the rural mental health clinician's capacity to provide services to Indigenous peoples. Not only is it highly qualified but it is also from the perspective group who is being written about – in line with Recovery values. This rich resource, especially Part 4, presents a strong argument for culturally aware assessment that strongly overlaps with narrative assessment advocated within this guide.

I don't believe I need to attempt to summarise this excellent resource here, and I truly believe that it should be regarded as a **primary resource** for OPMH clinician. I believe *Working Together* should be studied in depth. I would like, however, to draw out some themes from that book which can elevate the deeper applied knowledge of the importance of Identity as a theme of Recovery-oriented work.

As is outlined in *Working Together*, there are many principles involved in competent culturally sensitive assessment. The clinician's critical thinking skills needs to reveal depth, sensitivity, training and wisdom, or in the words of the book:

"self-exploration, critical self-reflection and recognition of the implications of the power differentials inherent in the

role of clinicians and clients".

This self-awareness, as mentioned elsewhere in our book, is a sign of a mature and person-centred mental health clinician.

Further, within *Working Together* the authors draw from the literature (p278) on Culturally competent assessment that includes:

- an exploration of the client's worldview and understanding of his or her problems;
- an understanding of the client's family background;
- cultural explanations of illness for the individual;
- cultural elements of the client–practitioner relationship that reflect a clear understanding of the practitioner's insight into their own positioning.

These approaches are set, throughout this work, in narrative assessment styles. For example, on p279, culturally competent assessment requires that clinicians:

"...undertake a comprehensive interview with their client before deciding on the assessment processes and use of any formal testing (if that seems appropriate)."

I recall a mental health assessment where I involved an Aboriginal Health worker after learning of the consumer's risk of homelessness, bereavement and health concerns. The worker organised emergency accommodation and help with the treatment. But further, she organised cultural activities with particular, sacred meanings appropriate to this consumer's need. Not only did this provide Connectedness, but it also helped with Hope, Identity, and Meaning. Culturally sensitive assessment can indeed facilitate the Recovery process and values in this way.

What Indigenous Perspectives contribute to Recovery in wider OPMH

Family kinship bonds are often strong in Indigenous societies in ways Western societies seem to have forgotten. It is anything but a nuclear family model and older community members remain influential, respected and very involved. Some older persons are often addressed as "Aunty" or "Uncle", and "Elder" is a title of respect and revere.

Social aging is profoundly influenced by the *perception* of aging that is part of a society's culture. "If a society views aging positively, the social aging experienced by individuals in that society will be more positive and enjoyable than in a society that views aging negatively." (Hooyman & Kiyak, 2011).

> Not only do health workers need to understand these roles and relationships, but actually we could learn from this perspective in understanding how to treat older persons in general. In the words of a psychiatrist who participated in my focus group research (Appendix 1):
>
> *"It needs to be one of the criteria learned to have respect for older people and in fact respect for elders, almost in that traditional sense of acknowledging all the older people that have come before us and that's why we're here now."*

While this is a white Anglo-Australian view about Aboriginal and Torres Strait Islander perspectives on Ageing, it may contribute much to the essential attitudes that OPMH clinicians put upon older persons. Respect for the personhood and identity of the older person supports, rather than works against, the chance that the older person may regain their sense of self, and get back to them.

The perspectives throughout *Working Together* help the clinician shift from 'discourses of distress' to 'discourses of hope' (p. 286). There are therefore clear overlaps between culturally-competent assessment and Recovery themes. Although the medical model may have predominance within the context where you work, as a clinician you can contribute significant awareness to consumers by understanding and applying Recovery values overlaps significantly with cultural competence.

Social and Emotional Wellbeing

In OPMH, Aboriginal and Torres Strait Islanders are often included from age 45, due in part to life expectancy, illness and quality of life issues. Rural and remote clinicians will likely have consumers who are older Aboriginal or Torres Strait Islanders, at some point. Some may be Elders, or call themselves Elders. Elders in Indigenous cultures have status that separates them in terms of their roles in the community, with a degree of respect for Elders services may fail to recognise

Some key concepts of working with Indigenous older peoples include:

- The knowledge and understanding of historical abuse by services, which is linked to distrust or at least a healthy scepticism of Anglo-Australian systems including Health systems
- The critical importance of incorporating family support
- Cultural differences in communication styles which can have a major impact on assessment outcomes
- The importance of liaison through an Aboriginal Health Worker or Aboriginal Mental Health worker if available, or at a district level clinical supervision through Aboriginal district level clinical supervisors
- That terminology should be nuanced such as the term "Mental Health" being replaced with "Social and Emotional Wellbeing"

The Stolen Generations

Australia's history of intentionally attempting to destroy the cultural transfer of knowledge from Indigenous mothers to their children by forcibly separating the children from their families, community and culture has a deep, ongoing legacy today. For example, policies of removing mixed-race children if the mothers were Aboriginal but leaving the children in place if the mother was white and the father was Aboriginal demonstrate the aim of breaking Aboriginal cultural transfer as mothers were viewed as the conduits of early cultural training.

Not only have many Aboriginals lives been caused intergenerational trauma with destructive impacts across generations, but cultural Darwinism continues to be an issue where health care providers attempt to provide care through the lens of their bias. These two issues – the history and the *current* bias, combine to generate distrust for western-based health, welfare and government service.

Racial bias is a potent confounder of assessment and it should be recognised and addressed. People from Aboriginal and Torres Strait Islander descent may have particular ways of communicating or being that might be misinterpreted. For example, eye to eye contact may mean different things to the assessor than it can to the consumer. Please read Part 4 of *Working Together* for detail on these issues.

One important way of achieving this recognition may be through liaison with Aboriginal health. The goal is to promote equality, accuracy and cultural safety in the conduct of the assessment. Although the mental health worker may consider themselves mindful on these issues, the awareness is from an Australian medical model. Clinician's awareness of their own racial bias is an essential area of reflection in supervision and support, and provides one pathway to personal and professional growth.

Cultural and Spiritual Considerations

Consider how deeply our cultural heritage impacts our response to any given situation. Similarly, clients from cultures different from the assessors' will react to problems in a way that is at least partly shaped by their cultural roots. The risk is that we as clinicians will see behaviour that appears bizarre or pathological to us, and fail to recognise that it is a culturally consistent behavioural response in the client. Add to this the possibility of cultural nuances in appearance, language, education, expressions of emotion and general behaviour. There is a risk that cultural differences can affect reliability of our assessment.

For example, a Mediterranean matriarch may have a certain style of response to a crisis that seems disproportionate to the clinician, and the clinician needs to become informed, recognise, try to appreciate and acknowledge cultural differences. This awareness also can include spiritual expressions, such as in the case where some see, sense or feel the spirits of their departed nearby in the case of recent grief and loss.

> Would *you* describe culturally appropriate spiritual experiences of a deceased loved-one as hallucinations?

Sexism, Bias, and the awareness of abuse

Along with Ageism and racism, sexism will blind the assessor from accurately recording what they see. It may occur, for example, in an assumption that an older person's anxiety, aggression or depression can be discounted or ignored through clinician's view of 'typical' aspects of a person's gender, which is extremely hazardous to the quality and validity of assessment.

However there is also a significant risk in the attempt to be too 'objective' – too dry. As a clinician, as a human being, you have insight, intuitive and other hard-to-define factors in play all the time. Awareness of your reactions can be developed in supervision. They are underpinned by social and personal values and your personal history.

To be succinct: Sometimes warning bells are triggered. For example, you may have observed someone as deferring, as someone else continually interrupted and spoke for them. Did you feel uncomfortable, looking back? Did you wonder about power and control issues? Did you feel to ask the other person to please refrain from answering for the person?

Domestic violence, always about power and control, is an issue that requires great sensitivity at assessment. For example, you may notice a client may gloss over certain details in a topic, or their voice may trail off on a certain point. At this stage it would be proper to wonder why you find particular details seemed sketchy, in contrast to generalising it by simply documenting "tangential thought form". It presents a dilemma because the clinician is part of a health service which seeks to treat outward symptoms of poor coping, and it may appear outside the capacity of the health system to respond to overarching issues of power and control within a relationship.

In the UK, there have been significant reforms around elder abuse, and toward statutory protection of vulnerable adults (safeguarding) for some time. Recently in Australia political leaders have begun to comment on these types of reforms. I noticed a new pamphlet just the other day about recognising signs of elder abuse. With arrival of these types of reforms comes a significant demand for clinical and professional competency toward understanding what constitutes the types of elder abuse, and the responsibility to intervene.

This is an important historical problem. From the early days of mental health internationally, diagnosis has been sometimes abused by family as a technique of manipulation and control within interpersonal power relationships. Some examples:
- a family may want someone to move into aged care very early; or
- where extended families with chaotic living arrangements impact upon the wellbeing of the consumer; or
- where complex bereavement finally triggers a reaction to family history of abuse and/or control against the consumer.

These are complex issues. Great care needs to be taken in the assessment that vulnerable older people's subjection to power relationships are identified, and that the impact of the assessment on the rights and psychological safety of the client is considered.

Feeling that you can explore your provision of professional service can make you more aware of your own responses and open to new experiences as you encounter the wide experiences of diversity. There are many occasions where personal bias needs to be noticed, acknowledged, explored and resolved and with a trusted supervisor. It will improve your work and make you more responsive and aware.

Bias about class, disability, sexual orientation, home address, medical history, family background, religion, criminal history or socio-economic status can interfere with the quality of assessment. All of these biases can be even more powerful when combined with insensitive appraisal of old age. In undertaking the

MSE, it is your job to observe and document without bias, although it is essential to recognise your sensitivity/issues in a safe place, namely supervision. It is competent practice to reflect on feelings you may have glossed over or that produces emotive responses within you, and to explore these, perhaps opening the door to a fairer and more balanced assessment.

> Consider generalisations you make and how they might affect assessments

To ignore the cultural dimension at play in assessment, and to ignore analysis of power relationships is to disregard Meaning, Empowerment and the person's Identity. It is not possible to describe your assessment as Recovery-oriented in this case.

Ageism, Risk, Rights and Responsibility

An assumption that depression is a function of age is wrong and discriminatory, but another more subtle way that Ageism can interfere with competent assessment in Mental Health is in the assessment of risk. Manifestations of risk must be taken very seriously in Older Persons Mental Health. Consider the following scenarios.

1. Is it possible that a lovely, diminutive and gentle lady poses a risk to her husband when her mental state fluctuates? (She had repeatedly threatened him with a knife, and recently walked up behind him with it ready to hurt him.)

2. When that kind, softly spoken gentleman says he has been walking near the railroad track, and has had thoughts of ending it all, can he really be at risk?

It is vitally important to do proper risk assessment!

One confusing factor might be around values the clinician holds about the right to die with dignity, and the issue of *legalisation* of Euthanasia. However, when someone is depressed and wishes to die, these issues might seem to interact. It is important to remember that depression is often treatable. A decision for a mental health clinician to overlook risk in depression because of personal views about assisted suicide or even the wish of the depressed consumer would be to fail their responsibility to the consumer and to fail in the clinician's Duty of Care. In any case, depression can diminish the person's legal ability to make an informed decision.

(This book is not intended to be the place for the *legalisation* debate, but for our purpose, the role for the clinician remains around management of mental illness, and easing of mental suffering.)

(Please read Risk Assessment in the Skills section for more information about this process)

Record keeping

It is important to be mindful that what you write, *and the way you write it,* may one day be viewed by the consumer, family or even in a court. Keep it factual, objective, non-judgemental. Failing to note significant issues can be just as problematic as recording prejudicial, ageist or wrong information. Laws exist that allow the person to request health information about them. Therefore, observations need to be brief, but respectful, show a compassionate attitude. You may find, for example that recording "Delusional. Nighttime paranoia, insufficient supports" may send a different message than "Recurrent aggression reported at night also involving delusional ideas about his wife being unfaithful. She reports secondary grief." What to write down can be a complicated issue and requires a thoughtful approach.

MEANING

The Recovery value around Meaning is about personal resolution and adaptation. The consumer's understanding of their experience of mental health and the meaning and purpose of their life underpin feeling well. It adds a context through which they can navigate and find support. Meaning is an individual perspective but may be strongly associated with wider social perspectives including for example: cultural and spiritual perspectives; faith (or lack of
faith) in the medical model and the clinician; levels of education; and social engagement.

> Something in the consumer's development underpinned their normal responses to stress. Then a new crisis or grief has come along and turned their world upside down. How does medication help this? Is it sufficient?

Depression can be linked to issues of meaning in life, but also bereavement, anxiety, dissociative states, psychosis and the adaptation to organic changes including stroke and dementia all may have strong elements linked to the meaning of life and life's learning, value and experiences.

> A retired army nurse who I was assessing was unhappy with the medical and nursing care she was receiving. The clichéd comment that I had heard (from another nurse) about nurses making the most difficult patients echoed in my head.
>
> As the narrative assessment continued, much was intimated about the level of trauma experienced in the army hospital tent. Upon investigation I learned of other symptoms of trauma. Anger and high anxiety were just some of the symptoms present. Flashbacks, constant sleep impacts and agoraphobia also played a role.
>
> The lady seemed to appreciate the way the narrative assessment got past the presenting issues, judgemental ideas and clichés and acknowledged the meaning and impacts of her sacrifices over the years.

For the consumer to adapt in Recovery is often linked to establishing or finding new meaning in life. However, in keeping with their stage of life, many older people tend to be more focussed on what has been achieved rather than their potentialities. Broader ideas that may have found resonance with them many decades ago may be very hard to simply turn around.

However, it should not be assumed that adaptation – including revisiting meaning – is a fruitless exercise in older people. With older people, as with anyone else, the presence of a crisis – even grief and loss (along with the pain) – also presents a beautiful opportunity to grow, to adapt and change. It is said that change is tough: Many older people (maybe with your support) can find that they are able to face change, and this is usually linked to finding new meanings.

Bereavement

Bereavement is a process of adaptation to grief and loss, and certainly involves revisiting our views of life and the world. Normally, we walk around very comfortably ignorant of the many threats to our existence, physical and psychological health, accepting "blinders" that protect us from the naked stark realities of life. Trauma, death, grief and other losses tear these blinders away. The meaning of our world is called into question due to the sudden lack of wholeness or safety that we enjoyed in our self-imposed ignorance.

These blinders are both normal and healthy, enabling us to function. However when they are lost, we may have to go through a number of stages toward adaptation.

Firstly, we may enter a period of shock, where the reality of the change is not intellectually or emotionally accepted. This period may be characterised by denial, disbelief and confusion. Next, we become aware of the pain of loss, but try to account for it using other emotions – we may be consumed by anger, guilt or sadness. Gradually we may question these responses and enter a period of disorganisation, where we acknowledge the pain and begin to feel that we may never feel any different. Finally we may enter a reorganisation phase, where we build a scaffold around the pain, begin to deal with life again, being able to remember the loss but also carry on with life. This latter stage usually involves changes in our meaning in life and our world view.

Older people may lose many friends, and will lose life partners and even outlive their children. They may lose their independence, and some of their dignity may be compromised with changes in bodily functions. Assessment may be requested during any of the adaptive phases outlined above. (It is not linear – these phases may happen in different ways at the same time, making the picture more complex).

Clinician's attitudes to older people experiencing grief, will have a lot to do with how useful the clinician is to the person. I have seen situations where an older person's grief responses have been confused with dementia, psychosis, and most often, depression. Bereavement is simply a sign that the loss is meaningful and the person needs reflective support toward personal adjustment with understanding and acceptance.

It is for the person to adapt meaning to their new situation and a Recovery sensitive clinician will support reflection to help the person recover from the loss. The medical model will frequently apply medication to the person. Where an older person loses sleep or can't eat at the death of their life partner, there are implications for and against taking medication.
This may be ok in terms of taking the edge off the symptoms; however no pill can ever *replace* compassionate understanding and support until the adaptation is made.

Further, bereavement *can* trigger a clinical depression

(e.g. melancholic depression). Medication can become the best treatment option, without which the person does not or cannot get benefit from the clinician's compassionate understanding and support. In any case, a Recovery-oriented clinician will provide support and compassion, assess what social and emotional supports are available in the person's life, and triage the person in preparation for the psychogeriatrician's visit to help the person toward Recovery.

Positive clinician responses to bereavement assess or ensure that the person:
- has someone to listen to them with understanding;
- they are eating, sleeping and looking after themselves;
- they are not too isolated;
- they have time to grieve.

These are things that a Recovery-aware clinician may encourage and facilitate among the person's support systems.

Erik Erikson's Theory of Human Development

'Services ought to have not only a social view but also a psycho-social developmental model'
OPMH Psychiatric Specialist, Focus Group (Appendix 1)

Further to theoretical perspectives on Ageing, one major theoretical perspective that helps us to understand how and why older people may feel things they feel is Erikson's theory of human development. This can be extremely useful in helping the clinician differentiate between symptoms of depression and disempowering perspectives that may seem simply realistic to the person, based on the sum of their life experiences.

Erikson proposed a series of developmental stages that occur at particular ages over the person's lifetime. During these essential stages an individual develops beneficial or pathological personality traits or "virtues" or "problems" that develop when the person faces the challenges or crises of each stage.

In OPMH we will not only be interested in the latter stages, but how the person has adapted to crises and achieved satisfaction within earlier stages, as each stage is influenced by successful achievement of earlier stages – in a sense building the person step by step, although accomplishment in each stage is not locked in and can be addressed at later stages.

The eight stages with associated ages are as follows:
1. Hope: Trust vs. Mistrust (oral-sensory, infancy, 0–2 years)
2. Will: Autonomy vs. Shame/Doubt (early childhood, 2–4 years)
3. Purpose: Initiative vs. Guilt (locomotor-genital, preschool, 4–5 years)
4. Competence: Industry vs. Inferiority (latency, school age, 5–12 years)
5. Fidelity: Identity vs. Role Confusion (adolescence, 13–19 years)
6. Love: Intimacy vs. Isolation (early adulthood, 20-39 years)
7. Care: Generativity vs. Stagnation (adulthood, 40–64 years)
8. Wisdom: ego integrity vs. despair (maturity,

65 – death)

By the age of retirement (around 65), for example, the person enters the stage described as "Integrity vs Despair". The way the person enters this stage is strongly influenced by their achievements in the "Generativity vs Stagnation" and earlier stages. So if the person's sense of productivity has been compromised by illness or loss, including issues of self blame from poor choices, alcohol dependence, or a business that went bad, the person enters retirement with their sense of integrity compromised, resulting in despair. It can be much worse when poor relationships with adult children resulted from difficulties in prior stages. If, on the other hand, they have fostered and develop virtues in their earlier life, their sense of integrity will remain intact.

Erikson's wife Joan extended this by observing a ninth stage when she herself was in her 90's, (from the perspective of her own experience.) She observed that in this stage the person faces new and unique difficulties that require them to re-evaluate their previous collective wisdom.

In therapy, Erikson's developmental perspective may provide a platform for cognitively reframing and challenging perspectives to alleviate issues of both mood and adaptation. In Recovery terms this relates to looking at strengths and acknowledging the crises to help the person re-evaluate meaning in life. It may be used to add contextual understanding to what from an external perspective to look like depression or poor functioning.

A man in his 80's was referred for depression, suffered from emphysema and circulatory problems that limited his mobility. He had a lot of trouble tolerating his C-PAP mask. He was regarded as a Casanova amongst nursing staff who described that he behaved sexually inappropriately toward the nurses.

In learning about his social and developmental history, he disclosed that his father, who had brought the family to Australia from southern Europe, had died early, and as he was the oldest child, responsibility fell to him to virtually run the family farm at 11 years old. Although his mother was present, her persistent problems with alcohol, harsh discipline and a series of relationships with men interfered with how supportive she had been in his eyes. I also learned that his father had been quite verbally abusive of her while he was alive.

Although sustained reduction of O2 can of course lead to depression, he didn't seem depressed when I spoke with him. There was certainly nothing like *anergia*. The predominant thought content in his mental state seemed to be around disdain for family and particularly toward women. He said he enjoyed talking to me and didn't mind the assessment.

Looking from a life stage perspective at the stage from ages 3-5 and 6-12, he faced major crises that seems to have interfered with his development of social skills. During his teen years, the effect of the problems became entrenched in his ego formation years, in a sense cementing that perspective in. My brief knowledge of Erikson came from university studies, plus childhood developmental perspectives when I worked in Early Intervention for family services helped me understand his problems as a result of trauma, DV and childhood neglect.

Where developmental challenges can be revisited, the person might make sense through a link to psychological symptoms, which can help the person adapt. Thinking back on the man in the vignette above, if he had a diagnosis based purely on current symptoms, it may have probably included an antisocial personality disorder diagnosis. While it is also true that the 'dice had been rolled a long time ago', without acknowledging developmental triggers it would have been difficult for him to see sense in adapting his behaviours.

To revisit the developmental perspective included asking him about positive masculine and feminine role models – respectful men and women that he admired, trying to draw out a strength-based perspective. It made use of psychoeducation about developmental challenges. He may at last have been able to acknowledge the hardship and abuse his mother lived through and thought differently about her.

I was able to reinforce boundaries with the nursing staff to decrease the risk of offences as well, and yet do so without outright condemnation of the consumer. Erikson's model helped me to better understand his perceived flaws as cause-and-effect of his development.

Recovery can be related to Erikson's theory in thinking about people with long-term involvement with mental health services and diagnosis. One interesting paper (Vogel-Scibilia et al, 2009) maps Erikson's eight stages to Recovery processes. In these Recovery-adapted stages, the stages are described as more fluid and less strictly age determined, and can be revisited toward resolution - a progressive adaptation after relapses, showing the hope and positive orientation of Recovery. From that paper:

> *"Much as the elderly often process their aging by reviewing their lives, the person in recovery may address feelings concerning the symptoms by talking about past relapses. This helps to produce closure for grief, demonstrate the utilization of a repertoire of coping skills and affirms the recovered life that has arisen."* (Vogel-Scibilia et al, 2009)

As the narrative engagement progresses, Erikson's theory can certainly be useful from a Recovery perspective in OPMH, and a way forward in evidence-based work. It's about the big picture of life, is replete with meaning, non-judgemental, and potentially useful in helping the consumer make sense of their experience.

MEANING: MAKING SENSE OF THE EXPERIENCE

Added to the sense of understanding the illness (in the Hope section) is the application of the experience to the value of finding meaning in what is happening. This may mean anything from tracing the causality of the situation to successfully placing the experience into to person's philosophy that implies some gain to the person or society.

> If you were really unwell, what would help you to make sense of the experience?

If you answered the above question with reflection on your role in your family, your achievements and crises in life, your philosophy and your spirituality, you are not alone. On a day-to-day level, making sense of the overall experience can be found through helping others who are suffering, learning about new hopes in treatment, and learning about others who have laboured against similar afflictions, which is about location of the self in relation to the shared experience of suffering.

Even where self-drive in recovery might be characteristic of a person's style, without this sense of location, it is hard for a person to take responsibility and control over Recovery.

There are things we as clinicians can do to aid in the making sense of the experience. The most obvious one is finding answers to and answering questions, for example about medication, side effects, how it can be useful. Similarly, a diagnosis may prompt a range of questions. While you sit with the person and try to help them find answers, they may be silently processing what is happening to them in novel and unpredictable ways. In fact, it is possibly not even the knowledge you deliver that is most important in this process, but the opportunity the consumer has to reflect on their situation. Talking about it helps.

In keeping with this, is it easy or difficult for you to talk about some theme like *death and dying* with a person who is facing these issues?

Sometimes differences in perspectives on these issues can be very confronting; however it is your role to serve the person – not to correct their understandings. In you simply reflecting their views, they gain the asset of a neutral sounding board. This can be a very healthy process as the person says things they don't normally say. I have a few tools I use to get people talking: For example I tend to take a dualistic approach to people's values. That is, I try to respect where they are coming from without necessarily feeling a need to agree or disagree with them on their values and beliefs. This promotes a sense of equality and allows one to see questions that might be worth exploring with them.

Another tool is to build on common beliefs. This allows a commonality to be enjoyed and experienced. Where there are differences, it is OK to leave them in the background. The greatest tool at your disposal however is genuine interest in their perspective and life experiences that have led to these views.

A negative example that touches on use of meaning was where I was talking to a group of young Mental Health clinicians sent from Sydney to help after the bushfires. I asked each of them in turn what they had learned since visiting the community of Tumbarumba.

One clinician said that her greatest impression was that farming caused global warming which caused these bushfires, so the fires were really "their fault". This rather abusive logic ignored the possibility that the people she was supposed to be there to help had suffered traumatic loss, and ignored her own absence of empathy. She put her own value judgements ahead those she was there to help and therefore came up with a very wrong answer in my view. This might be likened to the top-down values of previous disasters of human services and the "helping professions".

Understanding meaning does not equate to acceptance, so therefore it is not necessary for her to find fault in her clients in such an inappropriate way.

EMPOWERMENT

The man seemed to be feeling afraid of the assessment and what it meant for his independence. Over the psychogeriatric assessment much of the anxiety was dispelled through great engagement and responsiveness, however the fear had not been addressed.

Dr Williams remained focused up the client and picked up what the unease might be about. He *asked* the man if he had worries about the assessment. The man initially denied it, clearly not wishing to offend us, but eventually hinted at foregone conclusions and nursing home care.

The doctor addressed this man's concern. He exercised transparency agreeing that yes, there had been concerns that resulted in the assessment, but that as yet, there were no in-home supports tried, and that his assessment was not conclusive about needing nursing home care. He continued to address the man's worries, speaking about his choices. The varying nature of care was discussed and the man seemed relieved, not only that nursing home care was not a foregone conclusion, but also that his concern had been addressed.

Dr Williams didn't seem to use the language of rights and self-determination as I as a Social Worker tend to, however in practice he delivered these things to the awareness of consumers and was interested in empowerment. I recall him simply referring to "respect" and "Autonomy vs. Beneficence", which was a perspective he taught.

As a social worker, I was taught to think of mental health care in terms of empowerment long before I had ever heard of the Recovery movement. Empowerment is achieved, from the consumer's perspective, of having access to their rights to self-determination in care, receiving information about their care to help promote informed choice, and having their opinions valued and respected. In its simplest form it is acting in a way that shows a person that they and their opinions matter. It also involves focusing on strengths, linking the person into "Community Visitors" and consumer consultation, and to secure complaint mechanisms.

Empowerment also involves critical understanding of the consumer's agenda and facilitating it in such a way that helps them take personal responsibility and control of their lives. It therefore moves away from 'top-down' bandaid solutions to ones the consumer has ownership of, including self-management techniques.

Autonomy vs. Beneficence
At times, a consumer will be subject to unfair influence

by families who care and also service providers, whose agendas run counter to theirs. To be truly respectful and empowering, Recovery-focussed clinicians will also risk running counter to families as well as colleagues.

Many people, when faced with a significant change in a loved one's health, show a strong bias toward keeping their loved one *safe*. However, this can conflict with the drive to remain independent. Regardless of the presence of illness, a person's right to chose or decline medical care and other life choices including where to live **persists. It continues** until a number of conditions are met at which point further legal frameworks provide alternatives in decision-making.

Values of autonomy – where the independence of the person is emphasised – come into conflict with values of beneficence at that point. Added to this are historical factors of the relationship – for example, where a family are reacting to having seen the consumer drink too much alcohol in the past, and when the consumer has a fall, the family decide it is time their loved-one enters care. If thorough assessment finds the person retains most of their cognitive skill, reason and judgement, then the law, and by extension, the Guardianship Tribunal may find that the person's ability to choose is intact, despite the existence of various risks.

The mental state exam is a key part of collecting evidence of competence, along with history. Throughout this process, the Recovery-based clinician should acknowledge the persons right but also be quite transparent about the nature of the question as it has been posed, with sensitivity of course. Once the question of competence has been raised, it must be addressed, but in a way that is least harmful to the person's dignity. To be honest, truthful and yet respectful of rights can support empowerment.

Advocacy

The clinician will be the main point of contact with the consumer and the family, and their support systems. A lot rests on your willingness to speak up: If the consumer feels embattled by their family, and you try to assist, and the family then contacts your manager, and there is only you to speak for the consumer. (OPMH may often feel these types of tensions). Or when (all from personal experience):

- A consumer is tossed back and forth between the hospital and the mental health unit, it may be only you in a position to liaise with staff and enable better communication;
- A GP is adding medications to medications and not reducing them, and Polypharmacy could account for new symptoms;
- A nursing home staff member doesn't see a problem that a person in their care is depressed, and remarks that treatment is a "waste o' time really".

It's your job to be visible in your role, and your skills as an advocate will be exercised. Discretion helps, but does not mean backing down. Discretion means adapting to respectfully get your point across. Positive team relationships require respect of boundaries and an ability to act with moderation and temperance, but also a positive, respectful, trusting, confident and open stance that communicates that you respect other's rights and yourself as a worker. Assertiveness is a good foundation for a working relationship.

To be challenged is one of the pathways to true learning. In order to benefit from such a challenge, try to be aware of and comfortable with your own emotions while not feeling compelled to act on them (i.e. mindfulness!) This can make your responses a lot more relaxed and positive. Acceptance of your feelings doesn't mean being driven by them. To acknowledge discomfort – even though it may take the form of anxiety, anger or pain – is simply an indication that issues are important to you. Once acknowledged, the relaxation of anxieties can allow new solutions to spring to mind. This is the time for your learning. The team experience can be much more positive if viewed in this way.

Hope and Empowerment in Care Planning

The narrative, person-centred assessment style provides context for care planning, which is framed by Hope. "Care plans should be recovery-focused and consider clinical and personal recovery, and be developed in partnership with the consumer and carer." (NSW Health, 2017, p42)

This goes far beyond assessment. I remember a consumer whose family's agenda was so fixed that the rights of the person could only finally be exercised through a Guardianship Tribunal. In this instance (as in many) it was extremely important that the consumer realised that in fact the Tribunal was there to protect his rights as far as possible, not to end them. While I was not able to predict what the Tribunal would say, I responded to the issue by outlining its purpose to the consumer, from the Tribunal's own information. He felt much more hopeful at that news. The Tribunal found no cause for doing other than reinforcing his right to choose (to his relief), and our clinical relationship continued.

The current crisis brought about by the virus that causes Covid-19 has particular meaning and impact on the empowerment of older people - both those at home and those living in care.

My own family's experience involves one retired man living at home, (pre-Covid-19) - my father-in-law, who is a widower. Until recently he lived alone and saw family members, usually on a weekly basis. Fortunately prior to Covid his granddaughter moved in with her family which turns out to be a very positive impact and reduces his isolation and increases the care, while still protecting his sense of his own independence. He suffers from chronic illness (COPD) and has problems with his eyesight limiting his driving.

As a social model, his new shared family home follows a more integrated family arrangement, more like non-western family structures. Prior to his granddaughter moving her family in, he checked with the family if we thought the idea was ok? I for one told him it was an excellent idea because as he said he "never wants to go to an aged care facility", and, after all, it was his home and his decision.

We had often worried and wished we could be closer to him to help him have a better life. He loves having his great-grandchildren to play with and watch them grow. It is a great blessing because the problems of the aged care setting in Australia are mainly removed from him at this stage.

Then Covid entered the scene. My father-in-law tended to want to get out and about with his granddaughter, and despite the risks. We were able to persuade the granddaughter about the reality of the risks from our point of view. How long it took for them to change their behaviours, we may not ever know because we could not visit, but I believe that it was challenging for the granddaughter to outright decline to drive him anywhere, and there were visits to doctors etc., nevertheless I think we helped them understand our concerns.

In his case, my Father-in-law was very reluctant to change his behaviour without discussion and negotiation. Certainly he was in the high-risk category, but he didn't feel at risk. This is going to be just one of a range of responses where older people have choice. Ultimately his compliance with Covid-19 ingress upon personal freedoms was accepted under conditions of empowerment and with adequate supports.

Where older people are not given choice, or autonomy, through restrictions originating from concerns about Duty of Care, this is a major loss.

Advanced Care Directives, Covid-19 and legal rights

An often-overlooked aspect of empowerment is the implementation of Advanced Care Directives (ACD). I have worked with a few older persons with serious physical illness whose mood was strongly impacted because they felt damned to endure the health system "patching them up" with low quality of life, when they preferred to refuse treatment, although I was asked to assess this person for depression.

The SMHSOP intervention was to advocate, educate and to organise a meeting between the patient, the family and the hospital to address this concern. The person's mood immediately improved and was sustained by the eventual signing of the ACD form. Antidepressants were not needed after all. The person simply needed to feel their rights choose or deny medical care were respected. The ACD is now an entrenched, formalised process which has been difficult to obtain because of the corporate anxiety of health providers, yet even today the threat of a legal challenge often forces medical providers to respect decisions made under these legal mechanisms.

A counselling client who informed me that, because of Covid-19 she felt like "a prisoner in gaol" also revealed that she would much rather face the risk of dying than "to live like this". Normally the dignity of risk and right to choose is of primary concern - tribunals for example will not attempt to control someone who makes an informed decision to smoke cigarettes or drink alcohol even when the risks are clear.

Yet under Covid-19 conditions, agency appears limited by hospitals and aged care homes assumptions about protecting the residents. Usually in the past, isolation may have been imposed on the infectious, but not on everyone else. However under Covid-19 the response emphasises that a person may choose to put themselves at risk but the problem is around who else they infect. The virus seems to spread quickly and mortality seems to be very high in the older age group.

The World Health Organisation (WHO) published an

Interim guide (18 May 2020) called "Overview of public health and social measures in the context of COVID-19". On page 2 it states that "Mindful attention to the dual objectives of controlling COVID-19 and protecting communities from unintended consequences of response measures will help to safeguard health and protect well-being though all phases of response and recovery."

The WHO has recognised the "growing international consensus that all patients have the right ...to consent or refuse treatment..." (who.int/genomics/public/patientrights/en/ , accessed 29/06/2020), and Australia respects the right to refuse medical treatment. The Lockdown, with it's unintended impact on mental health and implication for autonomy and empowerment, has not as yet been tested in the Australian legal-medical system, and therefore it is likely that many nursing homes will employ a risk-averse, 'duty of care' policy that is more black and white, reductionist and paternalistic.

This current situation requires review if this standard becomes the norm, because it may also generally diminish the autonomy of the recipient of medical and heath care, within the more complacent nursing homes that are not routinely as mindful of autonomy of choice. This is a very unfortunate focus because impacts on mental health and related physical health can be massive in an environment of limited choice, an unintended consequence of the Covid-19 response.

Consumer Consultation

A goal of consumer consultation is delivery of a responsive, adaptable, and somewhat fluid conceptualisation of Recovery principles. We need to know what consumers think and how they feel about the services we provide.

The repeated implementation of consumer surveys has been problematic in the Community MH team I worked in. Almost no-one returned them. For this reason I designed my satisfaction survey to also be a discussion about Recovery values between myself and the consumer (in my private practice). It has been a wonderful experience for the consumer, as well as for myself, with positive emotions flowing. It was also tied to the pre-existing narrative and provided ideas for further discussion in many instances. I feel it in itself promoted engagement and empowered the person. (However, I know there are problems - the data is not "blind" and consumers might not feel free to give their actual honest feedback.)

Where people face questions, are asked to be on a panel, or to give feedback I think that we need to positively use the relationship to strengthen the process. And it is OK for them to also learn in the process. Otherwise the consumer is taking a significant risk, poorly supported, and seems to become alienated. The consultation can stagnate (as I have seen).

The nursing home industry is a good case in point. Residents often shared concerns with me but feared nursing home staff would react poorly to people who engage in consumer consultation. The issue is about building the relationship and sense of safety around consultation toward change (Russo and Wallcraft, 2011).

There is a high rate of prescription of psychoactive

drugs such as antipsychotics, benzodiazepines and antidepressants, and a very low application of other therapies or approaches to managing mental health issues in nursing homes. It is worth wondering about this in terms of chemical restraints v. the principle of least restrictive practice. It is reasonable to wonder how the cultural shift toward encouraging consumer consultation might generate antipathy toward consumers who speak out on these issues.

I believe Consumer Consultation will continue to struggle at a local level without significant protection for the consumers as well as significant research into how to link consumer responses to Recovery discussions and with open and honest feedback mechanisms and strong relationships.

EMPOWERMENT: UNDERSTANDING ILLNESS

This is another Recovery value important in OPMH. People often want the best information available about their affliction, including treatment options. This facilitates informed choice and is in line with Recovery values. It is, after all, about *them* and *their* mind and body. However, respecting this can require great care, because it definitely doesn't seem always in the best interest of the person to talk about risks, prognoses and worse-case scenarios. Delivering specific information about illness requires expert knowledge best supplied by the psychogeriatrician but as you go, you may find you also have some small added role in this and will gain knowledge that can be useful if gently shared, for example when someone asks a direct question about what you think.

Very frequently we humans tend to inappropriately attribute illness to some personal failing on our behalf. There may even be some truth in the persistent thoughts about blame. However these tend to prevent us from seeing the pathway forward toward adaptation.

The older person with illness may obtain much benefit from various perspectives on their situation, as a trigger to emotionally and intellectually processing and finally to adaptation. For example, links between physical factors and known psychological symptoms are useful conversations to have with people especially where they have no other explanation for their mental health impact than attribution to some failing of their character.

For example, links between:
- sleep apnoea and depression
- heart surgery and mood problems
- stroke and emotional lability (without corresponding depression)
- fluid in the lungs and anxiety feelings at night, where people typically go to sit in their armchairs at 2am for relief

...are some examples of useful knowledge that may help the person comprehend what is happening to them.

At the assessment phase, it is probably too early to teach psychoeducation. However, the noting of cognitive distortions and rumination about illness form an important part of the MSE. There is certainly hope of helping the person process these distortions, with or sometimes without medication following specialist assessment.

Psychoeducation and Trauma Informed Care

Where a person has a significant history of trauma, providing psychoeducation can be a Recovery-based, empowering CBT technique. In my counselling work I have seen clients become empowered by learning more about their bodies and minds, and most particularly, the stress arousal response. Understanding the 'fight or flight' response, what triggers it and how to think of it are good examples of this.

Learning that these functions are normal functions of the brain but a brain exposed to abnormal stress, and learning about why the whole thing functions as it does (i.e. the earliest response to recognising familiar dangers) can be incredibly empowering.

Many people with responses such as agoraphobia, flashbacks, anxiety responses, aggression, drug and alcohol self-medication issues and sleeping problems, for example see these symptoms as indications of their own 'poor' coping ability and there often is a lot of self-blame and poor self esteem silently attached to these issues.

I liken it to the low fuel warning light in my car. When it goes off, I don't focus on the tendency of the car to use up fuel. I don't pull over and avoid using fuel. I simply accept the warning and try to work out a solution and proceed. Herein lies the therapeutic value.

Psychoeducation is used particularly in Trauma-informed care, where learning about the Amygdala and Hypothalamus and their role in reviewing new information for correlations to known risk information as a normal process. Associated with this is understanding the corticotrophin and adrenaline response as a beginning point for people to understand their anxiety is often very helpful. The fight-or-flight and anxiety responses of the body come to be seen *in context* as the body's safety mechanism rather than a peculiar or fearful failing.

The person can learn respect for their bodily symptoms of stress, a step toward processing the issues. (You may wish to learn more about applying this perspective through studying trauma-informed care.)

Similar benefit can be delivered to people with upsetting, repetitive dreams, where they begin to understand how deep REM sleep allows the mind an opportunity to attempt to heal by processing unresolved feelings and events. Through learning to accept that it is the mind trying to heal itself, the person may be able to soothe themself at night when they wake up in distress, and in conjunction with mindfulness, move gradually toward a resolution.

Trauma-informed care is all about empowerment. It is about recognising that the consumer should control the flow of therapy. This is because their mind belongs to them, is their territory. Any therapist who goes dancing around in the dark memories of the person's past risks re-traumatising them, and simultaneously adds to their feeling of defeat by disempowering them. Providing psychoeducation, on the other hand, helps the person understand themself and gives them grounds to develop confidence in their emotional processes.

Attitudes to Illness vs Trauma-Informed Care

Trauma-informed care is therefore a strength-based perspective on illness and is empowering. Your attitude to illness will say a lot to the person you are assessing. For example:

Pitying – may tell the person that their situation is beyond hope, and a direct assault on the persons' sense of dignity. This may prevent satisfying connection and a sense of trust, and project bleak assumptions about the person's situation which may not be valid. Pity projects an unequal relationship. Even when someone is dying – quite often they might not need your pity. Especially since you're there to help, don't assume they need the extra burden of being pitied.

Officious – Portraying, in the role assessor, the roles of a medical 'functionary' or 'clerk', a mental health assessor can do much to disempower someone, even further traumatise someone who is expecting or badly in need of a warm supportive therapeutic connection. Relying on questionnaires and clipboards, little eye contact and warmth, using jargon, can add up to a misuse of power. How does it reduce power help recovery? Or does it? The average consumer seems to want to be treated like a human being! Emotions like fear and shame are what many are already struggling with, and a sense of connection can help. If you struggle to treat the person as you would treat someone you care about, this is an issue for reflection and supervision.

Distant: The person and their reactions is something to be feared and should be kept at arm's length.

Trauma-informed care: Looking beyond diagnostic profiles to see the real person and their strengths including in coping mechanisms (even ostensibly if 'maladaptive'). Promoting understanding of the link between the Mental State and what has happened to the person in their experiences can aid recovery.

EMPOWERMENT: DEALING WITH ILLNESS

Another nuanced OPMH Recovery value touches values around Empowerment is awareness of what people feel they need to help them cope. These coping techniques and mechanisms may mean the person can resume their life with relative independence.

In-home supports

One example is that older people may need information to help them access supports that help them stay at home. This is flavour-of-the month with government funding models because not only is it in line with many older people's wishes and best practice, it also helps take pressure off the demand for nursing home beds - a happy confluence of Recovery values and existing practice.

This may, for example, involve: Meals on Wheels, who can help monitor if someone is picking up the meals or doesn't answer the door unexpectedly; Home Care, which provides cleaning and maintenance labour but also a chance to speak to someone regularly; and the Red Cross's Telecross service, which gives people someone regular at set times to chat to at home. I have encountered situations where these services were needed for their primary and secondary benefits. It does not take long to introduce someone to these services and the services tend to be good at stepping in and making themselves useful. Facilitating practical and social supports is an example of Recovery-based OPMH work.

Compensatory techniques
Some older people with mild cognitive impairment find themselves making use of lists, diaries and calendars to help them keep on top of things. This may be useful to talk about with some consumers to help understand how they cope.

Continuation of social, networks, roles and meaningful activities
Meaningful activities may include sports (especially bowls), Lyons and Rotary, Freemasonry, CWA, Legacy, Probus, Red Hat, RSL, Clean Up Australia, Show societies, church, the local historical society, helping out with community events, volunteering with Meals-on-Wheels, Art societies, or something simple like fishing with a mate. Family History in particular has become very important to many older people over the last few years.

Social engagement is a predictor of wellness and coping. Unfortunately, some people disengage with the onset of cognitive changes or mental illness before they actually need to, out of feeling fearful of being noticed or a fear of failing in some way that is disproportionate to the risks they face. I tend to be inclined to identify concerns and 'sell' social engagement for it's many benefits. However, Recovery looks different from person to person. It is the Recovery-aware clinician's role therefore to open up about opportunities that help underpin wellness but to adapt the message to the wishes of the person.

Illness information

Helping people understand what is happening to them can help them to deal with it. This is an ongoing role as the person's needs for information change.

Self-help activities

The clients of my Tai Chi classes were in a social environment. The physical nature of Tai Chi can be lovely and helpful – and we reached a stage one day when we all experienced pleasant tingling, warm feelings as we worked the disciple. Tai Chi, Gentle Exercise, Art and Craft groups, Life-long Learners, Book clubs, and gardening groups all help a person maintain their wellness physically and intellectually, and give a person something to get up for in the morning where motivation may be lacking. I particularly like singing groups because of the endorphin release.

Being part of the world

Some hate reading the newspaper, but others regard it as an important part of their routine, and feel that it keeps their thinking up-to-date. I remember one chap who got his fill of the world through watching shows like Q&A, often tweeting away comments into the night. Others like talk-back radio. Being involved in the political process, whether at a local, state or national level is another opportunity for older people to connect with the world. Others will get involved on Election Day or as officials on the booths. Other variations on this is supervising exams, being involved in their church committees or pastoral care, or being involved in the teaching of things like music all are contributions that older people often engage in.

The Recovery-based clinician will value these things as empowering and understand that they indicate something very positive in the world of the person – a sense of involvement.

Counselling

If the person can find a counsellor who supports their processing of grief, trauma, struggles etc, especially a strength-based, trauma-informed and solution focussed counsellor, then it can be a useful technique toward underpinning recovery. Research shows that a major benefit of counselling is independent of therapeutic approach, the benefit being the narrative aspect, in debriefing.

In my satisfaction surveys, the respondents generally linked counselling with Recovery, except one person who attributed low mood to severe Rheumatism, and denied the psychological process of depression.

The Issues of Jargon

During the preparation of this book I mined the internet for definitions for specialist terms I have heard in my time as a clinician. The resulting glossary grew bigger and bigger, becoming huge! I presented this to the Focus Group as an issue and got a strong response: "Leave it out"! The psychiatrist cautioned against designing a guide that focussed on jargon:

> "If you go over to neuropsychology ...there's a huge

> *amount of information to learn and know. But it always comes back to what you observe. What do I see and what do I hear? That's the important point - that you notice and you write it down..."* (Appendix 1)

It was viewed that:

1. It is more useful, realistic and efficient to expect new clinicians to develop their observational skills than to focus on learning specialist jargon;
2. Consumers and families may not understand what is being said about them, potentially causing unneeded stress;
3. Jargon insidiously creeps into abuse of language with "Huge risks of error."

The overall feeling was that new clinicians need to be taught to sensitively engage in narrative assessment while making a range of simple, jargon-free observations. This is backed by other research - the emphasis on being jargon-free corresponds to better communication, transparency, equality and sensitivity to the experience of the person, and therefore has been linked to Recovery values (Trenoweth, 2017).

I have also realised how jargon represents a power relationship and that it can be very disempowering and therefore the opposite of Recovery-aware practice. Even explaining jargon as you use it can appear to set you up as an 'expert' decoding expert knowledge.

However, decoding others' jargon for the consumer may indeed reflect Recovery-based practice. The glossary may have value in helping the new clinician decode others observations as made in previous reports and letters. Toward this end, I have stubbornly left the glossary in, in a cut-down form. It's inclusion in this work is not a recommendation to learn all the terms by rote, but hopefully will be handy from time to time behind the scenes.

LEADERSHIP IN RECOVERY

Teaching a new paradigm of Psychogeriatric Care

The goals of culturally appropriate, trauma informed, recovery based, narrative assessment has been intertwined with the direction of reform at a state level, national level and throughout the world including academia. This represents reform on a massive scale which has been slow in OPMH. At a district level, the bureaucratic and efficiency requirements of operating a service can impede change. Inertia is also due to the spectre of retraining and difficulty with engaging consumers in consultation. This could explain the slow uptake of a Recovery-based model.

Recovery is value-based and thoughtful, requiring time, training and focus. However much of these values are common sense and are already operating to varying degrees. I have come to the conclusion that the simple inertia and fear of the new can account for a lot of it. That can be addressed simply through strength-based education of caring professionals about their natural caring tendencies with a little re-ordering of their work. Identifying what people are doing right already in the light of the Recovery values is the way forward.

The Role of Supervision and Mentoring in Learning

Clinical supervision is a form of supervision but most of the colleagues I worked with did not seek out professional supervision. One difference between the two forms of supervision is that professional supervision may be 'safely' external to workplace expedience, context and politics. This can translate to freedom to enlarge your understanding. I genuinely believe that my Social Work supervision allowed me to step away from where I work to help me process what I really care about as a professional. This allowed more passion to surface and helped me apply myself to what I was learning about Recovery. My advice would be for anyone to find professional supervision that can support your journey into Recovery focus. Hopefully you may receive very good Recovery-aware clinical supervision simultaneously.

Self-awareness in Assessment

To assess someone's mental state requires an awareness of your own thinking – a critical thinking skill. We try to remain objective, but it is an ideal that is often difficult to achieve.

> Consider:
> How do your own internal reactions impact the quality of assessment?

Can a clinician say their assessment is 'objective' if they have no sense of their own reactions manifest themselves? Having a sense of psychological safety in supervision means that a person can explore their responses without fear. It is about freedom to explore what you feel. (This is separate to problems of crossing professional boundaries.)

All relationships, even therapeutic ones, are a two way street. Values, feelings, morality and judgemental attitudes will all play a role in your response to the person – it's hard to be perfectly impartial. Consumers are sensitive to your responses, and will respond in kind.

Objectivism fades when we assess someone who reminds us of someone close. A personal connection from the past may trigger unexpected reactions and strong emotional responses within us, and may skew our observations of the client. It does and will happen – even to the most experienced clinician. This also is useful material to discuss with a trusted supervisor.

If you have noticed yourself speaking louder to someone who looks depressed and has poor eye contact – step back and reflect. That's how insight is gained. A great place to do this is in supervision. It's also great to learn from other clinicians to get a sense of their (and your) personal style and the pitfalls we all fall into.

Other Benefits of Supervision and Mentoring

Concepts of Mental Health, such as Recovery can be taught sequentially by supervisors or mentors, or in order of priority. Each supervisee should have opportunities to raise issues, questions not only for reflection but also for education. Recovery is well taught in the supervisory context because it is nothing if not *personally* appreciated in the context of reflections on clients. However there are other benefits to Supervision.

Self Care

A major concept that each mental health professional needs to understand is the concept of self care. Supervision is an important element of self care because of its element of debriefing. Every mental health clinician will encounter consumers whose feelings of grief, loss, fear, depression or their circumstances will resonate on a deeper level within the clinician. Countertransference, vicarious trauma and burnout are inevitable occupational hazards. Self care involves being open to the idea of support when these things occur.

When you notice that you no longer watch the news, that you avoid personal problems in your own personal circle of people, when you notice you have become cynical, it is time to rethink your working habits to a more psychologically safe level. But there is much you can do to protect yourself from these crises. It is about sharing feelings and seeking insight from trusted colleagues and supervisors. It is also about looking after yourself in a range of ways – taking holidays, enjoying your weekends, eating right, exercise and relaxation.

There are moments of a clinician's self care which are of great importance: When a consumer ends their life, for example; or a consumer relapses in their mental health, and the clinician suffers guilt and remorse. These are moments when a worker needs the support of a team, especially difficult when the worker is in a remote or solo role, or where there is no supportive team culture.

Contrasted to this natural grief on the part of the clinician, which is a function of simply caring, the institutional response can sometimes appear extremely callous. Often the institution is focussed upon accountability and adverse press, and does nothing for the clinician who faces a panel and questions about their involvement with the consumer. I experienced this myself, as other clinicians have, who told me about the challenge they faced of answering questions with little support – one describing a "Root Cause Analysis" as a 'kangaroo court'.

When accountability feels like blame and little support is offered, an external supervisor is an extremely valuable asset, as you then have an opportunity to explore what happened and your feelings about it in a safe and confidential environment.

Self care is to admit, to be armed with the perspective, that people make their own choices about suicide, that it is not the clinician's fault if someone ends their life. You may have done what you can, but the nature of our work is that we have an hour or two out of any week with any client, and what happens outside that timeframe cannot be attributed to your care if you were not there and that you simply did your best when you were. This needs to be discussed more in Health organisations.

Sharing of Knowledge

New up-to-date learning that is discovered by a clinician can flow into the system upwards as well as from other ways. Speaking up in clinical supervision can reveal gaps in knowledge to management – which is really education from the bottom up. Team meetings can also be opportunities to offer an in-service training session in important new concepts. I would encourage anyone who has learned anything from this book to share insights in this way.

Sources of learning and opportunities

It's an interesting and exciting time to be involved in OPMH. There are now courses coming onto the market offering training in Older Persons Mental Health. For example:

- Beyond Blue have launched a free e-Learning course aimed at training nursing home and community care staff in awareness of mental health problems in older people. It's "Professional Education to Aged Care (PEAC) program" began last year and has already had over 4000 participants!
- In NSW, HETI offers specialist graduate studies in OPMH
- NSW Health have produced a SMSHOP Recovery-focussed "Model of Care"
- Universities and Hospitals support OPMH learning and research (E.g., Monash University, St. Vincent's in Sydney)
- The International Psychogeriatric Association has eLearning and downloadable resources for their members
- The Australian Government has been collating tools in the form of their recommended "Psychogeriatric Assessment Scales (PAS) User Guide"

> If you are a rural clinician, there is opportunity to make use of long car journeys to clients. (One rural clinician does a lot of learning by downloading ebooks and playing them in audio format as he drives to appointments. A great idea!)

Section 2: Skills in Assessment

SKILLS IN ASSESSMENT: ONE CLINICIAN'S PERSPETIVE

A large part of the clinician's role is spent doing assessment. The quality of assessment depends upon the relationship between the clinician and client, which is what allows Recovery-informed values to be demonstrated. For this reason this book partly focuses on aspects of assessment skills. Assessment cannot be done without revealing something about the values, skill and knowledge of the clinician and the overall service.

So, the narrative assessment has commenced, with Recovery values and great care in engagement. The history and the consumer's point of view have been heard. It is time now to gather in specific assessment information.

This is not to suggest that the assessor suddenly disregards the values of the attitudinal section. Continue to pay attention to the person and do not become a robot-like tick-and-flick assessor, or the messages supporting Recovery are void or worse, ironically negated. Humour, sensitivity, reflection, and attention are parts of the ongoing engagement required throughout assessment.

Two questions that underpin much of the benefit of assessment refer to understanding 1) the ordinary baseline of a person's functioning and 2) the changes to this baseline functioning. The psychosocial history plus some specific functional historical data help provide the baseline, while the Mental State Examination (plus the other specific observations) are the snapshot that helps the assessor detect not only obvious pathological indicators but also more subtle changes from the person's baseline.

This skills section goes through some basic assessment steps including some functional areas and the MSE to help the new clinician prepare their assessment skills.

SLEEP

Sometimes overlooked in the mental health assessment, it is vital to holistic assessment and can provide clues to what is going on for a person, their mental state and physical and emotional wellbeing. Dr Williams often asked about sleep as part of the assessment, and taught that it is very important to learn in assessment. I have often transitioned from gathering the personal history to some more specific assessment steps via a couple of questions about sleep.

Sleep is an extremely important function that has a strong interaction with people's mental health. Discussions in the Knowledge section touch on specific impacts on sleep relating to illnesses: Sufferers of PTSD, depression, chronic illness, and dementia can all suffer particular sleep impacts. Sleep problems can also lead to further problems and risks – drug and alcohol problems, falls risks and the general wearing down of health.

The classic assumption goes that about eight hours is a good level of sleep for most people. This is probably culturally defined, and probably ignores the fact that teenagers need more and many older people simply require less – even if some make up for it with a 'nanny nap'.

As with other functional assessments, changes to their

baseline sleep pattern is important to learn about in comprehensive assessment. Changes in medication might also impact on peoples sleep cycles and may be important to spot, due to increased risks such as falls risk.

It may not be necessary to ask all the questions below. Start simple and proceed from there if needed. "Do you get good sleep?" People don't seem to mind discussing:
- how long they sleep;
- if they feel refreshed when they wake;
- whether they sleep through;
- how many times they get up during the night;
- and if they get straight back to sleep;
- if they make up sleep (eg do you enjoy a nap in the afternoon?)
- if they suffer from lethargy or daytime somnolence – daytime sleepiness
- if they are experiencing a reduced need for sleep (e.g. in hypomania/mania?)

Not all these questions are going to relate to every consumer. Start general and be more specific if needed. Do they suffer from Sleep Apnoea? Do they notice they wake at a certain time? It may also be worth exploring long-term impacts on their sleep habits – were they a shift worker, were they caring for a child with special needs for many years. Did these create patterns that became lasting habits? Some people may find their sleep patterns alter dramatically with the seasons.

A referral to a sleep specialist may be part of the care planning following a good mental health assessment where unaddressed sleep problems are identified.

DIET AND SELF CARE

In situations where the person lives alone, there may be little recognition of important changes to functional areas such as self-care and diet. One can observe the state of their home and themselves and ask if there has been a change in their self-care and diet. In a nursing home situation, solid data may be available to help you make your assessment about these issues. Again, it is an issue of baseline and changes. These functional changes may indicate a decline in organisational ability due to cognitive changes, delirium, depression, and psychotic and delusional states. They can provide clues to unmanaged illness.

Poor diet and poor nutrition can have follow-on impacts to mental health. Older people can be more vulnerable to these impacts and these issues should be addressed, including referral to dieticians and occupational therapists, and organisations such as Meals on Wheels.

Aspects of self care will be captured in sections of the mental state examination and are discussed in detail in the sections below. Changes to self care may be suggested by these observations and investigated further if necessary.

GATHERING MEDICAL AND PSYCHIATRIC HISTORY

It is very easy to fall short in the gathering of historical and current information that may have a massive impact on the understanding of what is happening to the person referred. Mobility can indicate a break in the continuity of the history. Depending on the person's presentation, it may be in order to seek correlating information from family members about medical and psychiatric history. Information about previous psychiatric inpatient care is very important. Of course, the incoming unified MyHealthRecord system may one day help supply complete records but it is vital not to assume that all the relevant data is necessarily present.

Requesting information from the current GP is essential but can have varying results: Some will supply longitudinal history while others will supply information about recent and current history. For the purpose of preparing for the psychogeriatrician's visit it is best to get an early start on gathering information. To aid in assessment, and where there is time before the psychogeriatric visit, the following list of pathology and, if indicated, scans can be of great benefit to holistic assessment. For that reason, I have included below a list of tests the Local Health District encourages SMHSOP clinicians to request from GPs prior to the visit:

Recommended work up prior to Psychogeriatrician Consultation

When the common causes of delirium (UTI's and other infections, dehydration, constipation, pain and recent changes in medication) are ruled out, the following tests might pick up causes of dysfunction, and are recommended prior to referral to the Psychogeriatrician

Routine Tests:
- Full blood count
- ESR
- B.S.L.
- Serum Calcium, Phosphate
- L.F.T.s
- E.U.C.s
- T.F.T.s
- Serum B12 /RBC Folate
- M.S.U.
- C.X.R. (if indicated)
- Cerebral CT Scan (if indicated e.g. first onset illness)
- TPHA (if indicated)

Figure 5: Recommended work up prior to Psychogeriatrician Consultation

Recent investigations sometimes have to do, depending on the situation. Of course, the comparison of current pathology results with earlier ones can help create a sense of baseline and variation. Those with a nursing background will probably be much more familiar with reading pathology reports, than social workers or other allied health. It is useful to learn about the typical format of pathology results. For example, they often show a reference range and then display results in **bold** or in red when the person's test results are outside the reference range of values.

MEDICATION HISTORY

Referrals that come through GP practices often provide a prescribed medication list but if you haven't got one, with the person's permission, it is certainly beneficial to obtain one. Discovering the current medication list and especially recent changes to it are vital to comprehensive mental health assessment.

However, medication lists may not always be 100% reliable as the person might not get all prescriptions from one source, the list may be out-of-date, and the person may not comply with doctors recommended use. It is important to get a feel for these types of issues. If you are in their kitchen, you might notice a plastic basket overflowing with many medications, remedies and supplements - which can be potent and interact with the medication.

Communication with the GP also can provide medical treatment history including treatment for mental health. Building a good relationship with the GP also is an opportunity to ask for pathology and CT scans if the person is likely to need assessment by the psychogeriatrician.

The following information is only based on my rough

understandings of issues that occurred in practice, and featured in various discussions over the years. The evidence base changes all the time and this learning may quickly exceed its use-by date, and anyway I am not a doctor or pharmacist nor do I have any specialised knowledge about drugs and their effects. These concepts should be discussed with a clinical leader or psychogeriatrician to enhance your own clinical knowledge. However, the ideas set out here may help the reader to conceptualise why gaining medication history is a serious part of the assessment.

Concept 1: Side Effects

All medications can produce side effects. Many are mild but should be reviewed by a medical professional. Psychotropic medications are potent medications and older people are particularly vulnerable to side effects from these. During assessment, psychomotor activity, gait, behaviour and facial expression can all tip the clinician off about potential side effects. There are some particularly important side effects of psychotropic medications which should be introduced to the new clinician. These sometimes can be serious considerations, even medical emergencies.

"Extrapyramidal" refers to motor functions of the brain that regulate such things as muscle tone and posture. "Extrapyramidal Symptoms" such as akathisia, bradykinesia, dyskinesia, dystonia, Parkinsonism, tardive Dyskinesia and tremor may be linked to the use of antipsychotics and other drugs and seen as triggering these side effects, particularly in older people.

Dystonia is a neurological movement disorder syndrome where sustained or repetitive muscle contractions result in twisting or a tremor and repetitive movements or abnormal postures. Any muscle in the body may be affected, including arms or legs, the jaw, tongue and throat (which can impair breathing - a medical emergency). Acute dystonia can appear soon after administration of antipsychotic medications such as Haloperidol.

Neuroleptic Malignant Syndrome is a life-threatening disorder where an adverse, sometimes rapid reaction to drugs occurs. Concern about this occurred once in my six years but was quickly assessed as otherwise by the psychogeriatrician, but it was a serious matter. Should you learn that a person has commenced a new medication and rapidly developed muscle rigidity, fever, autonomic instability (such as varying blood pressure) and delirium, this is a medical emergency and requires expert psychiatric assessment and treatment.

Many widely-used medications can produce psychiatric changes. Prednisone or other cortisone-like medications, for example, either delivered by injection or taken orally, can produce insomnia, excitation, and distractibility followed by depression, mania, hypomania, and in some cases psychosis. It is therefore important to get a full medication history. Another factor may be unregulated psychoactive substances such as herbal lithium which can have important interactions and side effects.

Concept 2: Issues around titration, timing and medication.

Titration is a regime of gradual reduction or gradual

increasing of medication to protect the consumer from being dosed with too much or conflicting medications. Some drugs are dangerous to cease without titration to the point that if you cease (e.g. cold turkey), permanent side-effects, seizures or even death can result.

An issue of risk around timing of medication occurs when someone has had a change of medication and there has not been a sufficient cross-titration from the previous medication before the new one was commenced (a polypharmacy risk). This may be because insufficient instruction was given by the prescriber, or because the person didn't follow the instructions, either through forgetting, a lack of understanding, or ignoring the instructions. If there has been a change in medication prior to onset of symptoms, try to gather information about timing issues.

Assessing clinicians also need to understand that changes from medication don't necessarily happen straight away, particularly with antidepressants. Desired effects, plus unwanted outcomes such as side effects, can occur rapidly or some weeks after. The diagram below is an example of unintended risk during transition to a new prescription. (This concept was explained to me by a clinical leader, but the graphic is my of own design).

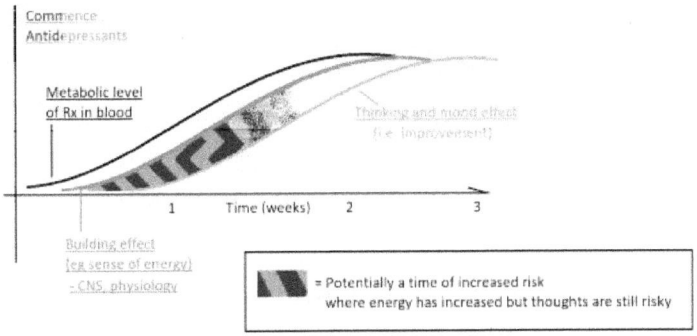

Figure 6: Increased risk concept during early period of a new antidepressant prescription

Concept 3: Polypharmacy

As discussed in the Falls section, medication can have serious implications for an older person's physical and social and emotional wellbeing. Side effects can be felt more strongly, the chance of Polypharmacy problems are more likely to occur, long-term management of mental health and general health conditions can have implications of build-up of medications in their systems, and dosing can need to be fine tuned to older person's metabolism, their livers, brains and waste elimination functions.

One definition of Polypharmacy I have heard is where people are on more than four daytime medications plus at least one psychotropic medication. Many older people are on a lot more than that. However, polypharmacy should not be defined simply by the number of drugs but by whether each is (or is still) necessary and whether there could be adverse or even dangerous interactions between them.

Sometimes it is simply because when a medication is added, no-one has thought about how long it should be used before it is ceased. This may be made more complicated by a breakdown in communication through changes to GP's as is often a feature of rural life.

It must impact many older people's health, not to mention the waste/ cost to the PBS. Thankfully pharmacists and doctors are increasingly aware of polypharmacy and recommendations for overall review sometimes follow psychogeriatric assessment.

Concept 4: Unintended effects

Sometimes a person has a predisposition to unintended reactions that cannot be known until the medication is trialled on them. For example, a bipolar disposition, without ever having been previously identified, may present elevated risks, should the person, in the depression phase, be medicated for unipolar (sad-only) depression. There may be a risk that the general lift affected by the anti-depressant may inadvertently 'push' the person with bipolar disorder into a manic phase of illness that they may have never experienced before. This can be a period of increased risk. Graphically it could be represented as follows:

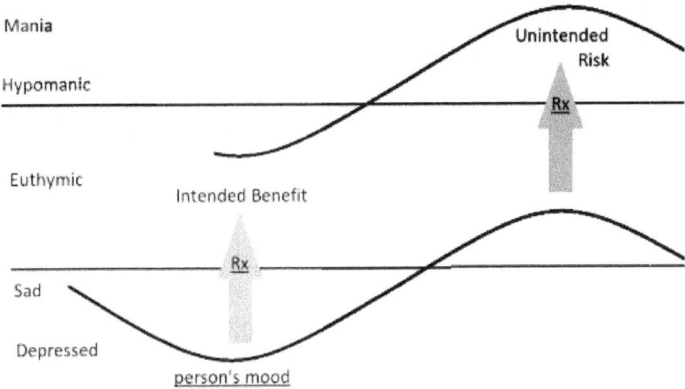

Figure 7: Undiagnosed Bipolar Risk with Antidepressants

When a consumer has been assessed and commenced on new medication, it is important that their support systems are aware of them and can communicate with the OPMH clinician about unforseen changes.

Concept 5: Where a non-psychiatrist has prescribed a psychoactive drug which appears not to be appropriate

This is a very delicate issue for the OPMH clinician, and really can damage relationships with prescribers if the clinician makes comments to consumers that are seen to undermine the GP's decision, made in good faith. There could also be legal ramifications for clinicians who challenge the doctor's knowledge without specialist medical authority and training, particularly to the ears of consumer and their carers. Where a problem is noticed, it may provide a rationale for prioritising psychogeriatric assessment and handling the case in the most diplomatic fashion the clinician can muster.

Examples of incorrect medications include prescriptions of antidepressants to manage mood disturbances without sufficient consideration of non-chemical therapies and antipsychotics where delirium may be insufficiently addressed.

Sometimes a person with Lewy Body dementia is given antidepressants and/or antipsychotics to manage mood or hallucinations and this can carry significant risk of symptoms worsening (including suicidal ideation). Few GPs may understand that anticholinesterase inhibitors are one of the few classes of drugs that can be safely prescribed in the presence of Lewy body dementia. Here again, specialist help is needed to resolve this situation.

Concept 6: Long-term prescriptions in older consumers

Older people who have been long-term consumers of psychotropic medications face risks to their general health. I have met consumers who, for example, have been on Lithium Carbonate for many years without review or monitoring, and whose tardive dyskinesia symptoms have not been noticed over a long time. There are risks of toxicity, even death, chronic kidney disease and hypothyroidism.

Whatever medications have been in place for a long time, these 'Graduates' of mental health services living into older age deserve specialist psychogeriatric review when they are located.

Concept 7: Increasing tolerance issues and increasing dependence.

Some medications become less effective over time. The relief people feel from Benzodiazepines can be very short – sometimes decreasing effectiveness after five daily doses in a row. However the person simply may feel they need more and more to get the relief from their symptoms. For this reason doctors coordinate prescribing to help reduce people's tendency to "doctor shop" for alternative accumulating levels of supply. Taking increasingly high doses can have other impacts on ones health.

RISK ASSESSMENT

It *is* vitally important to do proper risk assessment. If a person will not or cannot guarantee their safety, it is your duty of care to put systems in place that will keep them safe and provide them with treatment.

As discussed in the attitudinal section of this book, acute psychiatric illness in older people may look 'low risk' in the eyes of:

- I have heard a worker from an acute intake team describe a person at acute risk as a "cute little old guy" by the MHECS team, without consideration of recent addition of antipsychotics, the likely presence of Lewy Body symptoms and the expression of suicidal ideation.
- I have assessed a lady whose family member referrer worked in aged care, who forgot to mention that the lady had approached her partner from behind with a heavy blunt object and a will to use it (as the lady herself described to me).
- I have tried unsuccessfully to raise awareness of risk with nursing home staff about a man who had expressed to me a clear desire to end his life and had stolen razor blades from other residents.

The disingenuous 'cute' factor in disregarding risk of self harm, suicide or harm to others is a clear impact of ageism, as it is of unequal service.

Strength-based Mental Health care is required at this point, as is critical understanding. For example, where you ask a person what their protective factors are ("What keeps you safe?") and they say "My pets, they need me" that is a positive answer, as is "My family – I could never do anything to hurt them". Another strength-based aspect is a focus on the future. If the person is looking forward to going to Sydney to watch their granddaughter graduate in a month, future focus is a strength that can be evaluated to see if it guarantees their safety at that time.

Thus it is a balancing act but it's one in which you need to get a clear impression of risk. Where a person cannot identify any protective factors and doesn't sound future focussed, your critical skills should prompt you to explore if they 1) know who to ask for help to remain safe 2) feel that they could ask for help and 3) that they would ask for help. These helps may include emergency services and mental health care lines, going to the hospital, or telling their carer. Having the phone numbers, the person's guarantee, and the conversation about contingencies with agreement to follow it constitutes the safety plan.

A vital step in any initial assessment that detected elements of risk is that safety planning is undertaken. This may be framed by the question "How are you going to keep safe until we meet again?" Safety planning generally involves that each identified risk is answered for.

If a person will not or cannot guarantee their safety in this way, it is your duty to bridge the gap in their safety to put systems in place that will protect them until they have recovered to the degree that they are safe.

In OPMH, risk can also take on added dimensions. Malnutrition through anergia in depression, cognitive impacts, polypharmacy and the subtleties of the older person's metabolic risks of side effects all add special considerations to the meaning, immediacy and intensity of risk.

LEGAL ISSUES

I found that the most common, relevant legal issues in OPMH were regarding questions of who has been nominated as enduring guardian and/or power of attorney should the person's capacity is seen as temporarily or permanently impaired.

If you go online to the Guardianship Tribunal pages, it could be useful to look at 'Definitions' under the 'Quick Links' section. (In NSW, this is found at http://www.ncat.nsw.gov.au – other jurisdictions of course will have their own legal framework to consider.) If you then scroll down to 'Person Responsible' there is a definition:

"A person responsible is someone who has the authority to consent to treatment for an adult who is unable to give a valid consent to their own medical or dental treatment."

Below that is a link to a 'Person Responsible' fact sheet that clarifies the hierarchy and role of a Person Responsible under NSW law. It also lays out the types of treatment that can be consented to or where consent is required.

An Enduring Guardian is someone the person has previously appointed to make lifestyle, health and medical decisions for you when you are not capable of doing this for yourself due to reduced competency in decision making. Power of Attorney is where a person delegates the legal authority to a person to manage financial affairs on your behalf in situations of reduced competency. The next of kin will be the deceased's husband or wife, de facto partner, or parents.

It is only right that people who are unwell, who have a guardian, are protected from hasty decisions by having their guardian notified of intended service. It is a natural and legal right that people have choice in medical decisions and in choices of entering care, so how can the care plan be valid if their appointed guardian is not part of decision making? At times family members have strongly held views that contradict with the person, with medical advice, with other family members. During times of conflicting views it is doubly important that the guardian is involved.

Closely related to this are issues that follow the testing of competency over decision making in psychologically impaired people. At times the Guardianship Tribunal will be approached to help resolve complex issues of decision making, and the Tribunal will want to know how you have regarded the rights and desires of the person during your assessment.

With the currently growing awareness of Elder Abuse and the access to Tribunals that mental health clinicians can provide for consumers, the clinician is in an excellent position to help protect consumer from Elder Abuse. In my experience, where I have had suspicions that a campaign to get an older person into care could be motivated by greed, the person's competence and safety was called into question while family members were simultaneously withdrawing significant amounts from their parent's account. There are signs. It is at these times that the rights and independence of the person may need to be protected legally through application to the Tribunal about the person's right to stay at home and possibly financial management. Another possible use of Tribunal is where the care provided by family members is itself a risky thing in terms of making illness worse or preventing treatment. In these cases I have found that application to the Tribunal was not needed due to identifying common ground with the family and finding a workable solution.

With older people there is statistically a lowered risk that they happen to have outstanding arrest warrants for violent crime, at the time of assessment. However their legal history of course can still be relevant, to varying degrees. It can point to times of trauma in a person's life. It can point to feelings of unresolved guilt and anger, and of social exclusion. Much gentleness is required of the assessor should any of this come up.

If a person has had a long history of incarceration it can have implications for their coping ability in a non-institutionalised setting, their social and personal sense of adjustment and even their life expectancy and wellbeing. Older people who are homeless may have had complex histories that impact on their ability to settle into a home for very long. It is important not to be seen as being judgemental on these issues should they come up, or risk alienating the consumer.

CARE OF CHILDREN AND PETS

In this time of the post-nuclear family, where care of children is often shared with grandparents and where both parents need to work, it is expedient to understand what an essential admission to hospital might mean to the family. So if care of children, or children with disabilities, of pets and of livestock mean the person resists admission when they are unwell, it is part of the clinician's role to see that alternative arrangements can be made to assist admission. Usually family members are needed to fulfil this role. Questions might be "Who's usually at home?" and "Do you have any animals that you need to take care of?"

Sometimes the person will want to ask a trusted neighbour to keep an eye on their place while they are away. These questions support the person's connection to their life under Recovery principals.

In NSW, the RSPCA has a program of emergency care of pets of older people who have to enter mental health care. This is a *last resort* type of service and they will only help after all other possible avenues have been explored. They may board with vets, etc in remote areas but if the person is going to areas where the RSPCA has a kennel, such as in Orange, they may get housed there until the person returns home. The program is called "POOPs" – Pets of Older Persons.

DRUG AND ALCOHOL USE

Gathering information about how much the person drinks, what they drink, and how often they drink is an important step in assessment. When people have had long term addiction to alcohol and the impacts are becoming more obvious the symptoms may include wide-based gait (and balance issues), poor self care, malnutrition, liver problems, confabulation, social isolation (sometimes with secret connections that help maintain addiction).

If a person arrives in hospital after a fall and their mental state is unsteady you may be asked to assess them. The person may or may not have received assessment around alcohol use. This can be very important. The risk is that alcohol withdrawal can produce damaging seizures in the brain, and the person is likely to have a dangerous deficiency of B vitamins. (See the section on Alcohol-related brain damage for more information on Wernicke-Korsakoff and "alcoholic dementia".) It is therefore very important for the vulnerable patient to be given Vitamin B shots to support brain function when the alcohol supply is stopped.

An older person may sometime deny drinking regularly due to a misunderstanding about the number of standard drinks that they have thought is a problem. One fellow I knew read that less than two drinks standard drinks per day halved the risk of alcohol-related illness, less than four drinks reduced the risk from that episode of drinking. So although he at 74 years of age would limit himself to 6 drinks per night, he somehow rationalised that he was "pretty safe". He didn't recall reading that an older person is more than twice as vulnerable to risks, and he wasn't interested in change anyway. His family were increasingly worried because he had had a fall one night. However, all people who drink are at risk of falls and I couldn't see any other evidence to suggest that his agency on the issue of drinking could be used as a rationale to force him into care. Often I have found that where there is a strong alcohol history the family can have very strong feelings including grief, anger and hopelessness.

In terms of Recovery, the right to choose is very important, however once the question has been asked, we do have a duty of care to provide assessment around the person's safety and ability to choose their course and care for themself. Within this dilemma it is important not to react to family concerns or jump to conclusions at assessment. It there is need for Tribunal support, the person should have their rights compassionately supported throughout the process.

We tend to think about recreational drug use as a younger person's issue. However, in the USA, Woodstock happened in 1969. In Australia there are plenty of people who have been using pot since about then. This would put them into the OPMH age bracket. There was the history of very high prescribing rates of Valium in the 1960s and 1970s, there are issues of military personnel and transport workers being long-term users of "uppers" and "downers"- a variety of illicit drugs. It would be an ageist assumption to *not see* these issues as issues of OPMH.

THE MENTAL STATE EXAMINATION

The mental state exam is a *snapshot* gathering concise information from the clinician's observations about the affect, look, thoughts and behaviour of the person, reflecting their mental state *at the time of assessment*.

If, for example, nursing staff have reported that a client seems to be experiencing a change of behaviours around 4pm that they think is 'sundowning', and you happen to see the client at an earlier time of day, your role is to record in the MSE what your own observations tell you. The sundowning observation *is* important and should be recorded elsewhere in the assessment, such as in the history, presenting issues and in the functional assessment, with evidence gathered in a behaviour monitoring chart.

Using another example: In seeking corroborative evidence from family members regarding risks, you learn that a client has been talking about ending their life over the last few days, and that this is completely out of character for the client, however at MSE the client is future focussed, logical and concerned with their family, with no suicidal thoughts apparent at that moment and shows insight into a grieving process they have been going through. All this information would also go toward the careful risk assessment later on in the assessment process. However the MSE should accurately reflect thoughts at time of assessment.

The clinician gathers this information and synthesises it into a holistic assessment, which is used, under supervision, to prioritise access to further and more expert services. This snapshot can also be very useful for comparison's sake if a person's MSE is significantly different at another point in time.

The following points represent the key aspects of a mental state examination:
- appearance;
- behaviour during interview;
- affect;
- mood;
- speech;
- thought form;
- thought content;
- perception;
- cognition & intellectual functioning;
- insight;
- judgement.

They may be grouped or listed in slightly different ways but these are the key features of a systematic MSE.

How on earth will I begin to 'see' all these factors

By the time you get to the MSE in standardised comprehensive assessment forms (if you are working sequentially according to the forms) you probably have already observed much of the information about the person's mental state as you spent time with them. Your narrative, recovery-based story gathering will have helped with engagement, giving the consumer an opportunity to get over their initial reaction to you and the assessment process. So although you are getting to the MSE, a 'snapshot' of the current presentation, the gathering of MSE data should be very much part of the overall assessment – a wider process of observation.

One approach is to make one-word margin notes during the narrative assessment. After the assessment, collate these and reflect on what you have observed as you summarise it into the MSE section of the comprehensive assessment. You could attempt to learn the MSE section headings – and of course there are mnemonics out there – e.g. ASEPTIC stands for:
A – Appearance, attitude and behaviour
S – Speech
E – Emotion (mood and affect)
P – Perception (Hallucination and Illusion)
T – Thought content and process
I – Insight and judgement
C – Cognition

Perhaps when you observe something notable in the person's mental state something like ASEPTIC will trigger you to categorise and record the feature correctly. I *could* write that years of dedication, learning and practice are required to be able to observe and accurately record what is going on. I don't think of myself as a master of this process, but I have watched the psychogeriatricians during assessment and listened with amazement as they summarized their observations with great accuracy and skill on the Dictaphone as I drove them in the car. It would be great if we could all be so wise before we came to the role, but we often do our best learning 'on the job'! Therefore don't be phased about being new to the role – just make your observations, talk them through with your clinical supervisor, and let yourself develop the skills over time.

Mindful acceptance that you do get things wrong, that you are part of a team with a psychiatric specialist and clinical leaders to provide advice, and that your learning, particularly of technical terms, signs and symptoms will continue to develop as long as you keep working and reflecting, will help you relax and achieve competent clinical service.

One client will differ completely from the next in terms of their baseline affect, mood, risks, thoughts, expression and appearance we cannot easily always know what is normal for them, what is significant and what is irrelevant. The skill is simply to be familiar enough with the MSE to work through the key headings, noting observations you make as you engage with the client.

Getting to the point

Within the written assessment, your recorded answers do not need to be wordy – in fact the MSE lends itself to fairly brief, concise answers and the observations you record should be succinct. While you can quote one or two things the client says, there is a skill in brevity that gives the reader of the MSE quick path to understanding. It is counterproductive to get bogged down in rambling eloquence, with the amount of information the clinician has to compile.

It is not unreasonable to write up parts of the MSE immediately after assessment if possible. The format is organised, and with a little practice the clinician should be capturing key information extracted from the experience of the interview, quite quickly in simple, useful ways.

Some sample MSE results

The following tables are there to help a new clinician gain perspective on some typical examples of MSE presentations from my own jumbled recollections. I just thought that it might help a new clinician see how the short answers of the look in comparison from one diagnostic profile to the next. There are infinite possible variations of signs and symptoms and these tables are a sample only, based on memories I have had of different consumers presentations at MSE. Note the lack of reliance on jargon, the observational basis, and the short answers. To reiterate – this is not a guide – just some examples onl, based on a few observations over the years. There can be many other signs and symptoms not included in these examples so please do not regard it as gospel.

Sample MSE (Examples Only!!!)	Depressive	Melancholic Depressive	Psychotic Depressive	Bipolar Depression	Anxiousness	Trauma
Appearance (age gender +)	Slumped shoulders Downcast. Unkempt	Downcast. Unkempt. Loss of facial expression	Unkempt	Slightly untidy	Neat and tidy	Dishevelled Health problems
Attitude	Passive, Pessimistic	Reduced Eye contact. Pessimistic	Disgruntled	Challenging Help Seeking	Engaged	"Over-serviced"
Behaviour	Sat still	Restless	Wringing hands	Slight intoxication	Nervous Good eye contact	Anxious, some anger

Mood and Affect	Depressed Flat Labile	Flat, Weeping Anhedonia	Afraid, suspicious, bereft/torn	Aloof Bitterness	Acopia Teary at times	Challenging
Speech	Sparse	Morbid themed	calls key phrases repetitively Incomplete	Slow at times	Intense	Volubility at times
Thought process	Slowed	Ruminations	Perseverative. Fixed thinking. Blocked thinking.	Bleak NAD	Tends to fixed thinking on anxiety themes	Tangential Hyper-arousal
Thought content	Negative	Guilt Persecutory themes Risk (SI) themes	Self blame Nihilistic - Worries about contamination	Social isolation Low self esteem Unfulfilled	Neg ideas about coping ability	Low social worth/low self esteem. Suicidal –states nil intent
Perceptions	NAD (Nil Abnormality Detected)	NAD (waking)	Reports she "stinks" Somatic complaints	NAD	NAD	NAD
Cognition	NAD	Slowed thinking	NAD	NAD	NAD	Slowed thinking
Insight/judgement	Negative but NAD	Defeated, Hopeless	Clouded Hopeless	Hopeless and Helpless	Help seeking	Defiant yet helpless

Figure 8: Sample MSE profiles 1

Sample MSE (Example Only!!!)	Delirium	Alcohol-related vascular	Dementia	Dementia – Lewy Body	Parkinson's	Stroke	Bereavement
Appearance age gender +	Pyjamas unbuttoned	Poorly dressed Thin	Pyjamas	In wheelchair	Stooped	Leaning on armrest	Dressed in black
Attitude	Disinterest	Jovial, avoided depth in discussion	Passive	Variable	Engaging, apologetic	Engaging	Engaging
Behaviour	Psychomotor agitation	unsteady wide-based gait	Withdrawn Held assessors hand	Hit the table to make point	Small shuffling steps, Stiffness in limbs. Pill rolling	Leaning Left side weakness	Crying Wringing hands
Mood and Affect	Variable. Mourning state	Very friendly	Blank affect	Mood swings in assessment Angry affect	Drawn lips / expression	Anxious Lability – rapid changes	Lonely, sad depressed,
Speech	Rambling	Volubility	Quiet speech, Jumbled, continual stream	Loud	Slurred speech Varying volume, to very soft	Slurred	Soft
Thought process	Illogical, incoherent	Confabulat-ion	Disjointed Confusion	Perseveration	Logical	confusion	Mildly disorganised
Thought content	Farming/ history	Recalled long-term memories	'Word Salad'	Paranoia Angry	Appreciative Help seeking	Grief and loss themes	Fearful
Perceptions	Described "waking dream" Visual disturbance	ideas of wire inside holding body together	NAD / unable to assess	Lilliputian hallucinations, + cats	NAD	NAD	Spoke of feeling the deceased nearby
Cognition	Distracted Unable to do MMSE	Short-term memory impact	Poor concentration – very low MMSE	MMSE 21/30 Concentration effected	NAD	Reasoning and Memory impact	NAD (Nil formal testing)
Insight/Judgement	Very little	Nil	Nil	Nil insight into perceptions/ delusions	OK	Limited	Appropriate but family support not accessed

Figure 9: Sample MSE profiles 2

The following sections detail more about each aspect of the MSE.

APPEARANCE

(Physical description; Level of Personal Hygiene; Grooming)

The first category of MSE assessment, 'Appearance' is to observe and briefly record the outward physical aspects of the person. This can commence as first impressions are made at introductions and throughout the assessment. The physical environment is also relevant: e.g. ('75 year old woman, looks age, quite thin. Teary. In bed, fully dressed').

Discussion
Appearance can give clues to pathology. If someone is sweaty for example, and has trouble focussing, you may wonder if they have an infection associated with delirium. Low weight or obesity could be consistent with a depressive disorder, physical illness, anorexia nervosa, alcohol dependence or chronic anxiety.

Aspects such as dress and grooming, dental and other hygiene, apparent age, height and weight, and hearing and physical aids used can all be extremely relevant. You may make note of problems in skin condition, rashes, bandages, and pallor and noticeable aspects of complexion.

If someone is looking at you through very dirty glasses, you might wonder how organised their thinking is. Observing appearance can be a useful indicator of self care in particular, which involves a complex set of skills on various levels of brain function. Alternatively poor self care may also indicate much about mood problems such as depression. Unwashed, unkempt clothes, accompanied by poor hygiene including odour may reflect negative symptoms of schizophrenia.

A person whose buttons are torn or missing or they are regularly dressed in tracksuits may indicate difficulties with fine motor skills or executive planning.

Mania or hypomania may be present in the person wearing loud, colourful clothing or odd clothing choices (Be mindful of cultural bias here). It may be that their style has always been to wear odd or bright clothes, so corroboration will confirm the observation, or may cast light on cultural differences. Socially extreme clothing choices could also cast light on personality disorders which may be correlated with past trauma.

Looking at the whole person is as important as looking at details: For example, you may notice physical manifestations of long term problems with drugs or alcohol, which may be indicated via a package of signs like low body weight and other signs of malnutrition. Nicotine stains can indicate long term use of cigarettes. A characteristic odour should be recorded as it can accompany long-term alcohol dependence.

BEHAVIOUR DURING INTERVIEW

(Rapport; engagement; eye contact; psychomotor activity; interactions at assessment; facial expressions, posture, gestures; gait, unusual features)

This behavioural question is observations about the person's interactions to, or regardless of assessment. Broadly it covers what they do, their non-verbal communication, their attitude to assessment, their body language, and other physical movements both voluntary and involuntary.

Engagement and Rapport

Engagement is the way in which people express their entire self – physically, cognitively, and emotionally. Rapport is the existence of a positive emotional connection. Simple observations about the quality of engagement and rapport of the person tell a lot about their mental, psychological and social functioning. It also conveys much about the brain's wellness.

Engagement is reflected in the overall spoken and unspoken theme. Are they calm or aroused and agitated? Do they seem anxious, rubbing their forehead? In terms of body language, does the person come across as hostile, defensive or aggressive? Do they sit back and fold their arms, facing away from you, trying to keep control? Do they smile?

It is useful to note variations in rapport and engagement over the course of the assessment: eg "Engagement seemed stilted at first and Dawn's eyes were downcast, but she soon warmed and became quite open and friendly in her responses using good eye contact."

The ability to engage in interview can certainly be an indicator of wellness, and should be described. Common adverbs used may include willingly, amicably, reluctantly etc. Engagement (or lack of) can be a reflection of someone's depressive symptoms, negative symptoms of schizophrenia, their tendency toward isolation and likelihood of accessing supports, psychosis or delirium, their cognitive function, and any personality factors.

It is apt to wonder if the referred person views your presence as an intrusion. However, engagement may also reflect confidence issues with the mental health care process or their impression of the clinician. Gender, historical, cultural and social background of the client, the clinician and the mental health system can all influence engagement. General reluctance to discuss personal information with strangers may seem a very natural approach, especially as older people may have been raised in eras where a self-reliant 'chin up' culture was the first sign of coping.

Building Rapport

A terrific way to build trust is by just listening to clients in conversation. You could ask them if they grew up locally, and then ask them to comment on aspects of local history of the area, or the area they grew up in. Older people often enjoy sharing stories about conditions during their earlier life.

This storytelling can help the clinician build a clinical picture about their current thinking, their trauma history, literacy and education levels, family mental health history, beliefs and values, their memory functioning, medical history, current levels of confusion and a surprising variety of other bits of useful information. You can observe their expressions as their affects move through a range of responses, and experience their style of humour. These all form part of observations about people's mental state, and can be discreetly noted and explored in more detail during assessment and fleshed out when writing up the assessment.

A part of this is achieved through addressing initial concerns. Older clients have lived through eras when self-reliance was a very strong social value, and also when mental health problems were regarded as something to be ashamed of and deny, and mental health care was a very scary thing. Because mental health treatment and its social and legal implications have progressed significantly, an older person's views may be at odds with current service standards. For example, a fear of going into inpatient care may be around being left and forgotten inside a facility. Once you understand concerns, you can address them (eg "We now understand that often, if possible, the best place is for a person to recover is at home.")

Whatever the path that brought you to the client it becomes your role to present as trustworthy. You can do this by:
- Maintaining good eye contact and a responsive affect.
- Explaining who you are, what you do, and where you came from.
- Obtaining consent from the client, without which you cannot proceed unless immediate risk, duty of care, a delegation of consent or a legal order exists which overrides the decline of services
- Discussing the issue that has been raised, openly but gently and sensitively.
- Using everyday terms for things they may be experiencing that led to the referral.
- Highlighting normal and natural aspects of their responses where relevant.
- Introducing themes of hope
(eg I know a doctor who is very skilled and may be able to help you.)
- Being honest and responsive in conversation and addressing concerns

It is not uncommon for people to use gentle humour while rapport is building. This can be a promising sign; however it might be useful to consider if the person is casting up a wall of 'standard one liners' to put safe emotional distance between themselves and the assessor.

> Consider: How do *you* get people to

| open up and talk about themselves? |

Eye Contact

While on the topic of eye contact, it may be recalled that classically the eyes have been described as 'The windows to the soul'. Mood, fear, warmth, resilience, humour, sorrow, grief, engagement, confusion, anger and many other things can be communicated eye to eye. Avoiding eye contact can itself reveal a fear of disclosing something, a deep sense of shame or poor self esteem. This can be related to depression, as can teariness. Glancing around the room can reveal the person is responding to stimuli experienced as external (eg hallucination). Inability to focus may indicate delirium or attention and concentration difficulties ... or maybe just their nervousness at the prospect of assessment. Perhaps the person has autistic traits.

Many indigenous cultures around Australia have very unfamiliar styles of engagement to western people. For example, direct initial eye contact can be a mark of disrespect and so an Aboriginal person may feel that they are engaging well while a western-style assessment of this may erroneously suppose the person is disinterested or unwilling to be assessed.

Psychomotor Activity

When observing mental state it is important to notice what is going on physically for the person, noting indications of their overall activity and state of arousal. Their bodily behaviour may also demonstrate specific abnormal or involuntary movements, tremors, tics, hyperactivity, hypoactivity or dystonia. Further adjectives may also be noted: Eg slowed, repetitive, echopraxia (copying other's movements)

The global observation of arousal and activity may prompt descriptions such as hyperactivity or mania, which may be influenced by observations of other concurrent indications. Alternately a global impression of slowed physical responsiveness could attract a descriptor such as psychomotor retardation, a symptom of depression. These summary descriptions may be very apt but there may be alternative causes – for example, medication side effects can lead to any of the above states. Neurological disorders can also provide similar symptoms. Again the emphasis is that MSE is based on recording observation not jumping to the diagnosis.

For example, in noting abnormal movements, you can write "Mrs Jones right hand repetitively jerked to the left throughout the assessment", or "Jane squinted, her jaw moved and her tongue sat protruded (query tardive dyskinesia?)."

Interactions at Assessment

What is the reaction of the consumer to the assessment itself? Paranoid, cynical, or contemptuous? Is the consumer at ease, confrontational, inappropriate, or guarded? Their attitudinal response may be a summation of spoken cues and body language. It can be a reflection on the engagement and rapport skills, the consumer's view about yourself or your service, confidence, or attentiveness, alertness and underlying mental state; or a combination of any of these factors.

Facial Expressions

Facial expression is one dimension of the display of affect. Descriptors may include such as: Smiling, squinting, frowning, relaxed, tense, tearful, flushed or downcast. Adjectives could be added to these such as: Appropriate, variable, frozen.

Noting if the expression changes in relation to context is useful (E.g. Congruent, reactive, fixed). You could give additional detail: "Tearful, when discussing the passing of her son"

Gestures

Gestures are classically considered to be based in the same parts of the brain that support speech, and there is a strong relation to either informational gestures or communicational gestures, to language function. Informational gestures may show something independent of the spoken conversation, like rubbing a sore knee. Communicational gestures may involve symbolic hand movements or other bodily movements such as shrugging. Patting chest or heart may convey emotional distress

There are cultural and emotional dimensions to the use of gestures – For example, people using their hands to accentuate speech, people covering their mouth when they talk. People use gestures to communicate their mental state: Rubbing their forehead when stressed, rubbing the back of their neck when tired.

In mental health assessment, we want to observe any motions of the hands and body, without viewing all gestures as communicational or informational. Some people will:
- Reach for supports when walking due to anxiety about falling or poor balance
- Wring their hand wringing or grasp, in psy-

chomotor agitation,
- Do "Pill rolling" tremor in Parkinson's.
- Repetitive tactile motions as in punding.
- Do 'forbidden' sexualised or offensive gestures.
- Increase their use of gestures due to a change in their wordfinding functioning
- Rest their head on a "psychological pillow" in Catatonia.

Tremors and tics may also be noted in this section of the MSE, as well as any damping or loss of control. These types of physical actions may say much about brain pathology, medication side effects and/or mental state without the gestures being necessarily, or wholly communication or information based. In the case of Tardive Dyskinesia, or Dystonia it is vital to have the person assessed by the psychogeriatrician as soon as possible. In the more extreme cases these situations can lead to a medical emergencies or irreversible problems.

Psychomotor retardation, muscular stiffness as in Parkinson's, akinesia, catatonia, and negative symptoms of Schizophrenia may all show forms of a lack of or an inhibition of gestures. This should therefore be noted as part of the assessment.

Posture

Posture, or the position that a person holds their body when standing or sitting, may be observed when the person enters the room and throughout the interview.

Identifying posture (e.g. slouched, stooped, erect) can say something about mood, ease, self-esteem, self care and alertness – therefore about the mental and emotional state. Leaning can imply tiredness, and possibly something about the person's quality of sleep. Posture can convey subtle information about the person's social standing or their attitude, confidence in interpersonal relations or personality traits.

From a communications perspective, posture can convey particular messages. Someone leaning forward may be communicating anger, for example, while someone sitting back with a relaxed open posture may exude confidence. An open posture is one where the person is seen to not cover vulnerable areas of their body such as their throat, while a closed posture is more self-protective.

There are many other important observations of posture. Favouring one side or the other or poor balance can indicate other pathological situations such stroke. Stoop is a feature of Parkinsonism. Hunched posture can be a feature of Lewy body dementia. Kyphotic posture or curvature of the spine is a feature of Osteoporosis.

Gait

An Older Persons Mental Health clinician will want to observe the way a person's spontaneous walking style and features. Conditions such as Parkinson's, dementia, and chronic alcoholism and others have distinct impacts on gait. Depression can trigger psychomotor slowing in walking, some Parkinsonism, and also greater awareness of pain which can affect gait. Ataxia and some Parkinsonism can be a sign of psychosis and negative symptoms of schizophrenia, and medication side effects can certainly create a wide range of impacts on gait. Polypharmacy creates balance problems and increased risk of falls.

Observations of gait may include length of stride, difficulty initiating and stopping walking, difficulty turning, particular patterns, the person's sense of control and confidence, use of aides, steadiness. Posture and centre of gravity can say much about pathological situation. A shuffle is significant as are other patterns. Assessing gait can be a highly specialised skill and well beyond the new clinician to interpret specific gaits, but the object is to learn to observe gait, usually as the person enters and leaves the assessment.

Apraxia is where intentional or planning aspects of movement are impaired – i.e. the physical capacity may be present but the initiation of walking is not.

Some specific gaits: Ataxic gait features an abnormal, uncoordinated gait affecting stride length and tandem gait. "Magnetic feet" looks as if the feet are stuck to the ground. Parkinsonian gait is characterised by slow, small shuffling steps (petit pas) with reduced arm swing and a stooped posture. The person is therefore leaning forward and their may be difficulty starting walking and stopping.

MOOD AND AFFECT

A sense of wellbeing can say much about a person's internal mental functioning, and about changes to this functioning. For this reason, assessment involves consideration of emotional state – indicated by studying the person's mood and affect.

To conceptualise mood and affect in MSE, affect relates to the non-verbal: external, visible or behavioural observations of the way someone is feeling – the mood "as written on the person's face". Mood tends to be more about self-reported manifestations of the way the person is feeling, both described spontaneously and in response to inquiry. Mood can also be conveyed by more subtle cues throughout the assessment.

The quality of the clinician's own use of language comes into use in identifying mood and affect: A good vocabulary of adjectives is useful, and the clinician should not shy away from learning more of these descriptive terms and how they may be understood.

Although mood can change over the course of the assessment, mood is considered more longitudinally prevailing, while affect can shift in the context of the interview: The range of affect changes over the interview can provide useful clues to prevailing mood. Observations about the depth of mood, how long the person has struggled with the feelings, and how much or how often it changes are critical descriptions of mood.

When a change in mood or in affect is noted during assessment, consider the context of the changes. Could it be that the person's sense of hope, for example, is improved by the development of a supportive therapeutic relationship? Or, did certain contexts trigger anger?

Terms that are often used to describe mood in MSE include: neutral, sad, angry, fearful, apathetic, remorseful, euthymic, dysthymic, anxious, panicky, euphoric, suspicious, shamed, guilty, embarrassed etc. Blanket, generalised terms such as "disturbed" or "agitated" are not as useful without more descriptive terms. Sometimes people feel inadequate to describe their mood (i.e. Alexithymic).

Often the things people say about their mood is at variance with what seems to be conveyed through their affect and body language. Situations where this may arise may include where cultural and generational norms around mental health impel the person to express self-reliance when in fact their inner resources are depleted. This relationship to mood is often described as appropriateness of affect, or incongruous affect. On the other hand, it could say something about the person's insight.

Common terms describing affect changes include: reactive, variable, explosive, blunted (too little responsiveness), flat, restricted, fixed, stable, labile (rapidly changing, especially toward teariness) and nonresponsive. Terms to describe general affective states include such as: normal, ecstatic, bland, expansive, elevated, calm, irritable, and depressed. Descriptors of intensity of affect include heightened or over-dramatic.

SPEECH

Speech, so central to human functions, relies on a wide range of aspects of the brain function as well as our social, cognitive, emotional and interpersonal adaptation. Nuanced observation of speech can indicate the presence of grief, depression, anxiety, schizophrenia, trauma, or if there are significant changes to a person's cognition. It can hint at whether the person is feeling pressured, and can communicate content, style and themes in thinking.

Many mental health and other pathological situations can be identified partly through observation of spontaneous behavioural aspects of speech, or detected during cognitive testing. The overall pattern of speech can also be a useful observation. For example, people with mania may demonstrate pressured speech that can also be rapid and loud. People with depression may tend to speak slowly, sparsely and softly, with latency of speech that may reflect slowness of thinking or hesitation.

Dimensions of a person's speech can include:
- General ability – i.e. ease of conversation, articulation, spontaneity, latency
- Quality – slurring, stuttering, unique qualities
- Quantity – mute, minimal speech, volubility, verbosity

- Rate – rapid, pressured, reduced tempo, rhythm
- Volume – loud, normal, soft, variable
- Tonality – monotonous, prosody (sing-song tonality), tremulous, range of intonation, pitch
- Speech-based features of thought forms: tangentialism, circumstantial speech, thought blocking, derailment, disorganized, absent speech.

Some more specific descriptors of speech include: Speech agnosia, aphasia, aphonia, acquired apraxia, cluttered speech, word salad, dysarthria, echolalia, palilalia, mutism, neologisms, whispering and stuttering.

Perseveration can be noted to occur in speech, as can circumstantiality and tangentiality; however what is being noted here is speech and may be more fully recorded under the Thought Form section in the MSE.

There are certain cultural and linguistic considerations that may need to be taken into account during assessment: For example, people from Glasgow in Scotland may be more musical in prosody than people from Edinburgh, who tend to incorporate a more even, flat tonality into speech, relatively speaking. This of course is not to suggest people from Edinburgh are more depressed!

Communication difficulties may be acute or it may be from developmental or lifelong difficulties, or aspects of personality (e.g. shyness may play a role), and should be noted as such.

THOUGHT FORM

Thought form refers to observations of the way thinking is formulated or structured through listening to the things the person says, and listening for styles of thinking and pathological clues, as reflected in their speech. It would not be adequate to simply use diagnoses to describe thought form (eg: psychosis; dementia). It is the features of the spoken expression that give definition. A formal thought disorder is any noted disorder in the language, communication and content of thoughts as expressed.

When people's speech is clear, sensible and easy to follow, their thought form could be described as coherent. If the observer can easily follow the flow of thought it would be logical. Logic can be subtle – For example inferred emotional and physical pain states may be supported by speech and by non-verbal hints, and the flow of conversation may seem to have internal logic when looking holistically at the person. Therefore thought form can be thought of as the 'meta' view of what the person is *saying* - but is measured by tempo, quantity and continuity of thought in speech.

Tempo includes retarded or inhibited thinking (as in slowed or delayed responses in dementia or depression) or the opposite: racing thoughts may occur in anxiety and flight of ideas is suggestive of manic functioning.

Poverty of thought may occur with dementia, depression or psychotic illnesses when there are few ideas expressed. Thought blocking occurs when the person suddenly stops talking mid-sentence and cannot recover continuity of that sentence. Others may demonstrate a flood of thoughts. Concrete thinking is an absence of depth in the person's capacity to discuss abstract ideas, such as when a person describes what happened in a given situation, whereas an abstract thinker can consider different perspectives on what happened.

Continuity relates to the goal directedness of thought. Examples include:
- Circumstantial thinking is evident in anxiety, where people go a circuitous route to get their point across. This means they may include many themes before they return to the conclusion of their original idea.
- Tangentiality is different – the person does not return to the original point but jumps from theme to theme at connections between points. (I.e. 'off on a tangent').
- Tangentiality also can be further described as involving derailment of thought, or knight's move thinking, when the links between ideas seem obscure. The person may be able to explain how they got from one idea to the other, and when you hear it, it may make sense in a peculiar way.
- Fusion is where concepts are melted together.
- Loosening of associations is similar, except that the observer cannot observe the connections between themes as the person jumps from theme to

theme. Where speech consisted of a senseless jumble of words and sentences this is described using the terms Word Salad, Schizophasia, Paraphrasia or Verbigeration
- People can show perseveration in their speech, repeating a limited range of ideas.

Neologisms are where people create words to convey meanings (Such as when Homer Simpson, defending a word he had just made up while playing scrabble, by saying it is a perfectly 'cromunlent' word. If you're going to cheat at scrabble you may as well do it with style!) Confabulation, often seen in people with alcohol induced dementia, is where gaps in the memory are filled in with seemingly random ideas (sometimes fabulous idea), keeping interest of the listener without sufficient recall occurring. Where people fill in gaps in their recall or associations with rhyming words with no obvious meaning, it is termed clang associations. One client, who had a strong history of alcohol use, could spontaneously limerick for as long as he held the listener's attention, which was amazing to hear, however as he tired he tended to rely on neologisms until the limericks became a rhyming jumble.

THOUGHT CONTENT

This part of the MSE captures the general content of thoughts as expressed throughout the assessment as well as responses to specific questions, particularly the assessment of the presence of suicidal thoughts. Similarly, asking about thoughts of harm to self or others is highly important. Typically a suicide risk assessment will involve asking if the person has any thoughts of ending their life, asking how often they come, when these thoughts typically appear, do they have any specific plans to do so, and what keeps them safe – what their reasons for living are. Of course, if the person flatly denies risk, that will affect the flow of the conversation. If the person responds "very rarely", you might discuss how fleeting thoughts sometimes occur to most people occasionally. You might still ask about protective factors.

The general tone of thoughts (e.g. "sad" as captured under Mood) as well as emotional intensity and features such as the person's view of future (e.g. "Future focussed") can help corroborate the spoken content and contribute to the sense of reliability of the assessment of mental state. Therefore, capturing content of the person's conversation can be very useful, and also provides the opportunity to detect clinically significant features. Delusions may be mood-congruent, typical of manic or depressive psychoses, or mood-incongruent, as seen in schizophrenia.

Things to look out for include preoccupations, obsessions and delusions. Preoccupations are recurring themes of a minor intensity, for example Hypochondriasis. An overvalued idea is also characterised by lower intensity – a false belief that is held with some conviction. On the other hand, delusions are intense, fixed beliefs that have no rational basis in reality. Nihilistic delusions are those that where the person is overcome with an even which will result in their or other's death. Persecutory delusions are where one believes falsely that someone is trying to kill or harm them.

In older people, fixation on misplaced electricity bills or other minor concerns may have a nihilistic element, where the consequences become unthinkable and insurmountable. This may be related to depression with melancholia, where a person may dwell on perceived but unrealistic:
- money problems such as losing their pension
- worries over utilities and essential services being cut
- somatic obsessions and delusions, and
- shame over what their family may be thinking

Obsessions are where a person has thoughts that are dominated by persistent, often unwelcome and irrational ideas, desires, or mental images. Compulsive acts sometimes follow - compulsions are irresistible or very strong urges to perform repetitive stereotyped acts, often against their better judgement or will.

These ritualised actions are related to anxiety. Also related to anxiety are phobias, which are specific fears of a situation or thing that produce an intense anxiety response the person usually knows is unrealistic.

At MSE you may also notice specific themes that may be related to organic brain function: For example, an older person may be adept at talking about their long-term history where their retrograde memory is intact but their ability to lay down new memories is impaired. This can be related to dementia, and is clinically significant content to note.

- Ideas of reference which are false beliefs that an event pertains to the person. For example, a person believes they are receiving personal messages from car number plates or from the television.
- Ideas of influence where the person believes they caused an unrelated event. (for example, a person dies of illness, but the consumer feels they caused it through their thoughts)
- Grandiosity is where the content recurringly features really big, impractical or false ideas or the person's conception of their own greatness.
- Body dysmorphic disorder is characterized by an obsessive preoccupation that some aspect of one's own appearance is severely flawed and warrants exceptional measures to hide or fix it.

PERCEPTION

A hallucination is a sensory perception in the absence of any correlating external stimulus, and is experienced by the person as real. Hallucinations can occur in the five senses. Auditory, visual, tactile, olfactory (smell) or gustatory (taste) hallucinations can often occur in older persons with mental illness. Somatic hallucinations – affecting inner bodily sensations, are also common. Visual hallucinations may generally relate to organic problems, while psychotic disturbances tend to manifest in auditory hallucinations, but there is significant crossover. There are particular observations of perceptual disturbances in older people worth noting.

Screening for perceptual disturbance with a holistic perspective is critical not only for treatment of acute mental health illness, but because of the significant risk to older people from underlying organic pathology. In older people, perceptual disturbance can be common, especially in organic problems such as delirium and Lewy body dementia, or in people with impacts from long-term use of alcohol, or as a side-effect of medication.

The relationship of fear or distress to the themes of perceptual disturbance is important to note. It can be unexpected in some instances – for example, one lady with Lewy Body dementia reported seeing little (Lilliputian) humans with ugly faces and carrying big swords lined up along the kitchen bench during the assessment, but was not troubled by this. Another person had a delusion that staff members of her nursing home were giving her the wrong medication so they could kill and eat her. However her affect was matter-of-fact and not at all concerned. Often the opposite is true – the person's distress is obvious and important to note. It should be also investigated if the person feels that the perceptual disturbance is certain, or if they have insight into the reality of their perception.

In the older person suffering from depression with psychotic features, there is often a somatic component, which may be accompanied by nihilistic ideas. This can be a complex picture where for example, there may be realistic physical health impacts over which an acute mental health problem is laid, making the management of the physical health problem much more difficult and potentially life threatening. Illusions, where the person's false belief *is* related to reality, may accompany the somatoform hallucination, as fixed ideas about the meaning of the actual physical health situation.

Another type of perceptual disturbance is olfactory hallucinations. For example in conjunction a theme of guilt or self-loathing may be accompanied by a perception that the person stinks of faeces, where there is no apparent smell and the person has had a shower that day.

Other Perceptual Disturbances include:
- Déjà vu is a distortion of the person's sense of

time
- Depersonalization is a distortion of the sense of self (A dissociative symptom)
- Derealisation is a distortion of the sense of reality (A dissociative symptom)
- Pseudohallucination (for example as "voices in my head") is experienced in the person's inner world and can be akin to fantasy.

COGNITION & INTELLECTUAL FUNCTIONING

"RUDAS or 3MS/MMS completed No Yes N/A"

The prevalence of age-related brain changes in older people means that consideration of cognitive function is very common in Older Persons Mental Health. Cognitive function and ability interacts very closely with mental illness and mental disturbance. It can be an indication of changes in coping ability, for example. Symptoms that may appear acute actually indicate underlying changes to brain and functional ability.

Often these changes indicate chronic or progressive changes, which sometimes go counter to the acute focus in mental health. Cognitive indications can work the other way. For example: depression can precipitate a slowing of thought; mania can include racing thoughts; anxiety can trigger distraction, and poor concentration and can be part of psychosis.

Gathering information about cognitive changes is an important part of a SMHSOP mental health assessment. The approach does not aim to replace the role of Geriatric assessment by a dementia specialist. Psychogeriatric referral often occurs before a formal diagnosis of dementia has been made, or sometimes when the person has a recognised dementia, and a change in mood has been noticed by carers, or perhaps psychotropic drugs have been administered and unexpected results have occurred. For all these reasons, the SMHSOP clinician needs some basic skills in cognitive assessment and some understanding of changes to the brain.

Experiences of cognitive change

Cognitive changes, such as dementia, can occur slowly and insidiously, slightly below the immediate awareness of the family member. Close family members might barely notice changes in behaviour year upon year, without relating it specifically to long term changes in cognition, attributing deficits to "just getting old". This is possibly because recognising the changes has wider meaning to the relationship and the spouse's own wellbeing. Meanwhile, the person's cognition, personality, function and independence remain largely intact, but people naturally fear a creeping loss in their abilities, function and their independence, and reactions to the changes can quickly develop into a crisis.

It can be easy to confuse dementia (with mood and behavioural impacts) with treatable mental illnesses (with temporary cognitive impacts). For example, an older person who has been lying in bed for weeks due to depression may not be oriented to time and yet, despite a slowing of thought, may or may not be experiencing permanent cognitive problems.

When it is no longer possible to ignore cognitive changes, it usually amounts to a crisis, which can precipitate referral to mental health. These crises can be accompanied by grief and loss, depression, behavioural changes, relationship conflict, fear and paranoia, and psychotic disturbance. At this point in time, cognitive testing is a very sensitive issue. Fears about the loss of self and function are compounded by concerns about adequate self-care, competency (important in wills, medical and property decisions), relationship changes, health management, coping and safety, which all involve cognitive function.

> What might it be like to notice cognitive or functional brain changes in your life partner, or in yourself?

A fatalistic and ageist approach to these situations is to overgeneralise, and to roll these symptoms under one label. However more detailed assessment at intake helps to differentiate mild from more pervasive cognitive impact, and leads to a starting point in understanding what is going on, in preparation for the psychogeriatric assessment, toward best treatment.

Also, the *change* in cognitive ability is highly relevant. If through cultural, long-term biological or developmental impacts, the older person has not developed strong skills in one or more areas, it is very important to understand the history of the person's baseline, and record in the assessment these factors which have impact on cognitive scores. This requires great care, as the developmental and educational impacts can be a source of great shame and the person might find the assessment quite humiliating.

The Initial Narrative Cognitive Assessment

The typical MSE asks if the person is oriented in "time, place and person" (A common shorthand is "Oriented T/P/P"). Problems in recalling the date, time, where they are, the type of building they are in, who they and you are, can be a sign post to assessing the person's cognitive function. Achieving this part of the assessment may best be done reasonably discreetly during the narrative assessment – when you meet the person, introduce yourself and ask them their name, for example. It can be a discreet approach, if there is another person present (such as a relative), to ask the consumer who the other person is and what relation they are to them.

Initial observations of cognition during narrative assessment should note conscious states such as "Alert", "Drowsy", "Stupor", "Comatose". Changes over the course of the interview should also be noted – a variation in consciousness, for example, may indicate delirium, and might indicate a medical emergency, and then appropriate medical care needs to be sought. (Corroborative history might null the emergency if it's a problem that the person's doctor is aware of, and if the variability is consistent and a chronic problem.)

When it becomes apparent, either from referral information or due to suspicions you develop during assessment, a more formalised cognitive assessment tool can then be used if necessary.

Approaches to cognitive testing

Rapport and engagement process are underpinned at this point by preparing the consumer for what you're wanting them to do. To introduce the cognitive test,

I might try to find out if they like tests and puzzles, or if we've been discussing their life history, ask they liked school, and how far they went in school. If they were born overseas, did they study English as a second language? (All of these issues can be very sensitive issues, especially for people from marginalised groups, so tread softly.)

This kind of information is vital because many of the tests feature aspects of literacy, and as we are looking for changes in function and ability, poor initial literacy could bias assessment and should be noted on the test. Similarly, visual and hearing impairment could affect reliability of the test.

I might then introduce the test as follows:
"As part of my role I use a set of tests. A bit like school quizzes, some of them. They are designed to check our abilities in a lot of little ways. Some are easy, others a bit harder. Can we do these now?"

Some may find the testing very intrusive, or very frightening. They may fear that it is the process that means they may be forced into nursing home care. In some cases this fear is very well grounded and they may respond in grief. Some feel the opposite – they know they can still think ok in many ways, and they're interested to find out how they go, and sometimes people demonstrate aspects of denial or even a sense of belligerence, but they go ahead with it anyway.

Ultimately it remains a voluntary assessment dependent on the client's permission. Being a sensitive issue, the worker must retain humour, compassion and understanding to administer these tests. Also required are skills to respond appropriately to issues such as grief, fear and anxiety that may surface with these tests. Where the person is at reduced capacity to give informed consent, there is even more reason to be gentle, respectful, tactful, kind and as unobtrusive as possible.

In-depth, detailed MMSE

Aside from assessing consciousness and general orientation, the clinician assesses cognitive function using standardised tests to capture a snapshot in a range of areas such as: orientation, attention, learning and memory (registration, recall and general knowledge), visuospatial interpretation (with drawing ability), reasoning, perception, coordination, literacy and numeracy, and executive function (planning, abstraction and conceptual differentiation), and communication. These functions, and *changes* in these functional abilities, can have a strong interplay with mental wellbeing, and can also be among the indicators of illness.

In SHMSOP services, the MSE is augmented by use of one of a number of standardized tests. These aggregated tools measure cognitive functioning in a range of cognitive areas. With a high degree of overlap and with some significant differences between them, the RUDAS, the 3MS/MMS and the Addenbrooke's Cognitive Assessment are examples of well established instruments which have all been in used within SMHSOP and by visiting psychiatrists.

The cognitive assessment tests I had available in printed form were the 3MS/MMS, and the RUDAS. This 3MS/MMS measures a range of cognitive abilities, and provides a score out of 30 (MMS) and cuts the data a different way and adds more tests to provide a score out of 100. Baseline scores are provided which indicate likely cognitive impairment. Education, age and mood can influence the test results, with subjects of low education, advanced age and depression performing more poorly. Another well-known cognitive test is the Addenbrooke's Cognitive Examination, which comes with a useful explanatory document. It contains additional tests such as language tests, and perceptual tests.

Cognitive changes can lead to distress in the consumer as they feel frustration at not being able to understand or do things as they used to do. Very often this involves a sense of grief and loss, which requires adjustment and acceptance through love and support from those they care about to help them through. Often the grief and loss felt by the consumer and their family member as functional changes occur may evoke any one of a range of strong emotions: Blame, fear, guilt, anger and denial being common.

Alternatively, decline in brain function can precipitate specific degeneration in social and interpersonal ability that might look like standard, treatable mental health symptoms. Some examples of how cognitive problems may blend with mental health, functioning and wellbeing include:
- Brain injury, including frontal lobe damage through trauma: Inability to process anger, unresolved grief and loss, executive planning functions, acopia, relationship impacts, risk in driving with implications to independence, etc
- Brain starved of oxygen at birth: Impeded devel-

opment of social and intellectual capacity
- Dementia: Loss of independence and intellectual function, difficulty regulating emotions such as anxiety, loss of ability to communicate
- Chronic alcohol abuse: low initiative, poor balance, depression, self-neglect, incontinence
- Schizophrenia: Loss of intellectual function, emotional regulation, self care, communication/relationships. Hallucinations and delusions, risks such as from self-harm and suicide etc

A Mnemonic

The standardised tests contain fields for the consumer to write and draw in, and graphics and other written resources used in the test, so it's a bit difficult to get away from a formal examination toward a more narrative one. However, some familiarity with the various aspects of the tests can be useful. A Mnemonic I have heard goes as follows:

GOAL-CRAMP – it doesn't quite follow RUDAS and I wouldn't make this a high priority to learn but it may be useful at times.

G – general alertness and cooperation
O – orientation
A – attention tasks – WORLD spelt backwards and Serial Sevens
L – language – naming objects, repeat a phrase
C – calculation, division, subtraction
R – right hemisphere tasks – intersecting pentagons and clock face drawings
A – abstraction – proverbs and similarities
M – memory: Short term, historical (retrograde)
P – praxis: Wave goodbye and combing hair

Aspects of the Standardised Cognitive Exams

Orientation: The standardised tests revisit orientation, as discussed above, but in a more detailed manner, divided into temporal and spatial orientation, with scoring attached.

Attention and Concentration: Note the level of focus. Sustaining focus over the course of the interview can be quite wearing for the person whose attention and concentration is impaired. They may do well for the first few questions, then decline to participate further, saying they are tired, or even becoming generally less engaged. These may be indications of impairment of function.

Concentration is often assessed using a reasonably challenging test, such as spelling the word "WORLD" backwards, or counting backward from 100 by sevens. The latter is more useful, of course, if the person has difficulty with literacy. Both of these tasks require an ability to focus under pressure.

Memory: Memory is divided for assessment, into registration of new information, short-term recall, and long-term retrieval. Often a set of three words are read to the person, asking them to repeat them back (registration, laying down new memories). The person is asked to try to remember the words because they will be asked to recall them later in the test (short-term recall). Specific scoring for the person's ability to recall is usually detailed within the standardised test.

Longer-term memory can be assessed in terms of declarative memory and procedural memory. An example of assessment of declarative memory is asking general knowledge such as who is prime minister and which U.S. president was shot in the 1960's (Retrograde memory). Procedural memory is not part of some standardised testing, but is related to the RUDAS Praxis question, where the person is asked to watch and copy certain hand actions – although this is actually primarily a test of frontal functions.

Language: There are a number of language related tests common across various standardised instruments. They assess various aspects of language and communication as these are functionally significant. Consumers are variously asked to:
- repeat a simple sentence such as "no ifs, ands or buts"
- name familiar objects such as a pen or a wristwatch
- name drawn objects (Addenbrooke's – which is then used in a comprehension test)
- repeat certain words
- name as many four-legged animals or objects starting with the letter 'P' as you can within a 30 second timeframe
- name body parts the clinician points to on themselves
- follow three-stage commands (complex instructions)
- read the words "CLOSE YOUR EYES" and follow the instruction
- write a sentence of their own
- write something else, anything they like.
  (I sometimes get feedback: "This is stupid!", "Why don't you write something?")

Visuospatial functioning: This refers to the ability to perceive relationships of objects, essential to mobility and utility in the world. Driving vehicles, negotiating stairs and furniture, cooking etc all require this ability. The ability to recognise, copy and interpret three dimensional objects (or actually, drawings of them, such as the wireframe sketch of a cube) is therefore part of standardised testing, and may reveal much about the brain's health. Another common test is the intersecting pentagrams drawing, which is sufficiently complex to score in a detailed fashion by scoring the correct sides and corners of each pentagram as well as the correct number of corners in the intersection.

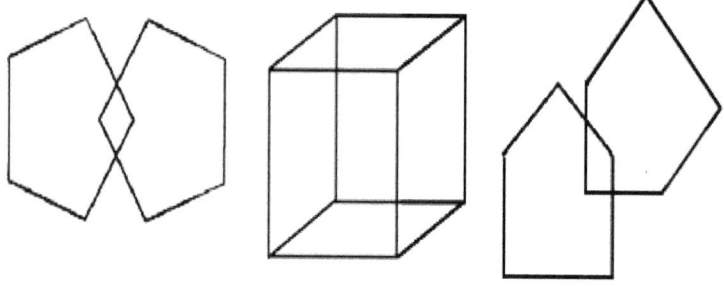

Figure 10: Intersecting pentagrams

The RUDAS features a Visuospatial Orientation question which asks the person to do such things as touching their left shoulder with their right hand.

On the 3MS/MMS there is extra space allowed for drawing tests and clock-drawing tests are mentioned. The clock face is complex and reproducing it involves planning ability. This test was originally used to assess visuo-constructive abilities is used because it can demonstrate impacts in a range of brain pathological situations. Interpretation of this type of neurological test is the domain of the psychogeriatrician, but a few possible outcomes are shown below:

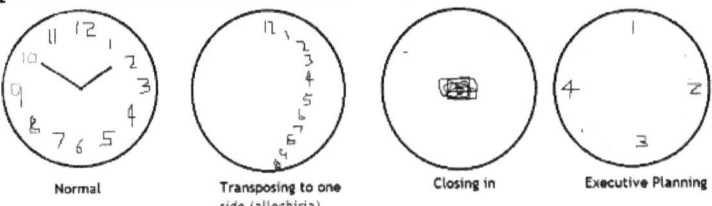

Figure 11: Clock face examples

Another common test is the trail marking test, a neuropsychological test of visual attention and task switching, where the person is asked to connect a set of numbered dots in sequence within a time limit.

The psychogeriatrician may use their preferred standardised test, plus other more specialised tests that the new SMHSOP clinician probably won't be aware of, providing a richer analysis of which parts of the brain may be being affected, functional impact and the best treatment options. For example a perseveration test, which involves copying and then extending a pattern, where the person may inadvertently repeat the last element:

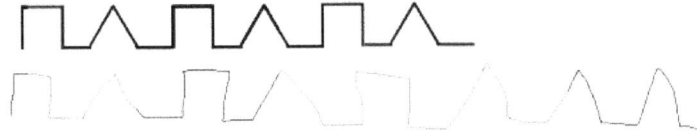

Figure 12: Perseveration test

Perceptual abilities: Some tests feature questions designed to test perception, such as in Addenbrooke's questions that ask the person to count dots without pointing to them, and recognising fragmented letters.

This can reveal deficits in visuoperception and executive function, which are common in people with a long history of alcoholism.

Executive Functioning: The higher orders of organised thought involving neurologically-based skills involving achieving goals and managing the self. It is assessed in cognitive testing by asking about conceptual similarities between things, and by means of a verbal fluency tasks. In the MMSE, the similarities question is threefold: Ask the person "How are an arm and a leg similar?"; "How are laughing and crying similar?"; "How are eating and sleeping similar?" Best answers are given within the test. Of course, people are going to put their answers in their own words. For example, "Eating and sleeping are both important for your health" will be conceptually correct but not the same as the answer "Vital for life". These tests represent a high standard of ability, and most people lose some points, it seems.

Abstraction and Conceptualisation: You may notice problems in abstraction and conceptualisation. Abstraction means deriving or perceiving deeper meaning beyond concrete ideas or observations. When people have deficits in this type of conceptualisation, they may only be able to give very literal answers. For example you may ask if an experience was enriching, and the person may say "I'm not rich". You could test abstract reasoning by asking the person the broader meaning behind a common proverb such as "The grass is always greener on the other side". These tests are not usually found in standardised tests.

There are many more very interesting and revealing

neurological tests that can examine specific function involving pathological situations including impacts in the Wernicke's area or Broca's area, parietal lobe or the frontal lobe, for example, by the psychogeriatrician.

INSIGHT AND JUDGMENT

Insight and judgement are at the crux of thorough assessment. Particularly around the client's discernment in questions of risk and protective factors, their choices about treatment adherence, and informed consent, compliance, and advanced care directives, the consumer's functioning in terms of insight and judgement is central. For example, a person's ability to make decisions about their care requires insight into their problem, as well as the judgment to make appropriate decisions.

Problems of insight and judgement might be observed throughout the assessment. For example, a person with chronic mental health problems may display, earlier in the assessment, a lack of concern about the capacity of their carer to cope with the burden of care. These issues can lead to pivotal concerns. Insight and judgement are at the pinnacle of organised thinking, and require abstract and conceptual ability applied to social, philosophical, ethical and personal values.

If mental health clinicians are going to help people when they at their most vulnerable, over their most difficult crisis, at times decisions about the person's well being will be inconsistent with the views of the person. This can overshadow the normal rights of the person. With progress toward recognising the consumer's voice in officially recognised recovery values, and principles of minimal restraint, this can now be clearly recognised as a potential personal tragedy. Decisions to transport someone under a schedule, or to monitor someone's compliance under a treatment order should be thoroughly documented as a matter of accountability to the client as much as to the state. In short, there must be a compelling rationale for action, transparently and clearly recorded.

Insight

Problems in insight are common in psychosis and dementia, and can have great impact on treatment planning and consent. Key issues are:

- Does the person understand the nature of their disturbance in mental state?
- Does the person understand the implications of their health decisions?
- Does the person understand your role and the reason for the assessment?
- Is their variability in their insight that may have implication on their wellbeing?

These issues can be canvassed by exploring the consumer's account of the problem and treatment options. If, in your clinical judgement, there are delusions or hallucinations, present, do they show insight into them?

When people have beliefs that are counter to one's own, it is generally accepted to be their right. In a clinical situation, there are more implications. However, many people live with mental illness by choice, independently in the community. This is their right under principles of minimal restraint, unless doing so places themselves or others at significant risk. The question has to be about risk, to them and to others.

Therefore, documenting clinical observations about insight needs to cover the key issues, but how that information is used in risk assessment may vary according to context.

Judgment

Judgement refers to problem-solving ability and application of sound thinking to practical problems. A question often posed is "what should you do if you see smoke coming out of a house?" In RUDAS, there is a question about what the person might do to cross a busy street. This requires higher order organised thought, planning and conceptualisation, and is useful because it can give a picture of whether the person has skills to keep safe. Does the answer show self-awareness, risk management ability, and social sense?

FALLS RISK

Standard #10 of the National Safety and Quality Health Service Standards is about recognising, assessing and managing falls risks. Screening for falls risks is mandatory and is considered best practice under ACSQHC. Often this is done before the OPMH worker has met the client. Significantly, however:
- 25% of people 65 and older fall each year.
- 50% of people 85 and older fall each year.
- 50% of people in living in an aged care setting fall each year.

Older people are particularly vulnerable to worse outcomes from falls than their younger counterparts. NSW Health Policy is aimed at reducing harm from falls for older people accessing clinical services and living in aged care. Communication with the multidisciplinary team and the client's support network can help identify risks.

Screening for falls risk

The Mental Health Functional Assessment form has falls risk identifying fields, and there are two further assessment tools: The Ontario Modified Stratify (Sydney Scoring) Falls Risk Screen; and the Falls Risk Assessment and Management Plan (FRAMP). These latter two tools facilitate time-series data collection and may require input from nursing and care staff, medical staff and occupational therapists. OPMH clinicians may contribute cognitive testing, delirium screening and mental state examination to falls risk assessment.

OPMH clinical role and falls risk

Older people, particularly those with frail health, may have a baseline of poor balance and falls risk. Health professionals supporting consumers in the OPMH age bands may be assisted in the management of falls risk through assessment and support, particularly in areas such as:

- Gathering historical information about falls during assessment.
- Assessing for cognitive impairment, Parkinsonism, dizziness, balance and gait issues.
- Being aware of the client's physical environment and requesting an OT assessment where cognitive changes, medication changes or delirium have put the client at increased risk.
- Assessing for delirium.
- Recognising implications of medications on falls risk: Antipsychotics, antidepressants, sedatives/hypnotics and opioid medications all increase falls risk, as do anticonvulsants, antiparkinsonians, antihypertensives, diuretics and hypoglycaemics. Additionally, consumers who take four or more medications as well as night sedation (Polypharmacy) are at increased falls risk, due to the older person's increased sensitivity to medication. Older people adjusting to an altered medication regime are especially vulnerable to side-effects, delirium and increased falls risk.
- For older people in particular, Benzodiazepams and other CNS-acting medications such as antipsychotics increase fall and fracture risk in older people.
- Extrapyramidal side effects are known to present greater complications to older people, including

aspects that may impact on falls risk.
- ❖ Reports of dizziness, changes in stability or steadiness, hypoglycaemic episodes can indicate falls risk.
- ❖ Clients with long-term history of alcohol and other drug problems may have Alcohol related brain injury (ARBI), which can lead problems of neuropathy and cerebellar ataxia, to falls and to accidents that further injure the brain.
- ❖ Recognising Postural Hypotension – a fall in blood pressure upon standing. Dizziness upon standing.
- ❖ Risks presented by clutter, squalor and hoarding. Home hazards, for which assessment by an OT would be indicated.
- ❖ Advocacy for clients who may require special management by care workers for reasons of restlessness, anxiousness, physical, somatic or psychological dependence, e.g. clients who may be incontinent, up a lot at night in the nursing home, or those who may frequently call on care staff.

Coordinating care

Contributing to planning for the client with falls risk in mind is an ongoing role for health providers. For example, if it is understood that a client's balance is already somewhat compromised, the addition of antidepressants could increase the risk of falls. If a SMH-SOP worker (or other consultant health worker) has assessed someone as a falls risk, assessment information should be made available to nursing / care staff and the GP.

Health Promotion

Encouraging clients to engage in health promotion activities that improve their fitness and balance is also a key to strengthening client's social and emotional wellbeing. NSW Health sponsored activities such as gentle exercise and Tai Chi are fantastic ways a OPMH worker can help their clients reduce their falls risk and also gain a wide range of other benefits.

Section 3: Practice-based Knowledge

KNOWLEDGE TO PRACTICE: ONE CLINICIAN'S PERSPECTIVE

The new clinician faces challenges of acquiring sufficient knowledge, but to the perspective of the consumer, the concerns are much more than academic. The following section, which is intended to correlate with the Knowledge part of competency, may point the way to issues for further research and discussion.

It looks at medication and at a few of the illness states that OPMH might regularly come across. Once again, it is largely experience based – my practice experience – and does not attempt to provide authoritative overviews of pathology, but attempts to consider Recovery perspectives in the discussion about pathological states.

I have started with a short quiz. Some of the answers are up for debate. While answering the following quiz I would ask you to also reflect on how a new clinician might feel about facing these kinds of issues. Consider perspectives of a consumer. Consider Recovery values. (It is not easy that the breadth of learning seems endless.)

FIRST, A QUICK QUIZ...

Quiz Question 1
An 85 year old woman confides with pleasure, during assessment, that she is pregnant. She hopes it lives, because as she observes she is quite old for a new mother. She says she lost a baby once before and was very sad as she "so wanted to have her own baby". She says she can feel it kicking. You may be seeing symptoms of:

a) Internal physical health problems involving her stomach, and delirium
b) A major depressive episode with mood-congruent delusions
c) Confusion in dementia, on a possible background of lifelong religiosity
d) Late-onset schizophrenia, with a Cotard delusion with a somatic dimension
e) Attention-getting behaviour – possibly an indication of a personality-based disorder
f) A rare form of late-life delayed pregnancy

(Continued)

Quiz Question 2
A 79 year old woman has been receiving help from her

GP to help manage pain, but nothing seems to work. The pain fluctuates dramatically, but no organic cause has been found. The GP commenced her on Avanza but she rapidly became agitated and suicidal, and tried to exit a moving vehicle. She appears to be having some cognitive decline, but this appears to fluctuate also. During MSE you ask about unusual thoughts, and she says no, but her partner says she talks about seeing small animals running through the house. She agrees with this, that it has been happening for a long time. This could indicate:

a) Diurnal symptoms of depression with extrapyramidal side-effects of an antidepressant
b) Delirium
c) Lewy-body Dementia symptoms

Quiz Question 3
During MSE, in cognitive testing a 80 year old farmer who has anxiety symptoms, does poorly on recall, but also particularly in written aspects of the test. Overall he gets 23/30. You might decide to: (Select any relevant answers)

a) Ask the GP if there is any recent pathology
b) Ask the client about his early life
c) See if there is a CT scan
d) Learn more about his worries about life on the farm

Quiz Question 4: Lingo
Match up the terms

Neologism	Mood
Partition	Hallucination

Lilliputian	Speech
Euthymic	Delusion

What can these terms described as?

Hints: Q1 – think Meaning in Recovery. Q2 – The value of authoritative specialised support Q3 – The value of narrative assessment. Q4 – Jargonese. Consider consumer's perspective.

PSYCHOTROPIC MEDICATIONS

An important area that I often struggled with as a social worker is having some level of understanding about the nature of the medications that are often prescribed to older people for behavioural, mood or other psychiatric symptoms. New OPMH clinicians, whether from nursing, social work, occupational therapy or psychology, or trained through a program such as the Aboriginal Mental Health degree, need access to some level of understanding about what these drug classes are and (some examples of non-generic brand labels):

Typical antipsychotic agents
Haloperidol   (Serenace)

Atypical antipsychotic agents
Aripiprazole   (Abilify)
Clozapine   (Clozaril)
Olanzapine   (Zyprexa)
Quetiapine   (Seroquel)
Risperidone   (Risperdal)

Antidepressants - Selective serotonin reuptake inhibitors (SSRIs)
Citalopram   (Celexa, Cipramil)
Paroxetine   (Paxil)

Sertraline (Zoloft)
Escitalopram (Lexapro)
Fluoxetine (Prozac)

Antidepressants - SNRIs
Desvenlafaxine (Pristiq)
Duloxetine (Cymbalta)
Venlafaxine (Effexor, Effexor XR)

Atypical Antidepressant
Mirtazapine (Avanza)

Tricyclic antidepressant drugs
Nortriptyline (Allegron, NortriTABS)

Mood Stabilizers
Sodium Valproate

SIDE-EFFECT ISSUES IN OPMH

The special issue of the sensitivity of older persons to side effects of these generally powerful medications is understood in OPMH services, but less so in GP services and even in general adult community mental health. Nevertheless these drugs are often prescribed (even to regulate behavioural problems in nursing homes).

Although these medications may produce excellent results at times, in instances of side effect reactions it will be useful for assessing clinicians to have some information about recognising side effects. The medications listed below are on the list either because they are often used in mental health, or they have significant implications for older people, or because their side-effects may overlap with mental health symptoms and attract referral to OPMH services.

This information is partially drawn from an excellent article from England called *Psychotropic Medication Use among Older Adults: What All Nurses Need to Know* (Lindsey, 2009). The research/knowledge base is developing all the time and there may be newer sources and more information, however I would recommend that Lindsey's article be studied by any mental health clinician who is starting work to with older people.

Not every person prescribed these drugs will experience these side effects, but at times you probably will be asked to assess someone displaying *dyskinesia* or *punding* (see Glossary) or some other side effect and it is important to be aware of the importance of gathering the medication history and the urgency of addressing new symptoms in these cases:

Drug group	Possible Major Adverse Effects in older people (For tables showing drugs and side effects, see Lindsey, 2009)
Typical antipsychotic agent	In my understanding tends to be used less these days in OPMH but in people with long-term prescriptions is still quite common. Side effects includes risks of extrapyramidal symptoms, tardive dyskinesia, neuroleptic malignant syndrome. Falls risks increase.
Atypical antipsychotic agents	sleep disturbance, overactivation, akathisia, neuroleptic malignant syndrome, tardive dyskinesia, deep venous thrombosis and pulmonary embolism, glucose dysregulation, seizures, hypotension (especially orthostatic), tachycardia, dysrhythmias, restlessness, akathisia, anxiety, extrapyramidal symptoms, agranulocytosis (the latter - see Clozapine) Falls risks increase.
Antidepressants - Selective serotonin reuptake inhibitors (SSRIs)	These medications have been indicated to have increased risk of serious side effects in older persons. Long list of side effect risks includes risks of suicidal behaviour, migraine, tremor, vertigo, hyponatremia, SIADH (syndrome of inappropriate antidiuretic hormone), increased risk of bleeding with co-administration of NSAIDs, aspirin, and warfarin Falls risks increase.
Antidepressants - Non-SSRIs	Have been indicated to have increased risk of serious side effects and falls risk in older

	persons.
Tricyclic antidepressant drugs	Increased side effect risks in older persons includes orthostatic hypertension, myocardial infarction, ataxia, extrapyramidal symptoms, seizures, glucose dysregulation, SIADH, sexual dysfunction, dry mouth, anorexia, constipation, nausea, vomiting, diarrhea, weight gain/loss, urinary retention, impotence, blood dyscrasia, increased levels in liver function test values, paresthesia, mydriasis Falls risks increase.
Benzodiazepines	Long-term use of benzodiazepines and use with other drugs such as Haliperidol presents increased side effects risks. The evidence for improvement in behavioural disturbances has been found to be unclear in a recent systematic review from the Cochrane library. The ride effect risk seemed to be lower to other psychotropic drugs (Zamal et al., 2017).
Antiparkinson's drugs	Although Parkinson's is not a primary presentation for an OPMH referral, you may be referred a client who is diagnosed with Parkinson's and a behavioural, mood or psychotic episode has developed after having been taking Sinemet. The following information is adapted from https://mentalhealthdaily.com/2016/02/11/sinemet-carbidopa-levodopa-side-effects-adverse-reactions-list/ Psychiatric symptoms may anxiety, appetite loss, confusion, delusions, depression, dizziness, dream disturbances, dyskinesia, hallucinations, impulse control problems, insomnia, memory deficits, psychosis, sleep disturbance and suicidal thoughts. Punding behaviours are also a feature of side-effect.
Mood Stabilizers	Sometimes being used as part of pain management, or for anti-seizure properties as well as for mood disturbance. May present interaction problems with other medication taken by older people, as well as the usual increased side effects risks and falls risks common to older person risks.

Cholinesterase Inhibitors	As discussed above, typical antipsychotics and some atypical antipsychotics have been shown to be quite risky in older people. If there is a presence of **Lewy Body dementia**, side effects can include significant behavioural changes including suicidality, side effects such as potentially fatal Neuroleptic Malignant Syndrome and other serious side effects. Benzodiazepines can also risk *paradoxical agitation* and sedation. (see Lewy Body Dementia Association (at https://www.lbda.org/sites/default/files/treatment.pdf)
Corticosteroids	In my work I was referred a client who had been treated with corticosteroids for back pain and who then developed mania with suicidal intent. The client had never been diagnosed with any type of mood disorder in the past. I did some research and learned that there is a strong evidence base for mania, depression and psychosis being triggered by corticosteroid treatment. Although the evidence has been around for some time, it doesn't seem to be well understood generally. From a review from Wiley online: "In the older literature, psychotic symptoms were reported in 58% of the 55 cases reviewed by Ling *et al.*14 Nearly 72% of their 55 cases included mood symptoms." (Kenna *et al.*, 2011) "In older patients, corticosteroid-induced dementia has been misdiagnosed as early Alzheimer's disease and can occur in patients who have not experienced a steroid psychosis and are free of mood symptoms" (Kenna *et al*, 2011)

Figure 13: Possible Major Adverse Drug Effects (OPMH)

The following sections give my impressions / practice-based understanding about clinical issues that apply to OPMH.

DEPRESSION

It is little wonder that depression is prioritised as one of the "Three D's" of Older Persons Mental Health. It affects older people frequently and presents subtly but importantly different in older people. Aetiology, signs and symptoms, the attitude of society, and all the impacts of illness upon the sufferer can be different than in general psychiatry, and treatment options require nuanced understanding. Overall, the consequences of treating an older person in the same way a younger person can be inappropriate – sometimes dangerous.

Consider factors that can lead to mood disorder in an older person. An older person may have endured a process of losing many friends and close family members, adding compounding grief to an impending awareness of their own mortality. Simultaneously the person is often left with increased isolation as there may simply not be as many close people around them to help them through. Complex health problems may also wear down their life-long experience and cultural understanding of resilience that tells them they should be able to cope.

Cultural/generational approaches to issues of depression such as sadness can create an issue of insight into the person's situation, and can lead to somatization such as unexplained aches and pains, changes in mood such as anger or changes in behaviour.

Other diseases and health states that can typically affect older persons can have strong manifestations in mood or behaviour. For example, you may meet people who have had open heart surgery who distinctly feel they should not be alive, or people whose heart condition leads to congestion build up in their chest around the same time every night and causes them to wake in an anxious state feeling as if they are drowning. Then there are hormonal changes such are thyroid function changes which can cause anxiety and agitation. Or tiny vascular events like mini-strokes that can impact a person's resilience and anergy and allow a pathway in for depressive feelings. Further, it is also possible that changes in mood hint at the presence of a disease state that may require treatment.

A young person on the other hand may have more resources of health and fitness to help them with their potential recovery, concerned family members ready to house and nurture them, and better adaptation to modern systems of support. These generalisations of course are not always the case, but they usefully demonstrate that there are groups of issues older people may be prone to suffering from.

The consequences that depression can precipitate can also be more serious for an older person. Whereas a younger person might not eat due to depression, lose body weight and sleep, but then bounce back with little long-term impact, the impacts on an older person of similar changes to appetite and sleep can have far reaching implications to their health.

The impact on sleep is an important feature of depression: Difficulty getting to sleep, disturbance of REM sleep (typically manifested by early morning waking around 2-3 am), difficulty getting to sleep and a generally poor quality of sleep with a lack of feeling refreshed can all be signs of depression. Sometimes these occurrences are related to Sleep Apnoea, which carries a major risk of co-morbid depression. (At MSE, while observing the physical surrounds you may notice a CPAP machine, which would prompt a question about whether or not the person is using it). Keep in mind that people often seem to need less sleep as they get older and that they often get refreshment in the form of a 'nanny nap' after lunch. These changes may not correlate with depression.

Society can be indifferent to older people with depression. TV shows hint at attitudes of society to older people in their mental health: "Grumpy Old Men" or "Mother and Son" can lead to uncomfortable amusement, but in Older Persons Mental Health, bias attitudes means overlooking symptoms of mood disorder. If clinicians find themselves attributing that an older person, for example generally looks sad due to their assumptions about how older people look, and fails to note it in the Mental State Exam, it means their attitudinal learning requires development. This is an issue for supervision.

The treatment of depression in older people using medications requires nuanced understanding as well, as the likelihood of extra-pyramidal side-effects (and also polypharmacy effects) are generally greater and need careful monitoring. Sometimes treatment can make matters worse for these reasons. Sometimes commencing on antidepressants can lead to a period of increased risk for a few weeks, as the sufferer finds new energy without yet having reassessed the negative thoughts involved in the depression. The clinician's role may involve monitoring mental state for a period from commencement or change in medication in conjunction with care provided by the psychiatric specialist.

MSE and Depression

Ageist assumptions can impact the reliability of MSE observations of depression, should the clinician expect older people to have extensive worries or have odd or 'doddery' behaviours, and therefore fail to note relevant observable features of depression. A cost of such ageist assumptions may be that treatable suffering may fail to be addressed.

MSE observations in depression in older people may take distinct forms. Observations of affect and posture are a beginning point. A sad countenance, wistful looks, teariness and worry lines may also be useful indicators. Older people can feature an 'Omega sign' on their forehead, intense worry lines above the centre of their eyebrows. Other physical manifestations of depression could include evidence of poor self care - broken or scratched glasses, crooked buttoning of their shirt, being dressed in sleep attire late in the day, and poor hygiene. Also, look for clues to the person's mental state in their physical surrounds, particularly if assessing them at their home or in their aged care bed.

Awareness of chronic impacts on MSE can help develop an accurate picture. For example, an extended history of sleep disturbance can be observed as signs of deep tiredness. Similarly, an extended period of poor self-care can feature extreme weight loss, and the person may appear very frail. Evidence of lack of self care may include ceasing to care for hair and reduced bathing, missing meals and medication. (Corroboration should be sought to establish that the lack of self-care represents a change from the person's typical baseline before diagnosis).

As with all depression, sadness, despair and negativity, and lowered sense of self-worth are components of mood disorder, as are persistent themes of hopelessness and helplessness. Suicidal ideation or simply a reduced passion for life, or a lack of motivation and energy can be indicators of depression. A slowing of speech and psychomotor activity are signs to look for.

Social withdrawal, ceasing hobbies and increased use of alcohol can be a feature of depression (possibly indicated by the smell of alcohol or other common signs). Social engagement is a very powerful indicator of wellness in older people, and withdrawal can be a indicator of depression, dementia or other illness states.

Slowing of thought due to depression can be indicated in the MMSE or other cognitive testing. There is a risk of misinterpretation of cognitive score in older people where an assumption of dementia may be made. Cognition can be in fact affected by depression.

Depressive illness states that are common in older people include Melancholic Depression, Depression with psychotic features, and Catatonia. Grief and Loss also can represent a depressive illness, but may be a situational crisis, depending on the sufferer's scale of impact, resources and supports.

GRIEF AND LOSS

Grief and Loss, which is very common in the older population, may have particular meaning in older people. As grief is often influenced by unresolved problems in relationships being bought into focus the grief may be very complex in nature. MSE presentations involving bereavement can appear extreme however the course of disturbance to mood can be hard to predict, fluctuating, short- or long-term and require understanding, empathy and support.

If there is a risk element in the things the grieving person says, a useful, balanced response may be to talk things over with the person to get a more in-depth sense of whether the person requires available support from their family to make it through a temporary risk (i.e. an expression of grief) or hospitalisation and further medical help to keep them safe until their acute risk is passed. As with all risk assessment, if the person states they will not harm themselves, can state protective factors, and the family believe they can manage risk while they support their loved one, often it will be better to leave the grieving person in their own community and with their own people.

Families often have contention within their bereavement. As many families seem to tear themselves apart over issues of end-of-life care, wills and inheritance, and redefinition of power relationships, I have come to consider such struggles as part of the grieving process, and from a systems-theoretical point of view, a necessary feature of families who are trying to reform after significant change in their structure. The older surviving person may indeed need a level of advocacy and protection when this is occurring.

Cultural and spiritual meanings can impact the course and expression of grief. To a narrow western-style analysis many cultural expressions of grief are poorly understood. In my experience, for example Aboriginal families going through grief feel and express their pain in ways that may appear quite contentious to outside observers. To me, this is a reflection of the closeness of family networks in Aboriginal cultures as much as anything. I.e., if a western-style family had the same closeness in extended family relationships as other many Aboriginal families, conflict would be as widespread at bereavement in the western-style family. Contention is very much a feature of family grief in western families, but is simply more visible in more extensive Aboriginal family styles. A clinician should avail themselves of support and supervision around cultural expressions of grief to truly understand.

Most significant life partners form part of an older person's support network, and when the partner is lost to the relationship, massive lifestyle readjustments may be required for long-term adaptation and resolution (or recovery from) of grief.

One significant risk is where a partner is watching their loved one go into care due to dementia. While the loss may be keenly felt in terms of impact to their interdependance and sadness about their own encroaching mortality, one often unexpected impact can take them by surprise. It is that as the changes begin to occur in their life partner, a feeling of demise of the relationship occurs. That is, something dies, while the partners are both still living. This unexpected grief can be prolonged and make them feel as if they are living in a slow-motion train crash.

Carer grief takes on new meaning when they visit their loved one in the nursing home, and the day comes that their partner fails to recognise them. The resulting grief can be very emotionally deep to the loving sufferer. Over process of time an adjustment may be found and adaptation made, however the situation is significant enough that when the person with dementia finally dies, the widowed partner may feel a peculiar emptiness as if they have already cried all their tears. This unexpected feeling can lead to some issues of guilt.

It is often felt that no parent should outlive their child. In situations where alcohol, drug problems and suicide have been part of an adult child's loss, an ageing parent is left with feelings of guilt as expressed in unresolved grief. Where there has been chronic or genetic illness in the child, guilt may also surface as a problem of depression. Where there has been domestic violence or other unresolved trauma that affected the child growing up, the guilt can become even more significant. Along with feelings of guilt can come anger and shame.

Another significant risk for Grief and Loss as a feature of depression is entry into care. Significant adaptation is required, and requires processing. Currently in Australia there is no systematic approach to enabling adaptation as older people go into care. Depression affects nearly half of people without and more than half of people with cognitive impairment, as they enter aged care. As with all episodes of grief, people often recall previous unresolved grief and the issues can be complex.

Grief and Loss can often be helped by counselling. Bereavement therapy is a component of CBT and other approaches such as reminiscing can be very helpful. Complex grief may require more skill on the part of the counsellor, and a trauma-informed approach may be particularly relevant. Other interventions such as advocacy and family work may be necessary. It is my belief that significant reduction in suffering can be made to people's wellness over time, through grief counselling. Sometimes the person just needs someone to reflect with them.

ERIK ERIKSON'S DEVELOPMENTAL STAGES

Erik Erikson's work on psychological development in humans (Identity and the Life Cycle (1959), Erik & Joan Erikson's The Life Cycle Completed (1998)), was nominated as an important theoretical perspective OPMH, which links crisis in formative developmental stages to the satisfaction or despair experienced in senior years.

These days I use Erikson's model of lifestage development as a reflection tool in counselling. Consumers often seem to find it fascinating as they see how their development might have been influenced by various factors at various stages.

Part of the usefulness of this reflection is that it can lead to some pretty telling interpretations of impacts on current adaptation, of unresolved crisis during earlier life stages.

Another benefit is that it normalises crises and casts them as a natural part of life and tha crisis trigger development. This perspective creates hope as crisis is transformed from being about permanent damage to being a path to growth.

I have found Erikson's stages a wonderful reflection tool in this way, particularly with older consumers. Using Erikson, crises in the years leading up to the 65 age band routinely feature the dilemma of "generativity vs stagnation". The abundant challenges of forced retirement, the desire to step back from mundane work into meaningful pursuits etc are part of this life-stage crisis.

After 65, "integrity vs. despair" life stage in the 65+ age group, looks at the challenge of reviewing old, unresolved lifestage challenges and failures as people assess their life's work. The "despair" as opposed to "depression" (and resulting overmedication) is framed by regrets about percieved failures.

Counselling can be helpful in the cognitive resolution. In assessment also, the Erikson perspective may help to differentiate between an acute depression and a long-term dysphoric baseline in an otherwise functional adult.

(continued)

From the focus group:
"The despair side of it is often confused with so called 'depression…'"
…so it's about the person's life and

> what is happening in their world,
> not a pathological flaw.

The Erikson approach is a wonderful foundation of psychological understanding, and was regarded as both sensitive and progressive by the Focus Group, activating and empowering the clinician to deliver of Person-Centred Care, and respectful of the person's life experience and the power of "connection" and "meaning" to the support of older people through Recovery-based care.

Situational Crisis

A situational crisis is a set of circumstances that impact upon mood. When observed at assessment that the depressive features are of less than two weeks duration, that they are not regularly reappearing and are tied to crises in the life of the sufferer, some benefit may be gained to the sufferer by nature of conducting assessment through the building of a therapeutic relationship and the chance of the person to reflect on the situation and it's impact. By all means, some short-term case management including talking therapy such as CBT can help the person move toward resolution.

Endogenous / Melancholic Depression

While talking therapies can help to challenge negative thinking styles, a predisposition to negativity can be a result of genetic factors or brain changes and cognitive processes. The term endogenous describes depression of a more serious nature with an organic underlying cause, as opposed to a reactive depression which tends to be externally triggered by situational crisis and adaptive problems. It is more common in older people than younger people and can be more difficult to treat.

In MSE, reports of bleakness and loss of motivation and energy (anergia) can indicate endogenous depression. The sufferer most probably will experience socially withdrawal. The sufferer may not be able to identify a causal trigger, as the depression may have arisen without an obvious external trigger. Should they be able to identify what triggered the depressive episode, their depression may seem disproportionately 'reactive', even to the sufferer (i.e. more intense, of longer duration.

In Older Persons Mental Health, occurrences of endogenous depression often are not an isolated incident in the life of the sufferer. Many treatments might have been tried in the past. The person may seem intensely interested in exploring the fixed nature of their depression and may have moved through a number of treatment options with negative opinions of treatment. They may be keen to explore new treatment options with an accompanying expression of hopelessness and otherwise express anhedonia (lack of ability to feel pleasure). There may be accompanying mood swings.

At MSE it is worth asking if the person feels better or worse in the mornings than as the day progresses. Where the person generally feels better as the day progresses, this might be described as "Diurnal Variation in Mood". This bit of history taking may help put current mental state observations into place.

A severe and often biologically based form of depression is classed as Melancholia or Melancholic Depression. It is used alongside the term 'Endogenous' to more serious depression, and is codified under DSM-IV to have the following features:

At least one of:

- Anhedonia
- Lack of mood reactivity (persistent low mood even with positive events), with
  thoughts content gives clues to persistent low mood.

And at least three of the following:

- Depression that is subjectively different from grief or loss
- Severe weight loss or loss of appetite
- Psychomotor agitation or retardation (slowed gestures and gait)
- Early morning awakening
- Excessive guilt / fixation on guilt themes
- Diurnal mood variation

Depression with Psychotic Features

There are a number of presenting features of severe depression in older people that can be classed as psychotic. In the MSE, thought form may include such observations as being fixed, tangentiality, derailment, neologisms, delusional and psychotic in relation to depression.

When distress, guilt themes and shame have crossed into self-loathing thoughts, delusions and fixations can often insidiously infiltrate thought content as observed during MSE. In older people, common versions may include ideas that they are physically or morally filthy. Sometimes the person may remorse that there is an odour of faeces that comes from within them and can't be washed away, when there is no odour apparent at assessment. Other obsessional themes of the body can be about physical illness or doubts about recovery and can take nihilistic forms. The intensity of these disproportionate ideas can certainly be a significant barrier to rehabilitation and recovery from actual current health situations.

In younger people, nihilistic ideas may take a form of extensive or horrible catastrophic events. In older people, nihilistic ideas may seem to the assessor as much smaller and more manageable in scale, however in the eyes of the person being assessed the themes present as insurmountable problems. Examples of this may include fixed worries about the electricity being disconnected, there being no money for food (when family members attest that this is not a problem), that the family are going to discover a terrible secret that will destroy them, that the water supply (or pump) is broken or poisoned. In some instances the person experiences a olfactory or taste-based hallucination of tainted water or food. It is reasonable to wonder, when a metallic taste is reported, if the person is experiencing sensitivity to some medication or some medical condition, or if the water does in fact taste odd, however it is also worth noting the association with other fixed thoughts and the corroboration of family members.

Another type of fixation observed in older people involved ideas of contagion. A person may worry if, for example, their family may 'catch' cancer from them. Also, that radiation risk from cancer treatment might kill their whole family (which may be a distortion of counsel they have received). Often the person cannot be reassured by counsel of nil or very low risk of such contagion taking place.

These presentations might be accompanied by other features such as extreme agitation, pleading and resignation. Odd behaviours can co-exist with delusional thought structures and may accord with these fixed beliefs.

Bipolar Depression
Another descriptor for the depression of generally sad people is the term 'Unipolar' – i.e. the orientation of the depression is one way (i.e. low mood). In contrast, there are a large group of people whose affective disorder ranges from low mood to a high within their depression. It is at the moment of the high when the person can feel invincible and omniscient. The highs can be greatly enjoyed by the person with bipolar depression – they are often powerful or creative people who do their best work when the sun of their high is shining, yet when the low comes, their whole being is shades of bleakness.

The times of high mood (eg the hypo-manic or *not-quite-manic* mood state,) are often tainted with negativity about a world that can't keep up with them, understand them or support their vision. There is commonly an impact upon self-esteem – the sufferer expresses wonderful ideas with incredible creativity, yet makes quietly despairing remarks about their ability to see their plans to fruition, or for others to help them.

Features of bipolar illness observed at MSE may include (on the high side): Elevated mood, verbose speech, loud and colourful clothing, expansive, overfriendliness, grandiose thinking, sexually inappropriate behaviour and speech, highly energy, excessive spending patterns, racing thoughts, inattentiveness to those around them, planning and scheming, rashly critical of others. During periods of low mood depressive features can be observed, sometimes characterised by a sense of bitterness or a fixation on personal failure against extremely high hopes the person has for himself or herself.

Although family history of bipolar illness is a strong predictor, the compassionate clinician does not overlook the psychosocial impacts that commonly precipitate or trigger depressive illness intertwined with genetic predisposition. Long-term stress can be a trigger for periods of decompensation. A background of childhood trauma can also be a large factor in the formation of problems in coping and with the sufferer's negative ideas.

Cycles in mood can be mild or major. There is bipolar I (includes mania with or without depression) and bipolar II (where depression and hypomania are features, without manic symptoms breaking through). Where cyclic symptoms are mild, the diagnosis of cyclothymic disorder might be used. Observations at the moment of assessment might make the one polar descriptor obvious, while the assessor must rely on history and corroborative evidence to understand about the opposite polar occurrence, duration and severity.

Anxiety is a common co-morbidity and therapies such as CBT can be useful. Substance use problems can be a common co-morbidity that brings complex problems of health and quality of life. Assessment of risk of suicide is essential, and can be started during understanding thought content at MSE. There are also other categories of illness with affective components (such as schizoaffective disorder), personality disorders, substance use disorders and medical conditions.

Some medications, for example corticosteroids, have been noted to carry a risk of triggering manic episodes, although this situation may not be considered bipolar depression. At times a previously undetected vulnerability to bipolar can, in conjunction with the introduction of non-mood stabilizer antidepressants, result in significant risk. Breakthrough mania and suicide risk can increase as the whole mood cycle tends to elevated.

Indications suggest that vulnerability to bipolar illness can intensify with age. With the aging population, a greater number of older people will have bipolar depression. This may include the 'graduates' – long-term survivors of illness, whose earlier treatment may have helped increase their life expectancy. This group face particular challenges involving the long-term effect of mood stabilizers such as lithium on the fitness and function of kidneys and liver.

There is a lot of misunderstanding around bipolar. Many people misdiagnose each other using the term bipolar. People whose mood changes rapidly many times within a day, for example, are often mislabelled "bipolar". In bipolar depression, changes in mood are more likely to occur over many weeks or months-long cycles. Seasonal mood disorder, where the change in seasons brings with it wide-ranging fluctuations in mood, can be a feature of bipolar vulnerability.

The class of anti-depressants used to treat bipolar are mood stabilizers – medication which limits the peaks and troughs of mood cycles. Some people don't like the effect of these medication because it can curtail both their energy, creativity and enjoyment during the peak mood cycle. This, along with stigma and concern about side effects of medication, can deter people from seeking treatment. There are many people living in the community with mental illness of many types, who have functional challenges but who *choose* to get by with minimal medication – as they have the right to. Although the mental health clinician has duty of care to ensure quality assessment, risk management and therapies are available, Recovery principles reiterate the right of the consumer to have their voice heard about their treatment choices.

DELIRIUM

Delirium, or acute confusional state, is a common, serious impact on mental health. It can affect anyone. Older people, by nature of other health vulnerability, tend to be more at risk of delirium, to the degree that it is considered one of the "Three D's" of Older Persons Mental Health. It can be a short-term impact affecting awareness, orientation, mood, perception, wellness and sense of control or hopelessness and is usually related to organic pathological problems. Medication changes or side effects can trigger delirium, and most classes of medication can cause these effects.

Dementia can increase the risk of delirium. Other mental illnesses states can have an element of delirium, particularly those with organic roots – for example alcohol related problems or dementia with Lewy Bodies. Delirium can interact with perception: For example, a vulnerable person with dementia might have a delirium response triggered (or made worse) simply by being moved into a different setting within a nursing home.

Features of delirium can include attention problems and disorganised thinking and behaviour. Perceptual disturbances like visual hallucinations: Seeing movement at the top corners of walls; shifting patterns on the walls; warping of walls; animals such as bugs or snakes moving on the floor, can all be effects of delirium. Sufferers may appear in a dream-like state or talk about experiencing dreams while awake.

It is said delirium can be fatal: It may be more concise to say that underlying causes of delirium, left untreated, can put the person in danger, particularly when there are no other visible signs or symptoms of health problems. For this reason, when there is a sudden onset in decline in mental state or fluctuations in mental state, it is essential to have the client fully medically assessed, including the collection of vital signs. An insidious risk from delirium is that due to extreme changes in mental state, people may be treated using heavy-hitting psychotropic drugs without having the underlying illness addressed.

Because delirium is common, serious and often unrecognised, it is an essential that mental health clinicians attend to the risk of delirium at assessment. To help identify delirium, screening tools should be applied to learn more about the course and historical development of symptoms, in conjunction with current mental state.

An issue of management delirium is that, with a longer-term fluctuating course, the symptoms can interplay with other effects on mental health over an extended period of time. For example, persistent recurring infections in a person with worsening dementia can make it difficult to differentiate whether treatment is effective (or even possibly making things worse). These situations can be particularly demanding on carers, particularly where there are accompanying behavioural issues.

DEMENTIA

In SMHSOP (Older Persons Mental Health, NSW Health) I was involved in the initial assessment of people over 65 years and older (for people of Aboriginal and Torres Strait Islander descent, from 45 years and older). People would be referred for assessment following a wide variety of behavioural, mood and cognitive changes, or due to the presence of increased risks. Generally I was involved in assessment of acute illness, but people with possible organic changes – including dementia – often presented prior to a dementia diagnosis. Some people with an existing dementia diagnosis, with a mixed picture possibly involving possible treatable acute mental illness also would be referred. In many cases the Psychogeriatrician may work in concert with the Geriatric specialist.

Therefore the Older Persons Mental Health clinician requires some foundational understanding of dementia for assessment purposes, although dementia lies outside the local definition of Mental Health services, strictly speaking.

My definition of dementia is it is a persistent disorder of brain function linked to changes in the physical brain, and is generally progressive in nature. It can cause death, but this can take a dozen years after a diagnosis is established – some people enjoy many years with a degree of independence, and may instead die first from other health situations.

There is no type of dementia where the changes are entirely uniform or shared by all sufferers. Many people have features that represent a mixture of types of dementia. It has been said that to a large extent an absolute diagnosis would require an autopsy – that the outward behavioural and functional signs require a high degree of interpretation.

Usually the identification of brain changes is a crisis for the family representing problems of adaptation within the family system. At these times the presence of a mental health clinical support can provide reassurance, but the journey of adaptation includes a grief process, and some family work can be very helpful as the family sort out what the change to the shape of their family means while the Psychogeriatric specialist provides leadership about the prognosis and care needs of the person.

There are often many questions to be addressed: For example, cognitive decline in dementia can involve increased risk of falls, as gait and balance are often affected. (In a house with many steps the safety of the person should be referred to the OT for assessment, consideration of accommodation strategies and a myriad of other even more personal decisions may need to be addressed by the person and the family.)

With other people, whose dementia doesn't impact insight, a sense of loss and dread may sometimes overcome them. While many areas of their mental functioning may remain intact, specific changes may present specific problems for them – resulting possibly in frustration, distress, agitation, grief, fear or anger responses from them. They may lose some of their ability to differentiate between a person trying to help them and a person trying to baby them, control them and even hurt them. There is some evidence of effective CBT – style interventions in certain conditions, and the family and carers of people often discover, through necessity, strategies for easing agitation. The provision of talking therapies, including CBT, Reminiscence, Family Systems and Bereavement therapies, can be important aspects of Recovery-based care of the person with dementia.

Quite often a GP may try to help manage the person's agitation or distress by prescribing psychotropic medication. It is useful to get the medication history and gather data about changes in mood and behaviour that may be in relation to medication changes. In older people in particular, in some instances medication can have the opposite to the desired effect, even increasing risk. The psychogeriatrician needs this data collected to provide the best guidance back to the GP.

Certain functional impacts may mean that the person finds it more difficult to filter, or to cope with various environmental stressors such as noise. Also, perception processed may be altered making functioning more difficult. For example – looking down poorly-lit stairs or seeing a wall painted completely white takes on a different perceptual experience and their coping ability may be disrupted by these elements. During assessment it may be useful to record the location of distress and look for environmental hazards and factors. There may be simple adaptations to the home environment that can be suggested. This can be part of Recovery-based care as well.

Following is some of the types of dementia and some observations and discussion. The topic is huge and specialised, and it can be difficult to predict what the clinician may encounter. In any case, my primary role was not dementia specific – I hope simply to discuss a range of dementias to help build clinical knowledge for MSE. Again, I am not an expert in dementia, but am passing on some little bits of practice-acquired understandings.

Alzheimer's

An impact of many dementias including Alzheimer's may include changes to memory. Many people continue to recall long-term memories but cannot consistently recall short-term memories – or can't lay down new memories (anterograde memory function).

Memory problems may involve other specific functions such as recognising particular objects or people, or finding words. Memory problems may impact functional roles such as self-care, and tasks such as cooking. For example a client was able to cook on the stove – she'd learned about that from her mother – but was confounded by newer technology, that she had previously been very competent with. Although cognitive testing may help identify problems, the narrative history taking of their experience is also particularly relevant.

In many instances, the person with Alzheimer's insight deteriorates so that they lose the sense of associated grief, becoming more adaptable to supports. Also, the person's initiative may decline. They may be therefore quite malleable to suggestions.

LEWY BODY DEMENTIA

Dr Williams taught that Lewy Bodies are quite common – they may be present in a quarter of all people with dementia. Functional impacts can be very different in those with Lewy Body Dementia than in other types of dementia – the memory is not usually impacted as strongly, but performance in memory tasks can fluctuate. Mood and agitation can also fluctuate. The picture can be very mixed and varied, however significant features of Dementia with Lewy Bodies are problems at MSE relating to executive function, attention and visuospatial functioning. Hallucinations can be accompanied by complex, developed delusions.

Some assessments I have been involved in often discovered hallucinations in the form of small animals, small children-sized people, and Lilliputian people. One person regularly saw "Pygmies from New Guinea" hacking at tree in the back yard. Another mentioned, when asked, that there were little people (think 3 inches high) armed with swords lined up all along the kitchen benches. Another person's carer commented that the person was always complaining about cats and children running through the lounge room, and yet another felt that she couldn't sit on the car seat because she doesn't want to "sit on the kid sitting there". She said they were usually in the back seats but one must have jumped into the front.

Often these hallucinations are described in an odd, matter-of-fact way. In Dementia with Lewy Bodies, I have noticed at MSE sometimes a strange disconnect of the content of delusions with what might be considered a typical emotional response had the delusion been true. In one case, a developed, complex delusion about care staff and doctors trying to murder the person was expressed with an emotional disconnectedness and no fear, which appeared odd and incongruent. When asked if the person felt fearful, they said yes with a smile, then shortly afterwards laughed about something unrelated.

Lewy Body dementia seems to be akin in many ways to a delirium state. Sundowning may be effect these organic states.

Frontotemporal Dementia

The varieties of progressive illnesses classified under the frontotemporal dementias precipitate a mixed and varied group of outward signs and symptoms. There may be changes in humour, unusual beliefs or obsessions. Memory deficits may be relatively slow to appear, but impulsivity and executive planning may be impacted, and an absence of insight.

Some people with these types of dementia can undergo seeming changes to their personality: They may become aggressive; or lose their capacity for empathy toward others; become disinterested in people; become disinhibited; and be socially and sexually inappropriate. At night time disorientation may increase and the person may be wandering around the house at night – the person is no longer restrained by social convention or ideas of safety and their natural curiosity leads them to wander – it is important to understand these elements of history.

There may be overindulgence in food or alcohol, poor self care and grooming, changes in sexual activity. They may not be able to recognise people or the use of objects. Some sufferers develop language difficulty – word-finding or understanding speech. Further, there may also be muscular stiffness and twitching.

Vascular Dementia

Vascular dementia is related to reduced supply of blood to the brain. At least some reduced blood flow is common in old age and can often be seen on a CT scan. This might be due to disease progressively affecting blood flow within the brain or can happen suddenly after strokes, or a mixture of these.

Often the picture of memory impairment differs from Alzheimer's dementia: The disease may not be insidiously progressive, but change quickly (e.g. if the effect is more stroke related). Memory difficulties may not even be significant, depending on where reduced blood flow occurs in the brain. Early warning signs might take the form of a slowing of thought not due to depression, although mood and behaviour can be impacted by vascular dementia. Also common may be difficulty in planning, attention and concentration, and some disinhibition.

Sometimes wandering can be a sign of vascular dementia, revealing confusion and disorientation. Balance can be affected and the person may walk with little steps. Vision loss can also play a part in this. Difficulties in speaking and understanding speech may be present and in advanced situations, word-finding difficulties.

Insight may be largely intact and understandably impact on mood may therefore reveal catastrophic reactions to loss of functioning. This anxiety and loss of confidence can accompany emotional lability, which may lead people to wonder if the person is suffering depression. However the lability can be less about mood and more about their ability to regulate emotional expression in the way they are used to doing.

In more advanced situations, the above features can be more severe, and memory loss becomes more obvious. Aggression, apathy and other personality changes and mood swings can become dominant features. Hallucinations can occur. There can also be a loss of urinary continence.

Alcohol-related brain damage

Often misnamed a dementia ARBD shares many symptoms with actual dementias, although excess consumption of alcohol – especially binge drinking – can trigger dementias such as vascular dementia. ARBD is a significant risk and vulnerable people are frequently not managed appropriately to that risk (See Jesse *et al*, 2017).

Some types of Alcohol-related brain damage include Wernicke-Korsakoff and "alcoholic dementia". An important issue for Older Person's clinicians to be aware of is that a person who is heavily reliant on alcohol for the majority of their calories who goes to hospital or into care for some reason, may have their usual supply of calories disrupted. Also, as the body attempts to flush out alcohol, water-soluble vitamins including thiamine get flushed out as well.

This is a significant risk to the person, as the absence of thiamine (vitamin B-1) in the diet is a cause of peripheral neuropathy and linked to eventual damage of myelin sheaths around nerves in the brain. This disrupts their function and interrupts transmission of nerve signals in the brain. To prevent this, people with known alcohol dependence issues are often given an injection of thiamine to protect brain health on admission.

After 2 or 3 days without alcohol, there is a strong risk of Alcohol Withdrawal Syndrome (AWS). Common psychiatric symptoms of AWS include illusions and delusions, hallucinations, paranoid ideas, anxiety, mood instability, combativeness and disinhibition. Awareness symptoms (including disorientation, delirium) and insomnia, agitation and irritability can also be common, as well as motor symptoms (especially tremors, gait and seizures) - a wide-based gait is common. Cognitive problems can develop, as can muscular weakness, asterixis, cerebellar ataxia, and chorea, and autonomic symptoms. (Jesse *et al*, 2017)

Memory problems of Korsakoff's sometimes severe include anterograde and retrograde amnesia. A common feature is confabulation, where the person invents memories as they speak, to cover gaps in their memory. These inventions are believed by the person, with conviction. This is consistent with a propensity toward poor insight.

Sufferers may be uncomfortable in direct sunlight and may prefer to be indoors in a darkened room. There may also be minimal content in conversation, blandness in expression, aphasia, agnosia, apraxia, reduced reactivity to context, and apathy. There may be a deficit in executive functions. With abstinence and thiamine from improved diet, people can make good progress toward recovery, and symptoms will probably not worsen.

Mixed Dementia

As noted the picture of signs and symptoms can often be very mixed, individualised and atypical. This could be partly related to the person's brain health involving any number of factors. At MSE it is probably most useful for the clinician to note the functional differences that can be detected through cognitive testing and the other factors, than to decide what type of brain changes may be driving the person's functional deterioration.

PARKINSON'S

Parkinson's is categorised as a progressive "movement disorder" and symptoms may slowly develop to include muscle rigidity, tremor, postural instability and bradykinesia. Parkinson's doesn't just affect movement. Non-motor symptoms such as pain, depression and problems with memory and sleep can also occur and have an impact on the day to day life of the person with Parkinson's, and sensory and emotional problems can also affect the person. Dementia is common usually in advanced stages of Parkinson's. The mental health clinician may therefore have less involvement with people with early Parkinson's per se, as management tends to fall under the geriatric specialty.

Parkinsonism is the characteristic movement disorder component that can appear in other illness states and dementia as well as in Parkinson's itself. A person is usually more likely to die of other problems than directly because of Parkinson's – they may live for a long time with it. They may present with slurred monotonous speech and a quiet voice, a fixed, mask-like facial expression, and handwriting that gets reduces in size as it goes.

Parkinsonian gait is characterised by a general slowness of movement (hypokinesia), and small, rapid, shuffling with a flattened foot strike. In the extreme cases there can be total loss of movement (akinesia). The patient has difficulty starting, but also has difficulty stopping after starting. The person is seen to lean forward due to stiffness and impaired balance and reliance on their centre of gravity, and there is reduced arm swing. There may be episodes of freezing mid stride when attempting to navigate a turn.

ANXIETY

Two perspectives: Anxiety is a widespread and common mental health problem of excess worry; *or* it is also an essential, built-in response to physical or psychological threats. If you look at it from the second perspective, it is a gift from nature that sometimes gets out of control and requires management to bring back into line with overall functioning.

From a solution-focussed (cognitive/counselling) perspective, there are three parts of anxiety – *bodily sensations* (signs and symptoms), *thoughts*, often misunderstandings, about what these sensations mean, and *avoidance behaviour* to escape from the sensations. This threefold view of anxiety is one where the aspects interact with each other and create a vicious circle that feeds on itself as it escalates. These can be helped through developing alternate cognitive responses and changing behaviour.

Generally, when these essential responses are felt without conscious appreciation of the trigger for the feelings, the person can feel they are very strange. Patterns of thinking develop that may be very critical of the self, including self-judgement and even shame. It is a large contributor to the tendency of many to self-medicate with alcohol and drugs, and anxiety can be immobilizing, socially and personally.

However, this behavioural /cognitive understanding involving oversensitivity to natural processes may overlook significant biological or organic triggers to anxiety. Thyroid function problems, for example, can be a major trigger for anxiety. Medication side effects might also play a role. Changes to life circumstances including increased isolation after the loss of a companion or exposure to prolonged stress can play a role. Another trigger, particularly relevant for older people, may be an increased sense of vulnerability due to changes in vision, balance or cognitive and functional ability. It cannot be ignored that some expressions made by the person with dementia may lead to feelings of vulnerability that may come hand in glove with changes to the brain.

In Older Persons Mental Health, it is possible to imagine a situation where the person had strategies for managing their anxiety – such as relying on their established status at work to help them manage their anxiety, which become subject to forced life changes such as retirement, and bring anxiety to the fore.

Although learning anxiety management skills is often effective, older people with dementia may not be able to remember the new skills being taught. Plus, as in the case of an older person anxious about being alone, may literally face challenges they never experienced before – it may be true, for example, that their children do not visit them enough and they become very attuned to generally feeling unsafe. Anxiety mixed with changes to the brain, body, medication and the socia environment is very complex.

Panic Attacks vs. Catastrophic Reactions

Lifelong panic attacks (usually started around age 8) and lower intensity anxiety attacks reflect situations where the person's inbuilt stress reactions have become consolidated with a network of negative thoughts about these symptoms of stress. Common triggers often play a role, and the person's sensitivity to internal responses are typified – e.g. an increased heart rate combined with the presence of a certain type of perceived threat. The cyclic nature of the relationship of symptoms of negative thought, and negative thoughts about symptoms leads to an escalation of stress until the body's stress response finally peaks. People often feel very ashamed of their panic attacks and a number of older people I have met who have had panic attacks have concealed or tried to conceal them for their whole life even from close family.

This can be differentiated from a catastrophic reaction – experienced like a panic attack in many ways, however catastrophic reactions can surface with unfamiliar negative life events and can reflect changes to coping ability such as might be found in the onset of dementia. The catastrophic reaction is highly relevant to MSE in Older Persons Mental Health practice as it may describe many instances of intense emotional disregulation and psychological arousal such as agitation, aggression and anxiety.

As in the case of anxiety attacks there is a feedback loop involved, including the way sensations of stress the body's reaction is interpreted – however this situation is not a life-long developmental pattern but more a feature of response to new threats. It is related to long-term coping ability, but one could say it is equally related to coping ability at the present moment, including any part of brain and functional changes.

Catastrophic reactions can be helped by altering the physical environment to remove sources of stress, carers understanding behavioural cues prior to the catastrophic responses, and responding to the onset of reaction with calmness, understanding and positive reassurance.

POST-TRAUMATIC STRESS DISORDER

PTSD is a group of symptoms that can occur as a stress response to intense acute or sustained physical or psychological threat. Combat, domestic violence, violent crime, sexual assault, and prolonged, frightening stress are examples of triggering events. A majority of people in the older age group will likely have been exposed to at least one traumatic incident in their life. Veterans of war, the majority being male, have a higher likelihood of trauma symptoms.

Symptoms of PTSD can increase with age, as challenges faced as part of the life cycle, such as the loss of loved ones, a job, independence and wellness can undermine coping strategies that have been used for years, and functional and cognitive decline can interplay with symptoms. Some coping mechanisms such as self-medication with alcohol will become problematic in old age.

Flashbacks to the triggering event are common accompanied by stress symptoms like panic, a racing heart, frightening thoughts and sweating. Avoiding thoughts or feelings about the trauma builds up an anxiety response and the person can develop avoidance behaviours of places or events that remind them of the trauma.

Poor sleep and bad dreams are common. The person may be easily startled, tense and emotionally labile. Anger may be a very prominent emotion, with self blame and guilt being common. Negative thoughts about the self and the world can lead to depression. Suicidality can be chronic and intense. This may be a factor in the increased statistical risk of suicide in older men.

Anxiety, anhedonia, detachment, alienation and dissociative experiences are common. Cognitive impacts may feature difficulty recalling aspects of the traumatic event (with some evidence suggesting that psychogenic non-epileptic seizures or "pseudo-seizures" can be related to dissociative features.)

The terrible legacy of the various Australian State's "Aboriginal Protection" acts of last century is that many Indigenous Australians are left with complex symptoms of trauma. Consumers I have met have recounted memories of their mothers being in terror when the 'Welfare' would suddenly arrive at the mission, and the children would flee into the bush. Much worse trauma happened to children who were extracted from their parent's care to be assimilated through religious-based institutions that are now notorious for the crimes that occurred in care. In rural sectors of Australia, where there are more Aboriginal and Torres Strait Islanders, the clinician will meet these clients. They often show reluctance to engage with people from health and welfare oriented government/business organisations. An important thing to understand is that trauma responses can be passed down from one generation to the next.

Older people may also have a lifetime of experience and wisdom that can increase their resilience in the face of their long-term stress response – not to say the symptoms necessarily disappear, just that there can be a shift in perspective. Cultural factors can also be confusing for the assessor as older people may retain values that guide them to play down the effects – such as ideas about bravery in war, parental discipline and domestic violence. There may be an erroneous attribution of symptoms to issues of health and aging.

Even so, co-morbidity with other mental and physical health conditions can be common, such as chronic alcoholism, pain and major depression. These can in turn correlate with poorer and chronic health outcomes and affect long-term brain health, arterial disorders, gastrointestinal complaints, dermatological problems, and musculoskeletal disorders.

Mental health conditions are very commonly triggered, at least in part, by trauma. There may of course be genetic and other factors but to respect the relationship of trauma to mental illness is usually to have a clearer understanding of the person's perspective and the clinical picture. As in all mental health care, it is crucial to handle the assessment process as sensitively and kindly as possible. It is not kind to ask the person endless questions about the trauma which has the potential for re-traumatising the consumer and trigger unnecessary suffering. During assessment, be sensitive of the impact of assessment upon the person. If a person feels more hopeless at the end of assessment then this may not have been a very sensitive process.

For example, if the person had a child out of wedlock when they were young, and it was adopted out, and they say something about not knowing who the father was – be sensitive. The principles of sexual assault support are just as relevant to the OPMH consumer as anyone else. Although we may not be trained in sexual assault, or be in a position to offer such, we can offer it by referral, and after asking if the person ever had the chance to talk these things over with a counsellor. Meanwhile, you as assessing clinician should understand and practice Trauma-informed Care.

PERSONALITY DISORDERS

A psychological definition around personality can be enduring behavioural and mental traits that distinguish between individual humans. Personality Disorders, which I think involve a social dimension, are somewhat controversial. It is used to account for poor impulse control, interpersonal problems and emotional regulation, and is a feature in around half of people with other serious mental health problems. I do not like the way the diagnosis tends to inevitably become a reason for compromised levels of service. A large correlation with suicide completion is found in the personality disorders, but this seems to be linked to unintended completion through misadventure.

The developmental impacts of neglect and abuse in the person's formative years is often a key feature. These situations may have led to highly reactive and often manipulative styles of interacting. When heightened risk factors and demanding and splitting behaviours precipitate contact with community mental health, the poor staff quite often also become reactive and divisive around the care of the person. (Transference?)

I remember reading an account by a person with a personality disorder diagnosis who attended an information seminar about mental health. She wrote that the speakers discussed schizophrenia, depression and almost all other diagnostic categories – except personality disorders. The point she was making was that personality disorder often puts people into the 'too hard' basket. This is consistent with my experience of the views even of psychiatrists in general adult community mental health.

The experience of working with people with diagnoses of personality disorder in OPMH uniquely reflects the experience of supporting these people under the community mental health model. Apparently, symptoms can improve with age. This fact calls into question a discriminatory premise of the personality disorder diagnosis – that personalities are fixed. I think of the changes in personality that I have been through since I was a teen, and I see that I will continue to change as long as I live. I know we can become less impulsive, probably less aggressive and somewhat less focussed on sexual priorities. On the other hand, among older people, antisocial and borderline personality traits become more visible.

Personality disorders are common but quite marginalised in mainstream mental health services, for a range of reasons, and while the same forces act in OPMH to create similar issues, I don't think these diagnoses are given out as readily. There is a dearth of diagnostic criteria if Personality Disorder specific to OPMH, and there is also a shortage of information available on behavioural and risk management approaches as well. One area of interest would be study of organic illness as a co-morbidity, and another could be the effect of grief and loss on the life expectancy and functioning of people with personality disorders at the loss of carer-companions.

Personality disorders don't have organic pathology but we know that trauma and neglect can affect the way the brain works, making people more reactive and with poor boundaries. Strong behavioural patterns can have great impact on the wellness of the person including their physical, mental and social health. For example, acopia and poorly managed distress can result in having been prescribed heavy doses of psychotropic drugs over many years, social isolation or long term patterns of self medication with drugs and alcohol.

Trauma informed care is, in my view, particularly relevant to people with personality disorder. It does the kindness of recognising the relevance of the person's experiences. It's about the normal function of a brain and the impact of exposure to abnormal circumstances.
In my view, these people need care and great kindness, but good boundaries need to be in place. Maybe I am oversensitive, but I remember feeling the pull of strong reactions to the person, and that reaction is something that needs to be acknowledged and managed. When you find yourself tempted to cross boundaries for a person, I invite you to step back and reflect, hopefully in supervision, about why. No worker is immune, and great care is required.

In my experience in OPMH, 'graduates' of a personality disorder diagnosis present with long-term and bizarre behavioural patterns. These people often evoke sympathy for the family members and carers who have been party to rather manipulative relationships. There were unfortunate staff members at the Nursing Home who were accused (and later cleared) of serious allegations, there were nursing setbacks – while trying to 'get people back on their feet while they can' which met with a stony refusal to cooperate, even at the expense of the person's health.

SCHIZOPHRENIA

There are many people who survive general schizophrenia (that usually develops in the early adult phase of life) into older age. Psychogeriatric support for these may be needed for medication review. Casework may assist the person transition into different stages of care, an aspect of Recovery-based care. I was never involved with assessing a person who would be diagnosed with Late-onset Schizophrenia, and I hear it's not common and even disputed as a diagnosis. I have spoken with psychogeriatricians who had experience of diagnosing it and saw value in its use. With many of the characteristics as general schizophrenia, key differences are: lower likelihood of negative symptoms of schizophrenia, development in the person's 60's, with stronger occurrence of positive symptoms. There are common *symptoms* to aspects of dementia.

APPENDIX 1: FOCUS GROUP – EVIDENCE FOR RECOVERY-BASED OPMH ASSESSMENT

Introduction

Across Australia, mental health services for older people (OPMH) have been developing unevenly, particularly in rural / remote areas. For example the Northern Territory combines it with dementia services in aged care units. (Northern Territory Government, 2017). NSW Health (2006) has recently completed a 10-year plan for SMHSOP, their OPMH. It included a survey (NSW Department of Health, 2011) requiring new SMHSOP clinicians to assess their own competence in 10 key areas of work under domains of Skill, Knowledge and Attitudinal learning. This aligns with wider understanding of measuring competency within similar domains of learning (eg ANMC, 2006). Under a variety of organisational structures and contexts around the country, new workers may experience varying degrees of support for learning this speciality.

The researcher became aware of learning needs as a new, Social Worker solo clinician in a remote rural location working with thin organisational support, experiencing difficulty in locating skill-related knowledge. A literature search found OPMH specialised texts mainly addressed knowledge and skill domains, without attitudinal learning. They were not integrated in their approach to the domains, and were not contextually relevant experience-focussed works.

Simultaneously the researcher became aware of a paper about Recovery concepts in OPMH (Daley et al., 2013), but at work found weak conceptualisation of Recovery as it applies in OPMH in discussions with management. Most published papers on Recovery at the time focussed on younger age groups (McKay et al, 2012).

Project Context

The idea of writing a practical Guide (called 'the Guide' in this document - currently under development) was formulated and some early draughts created. A research question developed: Does the Guide effectively integrate the domains of Knowledge, Skill and Attitudinal Learning to address core competencies of new OPMH Clinicians? A focus group-based qualitative research project was devised to ascertain if regional OPMH clinicians saw a need for a practice-oriented, experiential Guide, and to explore their views around content, including an integration of learning domains (which is quite complex), Recovery principles, it's design and distribution.

Method

A focus group is qualitative research where a small group of people are prompted to discuss issues from their point of view with other participants (Phan & Fitzgerald, 1996). This focus group could be described as an interpretive phenomenological approach, with certain nuances. It moves away from purely enquiring after the participant's own experiences, to responding to questions and prompts (See Appendix 1) about learning in relation to the Guide – a recursive process (Pietkiewicz & Smith, 2012).

Focus Group Questions and Prompts

The focus group was intended to research the following questions, with prompts if required.

A poster was displayed showing the integration of learning domains, and sharing sections from the Guide including: the Glossary (knowledge); training in relation to Mental State Exam (MSE) skills; or a discussion about ageism attitudes and how it might affect MSE might help participants think about integrated learning in this way.

Question 1: The Learning Curve (Your experience of learning in the role)

Prompts: What is the 'learning curve' like for a new Older Person's clinician?
How did you learn what you needed to learn?

Question 2: What learning is needed for competence in new clinicians
Prompts if required: Exploring the domains of Knowledge, Skill and Attitudinal Learning

Question 3: What do you think of the written Guide so far?
Prompts (if required): Structure; Potential barriers to use, or benefits?
How well does the Guide use integration of the domains?

Question 4: How best might learning be disseminated?
Prompts (if required): Downloadable vs. printed books; Cost level; Promotion; Knowledge Wiki's; YouTube Channel

Question 5: Is there anything else you would like to discuss?

A week prior to the day participants received: a draft of the Guide; questions for the Focus Group; and a scenario of a challenging situation; privacy, information and consent forms. At that point the Focus Group partially became a critical evaluation of a text containing pre-formed ideas and approaches to the problem of applied training.

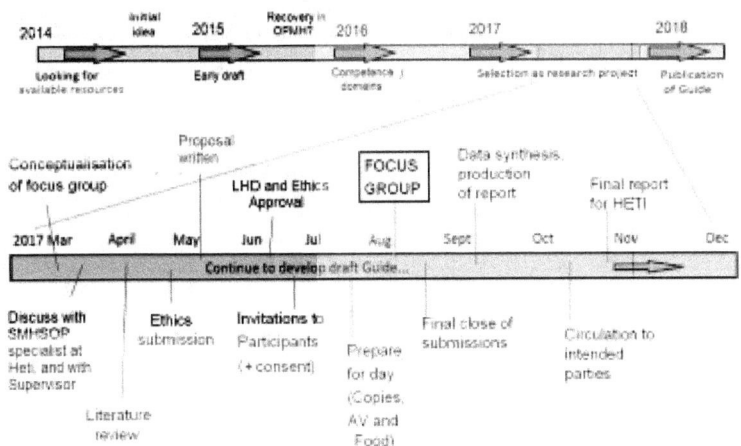

Figure 14: Focus Group project timeline

Participants

Participants were recruited from Albury Wodonga Health's nine OPMH clinicians through coordination with their operational manager. The selection of an Older Persons Mental Health team in a rural setting was intentional, with contextual similarities to the researcher's experience. However, many factors provided useful differences such as: Being connected to a cross-border health organization; Being a larger team with its own offices, clinical leadership and management; Being from a range of backgrounds; and having more specialist psychiatric support.

Analysis

This single focus group was digitally recorded and transcribed by a research assistant. The document was reviewed separately by the researcher and a mental health student. Observations were discussed and reflected upon. The researcher then utilised Microsoft Access and Excel to classify de-identified responses according to corresponding research questions and subthemes based on responses. Participants had the option of providing the researcher with additional input, however none was received.

Responses that covered more than one research question or sub-theme were duplicated to ensure the issues were fully included. Finally responses were grouped and then summarised into themes and sent to participants and to a supervising social worker for review.

Results

The hosting service provides coverage to older people within a population of 600,000 in North-East Victoria and South-East New South Wales. On the day (16/08/2017) the sample size was small (due to illness). Five clinicians participated at their facility. One was a psychiatrist, two were social workers, one mental health nurse, and other allied health mental health clinicians. Three participants were female, two male. All had greater than four years experience within the current team.

(Continued...)

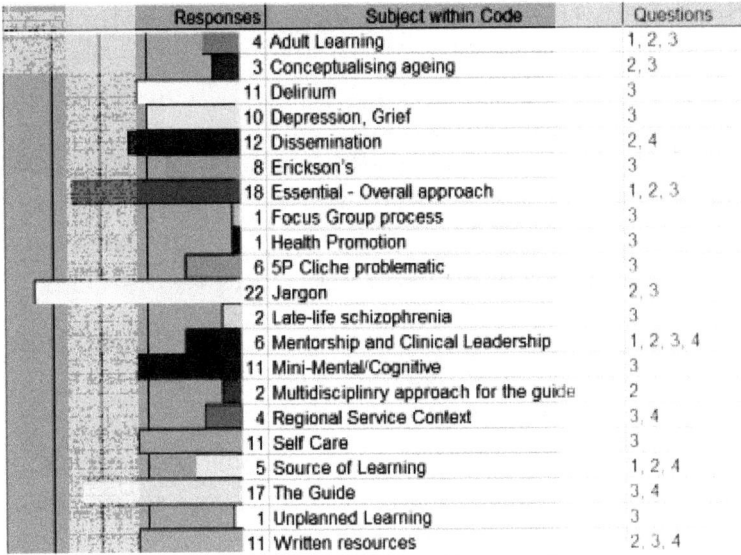

Responses	Subject within Code	Questions
4	Adult Learning	1, 2, 3
3	Conceptualising ageing	2, 3
11	Delirium	3
10	Depression, Grief	3
12	Dissemination	2, 4
8	Erickson's	3
18	Essential - Overall approach	1, 2, 3
1	Focus Group process	3
1	Health Promotion	3
6	5P Cliche problematic	3
22	Jargon	2, 3
2	Late-life schizophrenia	3
6	Mentorship and Clinical Leadership	1, 2, 3, 4
11	Mini-Mental/Cognitive	3
2	Multidisciplinry approach for the guide	2
4	Regional Service Context	3, 4
11	Self Care	3
5	Source of Learning	1, 2, 4
17	The Guide	3, 4
1	Unplanned Learning	3
11	Written resources	2, 3, 4

Figure 15: Themes, grouped with question numbers

Discussion

The results of the focus group were consistent with anticipated outcomes. Overall there were definite leaders, but every participant contributed. Although, unfortunately, the draft Guide that had been sent out had not been read by participants, it was an enriching focus group experience, with strong values expressed that concurred with the Guide, exceeding it in many instances. Attitudinal perspective, integrated with skills and knowledge, informed by an established model, and worker experience were seen as central to learning. Prompts were often redundant as to discussion of attitudinal learning, which was spontaneous, although usually discussed in terms of philosophical (or overall) approach.

As can be seen in Figure 15, the issues were numerous for a 90-minute discussion. Leading issues with quotations from the group (*in italics*) have been included below representing key themes.

Ageing and Ageism

"It needs to be one of the criteria learned to have respect for older people and in fact respect for elders, almost in that traditional sense of acknowledging all the older people that have come before us and that's why we're here now."

An aspect of attitudinal learning was raised around preconceived ideas about ageing:

"... when we've had allied health graduates coming through or nursing grads ... you can get people having to not just to understand the clinical skills in order to do an assessment or knowing what to look for, but also it's educating around what is the concept of ageing, how has that evolved, sensitivity around that."

For example, when other clinicians wish to transfer people simply because of reaching 65 years, without an age relating associated presentation: *"Sometimes we have mature clinicians in community settings that just don't get it..."*

It was felt that ageism can be evident in terms of people's ability to connect with the narrative, and is visible in limited thinking about treatment and therapeutic options.

Service Orientation/ Philosophy

Participants felt strongly that the overall philosophy of the service was an essential element of early learning and differentiated between their narrative-assessment style based psycho-social model and what they experienced elsewhere. One remarked:

"I worked in the inpatient unit before I came here ... here you get a much more comprehensive overview of what their

life, socioeconomic problems or all sorts of things. We are more holistic."

The group as a whole were very critical of *"silos"*, and of a strongly hierarchical leadership model, and *"assessment/ treatment/ discharge"* and *"medical model"* thinking. Differences were seen as a function of local leadership, distinct from departmental training like *"mandatory training"*.

Current and preceding leadership promoted that *"services ought to have not only a social view but also a psycho-developmental model"*. The group were strongly oriented to building working relationships through narrative understanding of the person, the systems around them and then having a coupled of psychosocial / medical approach. This was linked to rights, sensitivity toward consumers, valuing personal meanings, and valuing the narrative of the family and GP. The psychiatrist said *"I'm anti-scales, anti-tick boxes, I'm about talking to people."* In the rural context this meant working over great distances through educating GPs, working *"collaboratively"*, and recognising shared care across the community.

Although participants didn't respond explicitly to prompts about the Recovery model, narrative assessment merges with Recovery models. In Older Persons Mental Health It has been identified that a shared paradigm is needed, using both the Person-Centred Care (with a narrative emphasis) and Recovery models (McKay et al 2012).

Narrative assessment is also linked to culturally aware practice. Hall & Powell, (2011) point out that narrative assessment is not only kinder, but is linked to recovery by values like identity and meaning. Recovery values (e.g. CHIME) assist culturally sensitive practice through narrative engagement and the clinician can apply these to diverse cultural contexts. Connection is through listening and really hearing the person (Brijnath, 2015)

Mentoring and Leadership

Experiences of the 'learning curve' were mixed. Those who received less mentoring and clinical leadership agreed it was difficult, while recognising it as common within that regional profile. One recalled being handed a list of files of consumers in crisis and being told *"Off you go!"* Others benefited from a *"nurturing environment"* with *"a good mentor"*. They observed that a lack of leadership forced an accelerated learning curve. One clinician initially worked in a city-based OPMH service where she experienced a stifling level of oversight:

> "...the psychiatrist has to come out for the initial assessment and the review assessment so there's this hierarchy. You don't make any decision without the advice of the psychiatrist... In a way the overuse of the psychiatrists ... disempowers the clinicians to actually make clinical observations..."

Sources of Learning

It was observed that rural and remote clinicians struggle to access session-based training because of distance and caseload issues. Online pod casts, journal articles and other media were utilized including *"E-books"* played in the car when travelling long distances to appointments. It was remarked that city-based clinicians in high-pressure roles, and those with little autonomy within top-down *"hierarchical"* medical model leadership might also lack support in accessing critical attitudinal, skills and knowledge learning.

Self Care

Participants discussed the issue of self care as essential learning. Discussion was around: the dignity of risk; where you sit with someone's life choices; your role; doing the best you can; unpacking, debriefing or processing loss, particularly where the clinician feels isolated; transparent practice; feeling supported by a team; and feeling "it's okay to get it wrong".

Erikson

Erik & Joan Erikson's The Life Cycle Completed (Extended Version) (1998), was nominated as an important theoretical perspective of their approach and it was felt that a section should be included in the Guide about it. Correct understanding (and treatment) of depressive symptoms was through the impact of unresolved earlier life stages on current adaptation, added to losses that people suffer in later life. Using Erikson, impacts were discussed in terms of generativity vs stagnation, and especially integrity vs. despair (p 112-113), as opposed to oversimplified "depression" and overmedication.

"The despair side of it is often confused with so called 'depression'"

Their approach is seen as both sensitive and progressive, activating and empowering the clinician to deliver of Person-Centred Care. The issues offered seemed to evoke positive pride and passion in the participants, a sense of social justice, equality and respect.

Jargon

As a prompt, a Glossary were presented from the Guide. Responses favoured avoiding specialised jargon in training new clinicians:

4. It was viewed more useful, realistic and efficient to expect new clinicians to develop their observational skills than to focus on learning specialist jargon;
5. Consumers and families may not understand what is being said about them, potentially causing undue stress;
6. Jargon insidiously creeps into misuse of terms with "Huge risks of error."

The psychiatrist cautioned against designing a guide that focussed on jargon:

"If you go over to neuropsychology ...there's a huge amount of information to learn and know. But it always comes back to what you observe. What do I see and what do I hear? That's the important point - that you notice and you write it down..."

The overall feeling was that new clinicians need to be taught to sensitively engage in narrative assessment while making a range of simple, jargon-free observations. The emphasis on being jargon-free corresponds to better communication, transparency, equality and sensitivity to the experience of the person, and therefore has been linked to Recovery values (Trenoweth, 2017).

Illness (Knowledge, Attitudinal and Skill Domains)

Positive emphasis was made about inclusion of narrative-based and other cognitive testing, delirium screening, psychotic symptoms and depression in the Guide. Ideas about the integration of learning domains were clearly demonstrated: For example, cognitive testing is *"first and foremost a narrative cognitive assessment, then if needed, with screening tools"*.

Similar integration was demonstrated around depression knowledge, using attitudinal learning as well, including critique of medical-model mistreatment of grief and loss in the life stage.

The Guide

Participants, independent of professional background and their own learning curve, all supported the concept of a Guide. The popular view was that it should be a handy reference – not as a *"sort of mandatory learning unit."* It was viewed as being useful for new clinicians to think post assessment within a heuristic learning environment.

Multidisciplinary Approach

It was identified that new clinicians need training that crosses professional specialities and therefore participants share a list of books. They discussed capacity building so that *"people feel confident to operate in a role that isn't necessarily their natural skill set"*. Examples were given that a social worker needs to understand gait and medicines, while nurses need skills in narrative therapy.

Adult Learning

The experience-based nature of the Guide was supported. One participant, previously from a education background, proposed: *"... put in a bit about how adults learn, adult learning principles. Because it's not just about information... it's about experiences and all sorts of things..."*

The responsibility of new clinicians for their own

learning was mentioned, even where learning supports are less available. As far as uptake goes: "Some do, some don't" but the issue was that they are given the opportunity. Practice-based learning was acknowledged – "...in terms of knowledge-to-practise, it's actually having to go out and do the work."

Written Resources

There was a strong theme reflecting popularity of printed resources. Sharing of books, articles and reading lists is strong within their service, and they have formed a journal club. For many clinicians traditional printed books are favourite, with some foray into other formats.

Dissemination

In terms of dissemination, printed resources are still favoured, with (online?) journal articles and E-books also being utilized. Downloadable E-Books (e.g. through Amazon) had the most support compared to formats such as YouTube. Negative experiences of web searches included difficulty locating quality information: *"There is nothing exciting or sort of current, or it doesn't seem to stand up to our standards."*

A prompt was offered about issues of affordability – the response was appreciative but brief. The psychiatrist suggested the Guide be circulated to the faculty of old age within the RANZCP, to see if they might list it (List ref RANZCP 2017).

Strengths and limitations of the study

A weakness is that the focus group was small. It would be valuable to repeat the study in a variety of settings, and also consider running focus groups post-publication, to explore uptake issues, the quality and focus of the information, and the helpfulness of the Guide.

To a large extent the contrast between the training now available under participant's highly developed service philosophy of care and their previous experiences in other OPMH services correlated to the researcher's experience of wanting better orientation and training within his role. Their highly developed values correlated and extended the researcher's. In other words, researcher bias was aligned with their strongest responses, and the project appears not to be overly negatively invested, using this group as evidence. There are of course departures between the experience of the researcher and the participants: Hence, issues such as the approach to the Glossary (Jargon), Recovery, information about treatments, the Erikson model, and especially the way the Guide discusses supervision and self care mean considerable reflection of the current draft is in order. It seems it may have been better to conduct the research before writing drafts.

Possibly because no participants had previewed the sample Guide, there were areas of limited understanding: For example, cultural analysis was thin (aside from general approval of prompts about inclusion of Stolen Generations in the trauma section). Perhaps there should have been a stronger focus on OPMH cultural awareness in the prompts. An excellent resource in culturally awareness featuring a whole section on assessment in Aboriginal Health (Dudgeon, P., Milroy, H., & Walker R., 2014, especially Part 4) will therefore be discussed in the Guide. This rich resource presents a strong argument for culturally aware assessment that strongly overlaps with narrative assessment advocated by participants.

Similarly, little comment was made in response to prompts about Recovery in OPMH. This may indicate that Recovery has not conceptually integrated very deeply in OPMH. A recent publication by the NSW Mental Health Commission (2017, p19) called Living Well in Later Life discusses the difficulty which services have in adapting to Recovery principles. It briefly refers to the particular nuances of Recovery in OPMH, and expressions of Recovery in Nursing Care. The principles mentioned concur with those identified in Daley et al (2013). The person-centred approach is linked, as is reminiscence therapy, but narrative assessment is not. It was beyond the initial scope of this research to pull the various strands of Person-Centred Care, narrative therapy and Recovery into focus. Other aspects of Recovery, such as client consultation, were also not addressed.

Implications for clinical practice and future research

An interesting Human Resources business-focussed web article discusses how feeling pride and passion in one's work could reduce burnout (Hagel et al, 2014). It ties mentoring and leadership to sustaining passion. Improving morale can therefore improve care of the consumer. One participant stated they're 'a bit of a difficult personality in terms of whether I conform'. Certainly it is easy to see how a more vocal, empowered clinician will thrive in a philosophically reformed environment, as opposed to an environment of more legacy, hierarchical values. Further research could explore whether staff in a Mental Health service which has reformed values they engage passionately with, cope better, last longer and are more useful to consumers.

Further research is needed around culturally aware training in OPMH services. Also, as mentioned previously, the uptake of Recovery orientation is lagging in OPMH and it would be interesting to learn more about this.

Conclusion

Production of the Guide is an excellent opportunity to inject awareness of Recovery into OPMH services, and the Guide will be revised to maximise and focus Recovery values. The narrative approach suggested will also be advocated within the Guide toward a shared emphasis between Recovery principles and linked to culturally sensitive practice training resources. The group's values around the approach of the guide in being an overtly experience-based work, getting away from jargon, as supporting early specialist clinician learning, will also have an impact on the development of the Guide pre-publication.

The group's passionate philosophical approach maximises many aspects of a Recovery framework, including values like connection, identity, hope, transparency, and meaning. The participants did not yet conceptualise their approach as Recovery focussed or demonstrate consumer-led values as is part of Recovery frameworks, however this research suggests there may be potentially many excellent Person-Centred OPMH services and clinicians with embryonic Recovery values, needing awareness of this model.

Ethics Approval

Ethics approval was by Albury-Wodonga Human Research Ethics Committee prior to the focus group.

Competing interests

The author has stated that there are none. When the Guide is produced, the intellectual property will remain with the author unless otherwise stated.

APPENDIX 2: THOUGHTS ABOUT SETTING UP A SUPERVISION GROUP

Trauma-informed Group Supervision for Diverse and Isolated Counsellors

Australia is a huge place. Quite often services are sparse or inconsistent, and geography can isolate diverse counselling professionals which is a major factor in workplace retention and turnover (Nickson, Gair & Miles, 2016). Many workplaces support the idea of supervision, without providing sufficient access to supervision in rural and remote areas due to lack of resources (Ducat et al, 2015). Local supervision can be quite hard to obtain.

Many organisations, including publicly funded departments, are enmeshed with a risk-averse perspectives (Beddoe, 2010), which unrealistically seem to assume the coalface worker has responsibility or control over client choices and other negative outcomes, with the worker left feeling guilt and isolation. This silently draws the focus of the organisation away from a client focus and distorts the agenda of management. This subtle blaming culture is felt as services become more controlled, bureaucratized and accountability-focussed "The values and culture of an organisation set the expectations about the work." (Bell et al., 2003, p. 463)

Meanwhile the worker remains at the coalface trying to keep others well and safe. In this instance, an external group supervision process offers an alternative to workplace clinical supervision (which is often absent anyway) with its link to performance, and offers healing and hope. Perhaps we need to create opportunities for diverse, isolated professionals to meet together in a local group to engage in trauma-informed co-supervision and to provide mutual support, reflection on difficult cases, localised networking, knowledge sharing opportunities and cohesiveness. In other words, group supervision may help make up for many of the difficulties and risks of solo work.

Supervision is regarded as essential for those in mental health professions, but in many instances sufficient supervision is difficult to find, particularly in rural and remote areas, or where professionals are isolated with their organisational constraints. Isolation brings with it other risks. These may include burnout, vicarious trauma, losing connection with information sources or missing out on new information. At times clinicians may feel very alone and isolated.

The external supervision framework for diverse counselling professionals proposed here is designed to consolidate restorative approaches that support supervisees from various disciplines and contexts to address impact of vicarious trauma and other influences on their practice while retaining focus on their client's needs. It is a chance to attend to restorative functions of supervision in a climate that often seems inclined to define supervision as a process of performance measures and risk avoidance, so it offers healing and hope.

The move toward trauma informed care has been followed by questions of how to address vicarious trauma in the supervisory setting. If group supervision can positively address vicarious trauma through drawing upon the shared experience of dedicated professionals, a question arises: How might group supervision be incorporated with strength-based, mindfulness and trauma-informed principles?

Group supervision can be restorative similarly to individual supervision, but works through a shared lens of co-supervisors. This lens can create perspective on whether interpretation of a phenomenon is "objective" (using wider group reflections) or "subjective" (i.e. views of an individual supervisor) (Andersson, 2008), decreasing the likelihood of bias or blindspots. Group supervision can therefore increase emotional safety.

A group setting also allows inexperienced co-supervisors to gain perspective on how common feelings of inadequacy really are (Holloway & Johnston, 1985), and learn much about the restorative power of mindful reflection. It can be a safe place where self-disclosure is valued and the supervisee learns to trusts that awkwardness and shame are worth addressing. In a recent group discussion about supervision by experienced clinicians, one described supervision as "A safe place to get it wrong".

The next concern is to define *how* this program uses models to achieve restorative processes in an arena of work where vicarious trauma can result in physiological symptoms that resemble posttraumatic stress reactions in caring professionals (Bell et al., 2003). By extension, the application of trauma-informed care principles could promote psychological safety and a healthy sense of empowerment within its process.

Proctor's widely known model of Supervision is described as being about three functional aspects: Formative function, normative function, and restorative function (Beddoe, 2010). In formative function, training is provided to teach the supervisee things they had not understood. In normative, organisational standards are discussed. In restorative function, support is given. In the author's experience, the normative function tends to receive less reflection in external supervision; however the organisational context is never very far from the core of the issue. All three functions should be addressed in supervision.

This presents challenges to a trauma-informed group supervision model, where support is maximised and the supervisee should be regarded as an expert in their own process. In contrast the normative function especially may seem to highlight on shortcomings, even pathological flaws. It may induce stress and possibly re-traumatise the supervisee because of the realities of the institution.

A psychologically safe normative function of supervision approaches evaluation with both maturity and safe distance. This means acceptance of the reality and need for outcome measures and accountabilities, yet in the same moment acknowledging how contextual structures constrain, allow, and facilitated client focus, similar to the Seven Eyed Model of supervision (Hawkins and Shohet, 2012).

It is the professional's responsibility to ethically apply their best professional understanding to the work of helping the client, and in fact to *push back* when the organisation's drift toward self-protection encroaches on services to the client. Recognition of this differential can bring the whole process back to productive balance, reflection and restorative function.

Aside from where normative functions can be safely approached from the balanced, critical, strength-based perspective, evaluative responses need to be carefully regarded. This is could be a strength of external supervision, for it avoids confusion between performance measures and addressing problems in facing the pain incurred in the course of work (Bell et al 2003).

General Principles

Psychological Safety

It is vital that an atmosphere of psychological safety is generated throughout the supervision. In terms of general approaches, this can be created through several value statements and value-aware approaches which will define the group dynamic, such as is listed below:

Trauma-Informed Supervision

(including vicarious trauma)

Five key principles that have been identified for trauma-informed care are: Safety; Trustworthiness and Transparency; Choice; Collaboration and Mutuality; Empowerment (Fallot & Harris, 2006, p 9-14). A sixth could be added referring to awareness of Contextual issues such as Cultural, Historical, and Gender Issues.

This proposal argues for a psychologically safe co-supervision process based on these six principles. Peer support and Supervision are two identified strategies of addressing secondary traumatization in professionals, and this project is aimed at these two areas in combination. (SAMHSA 2014, p198). It is seen as essential that the co-supervisors also have opportunity to learn about and discuss what trauma-informed care is in an operational sense, in the safety of external supervision.

Psychological safety is a fundamental principle allowing processing and adjustment part of a trauma-informed approach. The supervisee (or other co-supervisors) may be experiencing grief, shame, confusion, anger, attraction, guilt, or a host of other emotions, which are feeling bound to their client's suffering. There may also be unexpected interaction with their own trauma from their past. It is impossible to know how much is vicariously transferred and how much is triggered. The supervision session is not a counselling session, and anyway counselling often runs counter to boundaries in trauma-informed care. In Trauma-informed care, the person (i.e. the supervisee in this instance) does not necessarily benefit from reliving or even being critiqued for the story (which is often re-traumatising).

In the present project is not suggested that co-supervisors assume control of personal healing, for this belongs to the supervisee, counter to ideas of catharsis or psychoanalytic perspectives. The supervisee simply needs to be supported and understood, with respect for their humanity, professionalism and intentions.

The "Good enough" Counsellor

The idea of the "good enough mother" is that a child naturally expresses it's outrage as a normal function of development and the mother does not start reacting but rather responds to feelings without a sense of failure, through her understanding (Hawkins & Shohet, 2006), and a supportive partner does not criticise her for her child's outcry. The supervisee needs to be shown similar grace and latitude to maximise their confidence and development. Attacks based on the client's/colleagues/institutions reactivity, any countertransference experienced, and the painful, awkward feelings that can result in the supervisee need to be responded to with trust, warmth and support.

"The supervisor's role is not just to reassure the worker, but to allow the emotional disturbance to be felt within the safer setting of the supervisory relationship, where it can be survived, reflected upon and learned from." (Hawkins & Shohet, 2006, p3).

Thankfulness/ Appreciation

It takes courage for a person to expose their tensions, self-doubts, dilemmas, ignorance and even shame. The bravery that is exercised in telling the story should be respected, as should the clinician's humanity. Expressing gratitude for their bravery is a beginning of restorative process.

Empathy

It is simply not possible that a human can do compassionate work without experiencing transference/ counter-transference/ and defensive responses to clients, and quite often. Respecting the desire of the clinician to excel as a professional requires acknowledgement of the *'There, but for the grace of God, go I'* principle. Empathy is recognition of shared human issues. Empathy does not require a lack of discernment, but rather a withholding of condemnation for the person sharing their story. Also, empathy cannot make any difference, or perhaps even really exist, without having been *expressed*. Expressions of empathy may start with positive statements such as: *"Yes, I can see* how challenging that must have been for any clinician...", taking issues of difficulty as generalised to the human experience.

Respect

Although co-supervising group members might not understand the perspective of the supervisee, they can express respect for the person and their perspective. This is an opportunity to study the way systems affect their issue, systems that may be quite outside the co-supervisor's awareness. Respect will, in this regard, operate counter to ignorance.

Curiosity

There are moments when wanting to know more is sparked by creativity and a novel take on the issue. Judiciously applied, curiosity can open doors to new perspectives. If questions are framed respectfully, curiosity can lead to moments of shared insight and illumination.

Mindful reflection

Mindfulness is the appreciative, non-judgemental awareness of our experience as it unfolds, in terms of thoughts, feelings and physical sensations. The act of noticing without further interpretation opens pathways to spontaneous, deeper processing. Becoming aware of feelings within, without having to act, creates a "friendly, detached attitude"... which permits us to decentre from our thoughts and therefore allow more creative options (Powell, 2009, p108): perspective has restorative power. In supervision, Mindfulness can be used to identify parallel processes. For example, as the supervisee tells their story, fear and unease may grow within a group member as a parallel process. The co-supervisor's mind might relating to times when they experienced similar fear. In reactive mode, they may take an attitude of bravado which, if expressed, seems to criticise the supervisee's response. Through mindful reflection, however, a co-supervisor feel similar fear, become mindfully aware of it, and in their turn simply acknowledge their own responses (without the need for making sense of it). Those experienced in mindfulness will probably catch on, which could have a positive impact on the group dynamic.

Reflective listening skills

(I.e. restating back to the person the issue plus the impact as revealed by the person) is closely related to mindfulness in this sense, however it is noticing *the other person's emotions* and reflecting it back to them (without further critique). This allows the person to feel connected to the hearer, and processing is vicariously supported in a similar sense as it is internally through mindfulness.

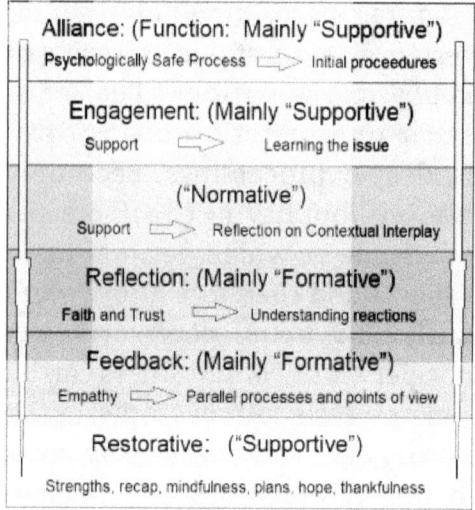

Figure 16: Strengths Sandwich - an Iterative Process of Trauma Informed Supervision

Strengths-sandwich Supervision

A focus on strengths may be quite difficult to find in a risk-averse organisation, yet it corresponds to psychological safety and trauma-informed care. Below is a brief form of the resource prepared for this project as a guide to strengths-based co-supervision.

The overall structure is intended to demonstrate a supportive 'strength-sandwich': The yellow representing the supportive structures (the bread), the green adding texture and context, the red being the reflection and feedback – the reflective 'meat', followed up by a final set of supportive techniques to keep the overall process intact.

Group design

Ideally the group will be from five to seven co-supervisors / supervisees. Because membership may include junior or trainee counsellors and newly employed graduates, a proposed standard is that membership is only available to counselling professionals who have signed on to professional associations with published ethical standards.

All group members, including the Chair and the selected supervisee, function as co-supervisors in the sense having a say in the flow of processes, the application of the General Principles, and the exercise of the group agreement. Although the Chair may hold the resource (below) as a prompt or rough guide to process, the term 'co-supervisor' points to shared responsibility for the process.

Ethical Considerations

Without breaking the confidentiality agreement of the group or identifying members (beyond agreed risk/ confidentiality standards), some seeking of support has to be acknowledged as being a likely occurrence from time to time. This possibility would of necessity be limited to consultation with their contracted professional supervisors, and discussed in regards to group supervision processes, group facilitation skills, the application of supervision models, personal impacts/ transference, and other similar, relevant processes.

Being professionally subject to a code of ethics as a minimum standard for participation strengthens the confidentiality agreement and also the way co-supervisors relate to each other. This will increase trust in the process. However situations involving harm, crime or unethical risk need to be managed, ultimately, to a professional standard, and each professional is implicitly responsible to see the issue addressed.

All groups go through phases and at times differences, disagreement and even conflict are a possibility, and if well managed, a healthy aspect of group process. At times personalities or ideas run counter and people may look to outside supervision for information and support. However, the group process as agreed needs to be both robust and respectful. If it truly is, and participants feel they can use assertiveness positively, internal confidence in the group's process may be strengthened as clinicians resolve issues inside the group.

The overall nature of the program could be viewed as somewhat radical as it attempts to balance hegemonic controls and over-reactivity of institutions, while still retaining a restorative focus and normative functions, delivered as safely as possible.

Contracting phase

The group needs to have the opportunity to participate in forming a working contract or agreement with standards and functions of the group.

One possibility is that co-supervisors have opportunity of being, in turn, Rotating Chair of the co-supervision process. The Chair is someone who invites, restates and summarises, and supervises and facilitates the flow of processes over the session. They referee the democratic prioritisation of issues and selection of who will be supervisee. Not every group member may feel comfortable being Chair initially so this could be negotiated.

Appropriate standards of confidentiality will also be identified in the initial session of the group and will be developed into a working supervision agreement, as well as other standards defined by co-supervisors. These may include etiquette, timeframes, application of the General Principles (above), avoiding counselling, and participation or other negotiated ideas.

Arrangement for Supervision/Support

There is potential that some extra leadership may be required should the group become aware of unmanaged risk, unethical behaviour, or harm (Falender & Shafranske, 2008, chapter 8). Conflict, group dynamics and transgression of the group agreement are also issues that may require qualified, ethical support. This should be negotiated early in the contracting phase. This could involve participation of an experienced supervisor who has experience in running group supervision, or a channel for consultation with one.

Starting Each Session

Each session, after welcoming each other, each co-supervisor will be invited to rate an issue affecting them, in terms of the weight and urgency for them. At this stage there is no need to discuss the issue, just to offer a rating from 1 to 10, 10 being most important. Next, the highest ranking issues are discussed to work out who is to be supervisee. Not every supervisee will be ready to share an issue, and this is perfectly acceptable – the choice remains theirs.

Starting Supervision

The next phase starts with the supervisee giving a brief history of the event and it's impacts. As this concludes, the Chair might invite participants to either ask respectful questions or provide empathetic feedback, even one by one in turn. This process also builds inclusiveness early, as a cornerstone of the group supervision process. This step brings focus and responsibility to the group early, and gives them permission to express their responses while they are fresh in their minds. It also may allow emotions to be expressed that then open up to reflective process.

During this phase, issues may begin to be explored in greater depth and the questions may sometimes lead off into tangents. There may be a gentle timekeeping role for the Chair during this phase. The Chair then also then adds their feedback and comments. The next step is the Chair paraphrasing the story. (It can be if the Chair has jotted down some keywords – to be destroyed at the end of the session.) After paraphrasing, the Chair may check that they have the story, impacts, questions and issues clearly framed. Once the person agrees, the next phase may begin.

Using the Prompts

The following table is intended to be a tool for the group to think about some of the approaches to supervision. It is a combination of Proctor's Functional Interactive Model, roles of supervision, and the Seven-Eyed Model of Supervision (Shohet and Hawkins, 1989).

It is not a list of points to raise – more it is a set of suggestions. Not every element must be used, and the sequence may differ (The advice is to keep to a 'Strength

Sandwich') format.

It is suggested that each group member familiarise themselves with it, which could strengthen group process. Although the Seven-Eyed model is followed sequentially for the most part in the following figure, Mode 7 appears out of order, which is fine. In the design of this resource it was felt that the contextual and cultural analysis of Mode 7 actually belongs in the middle, where, once addressed, it can be incorporated into the reflective/feedback phases and then supportively addressed within the restorative phase, not as an afterthought.

The roles are the headings in the table, the processes are listed down the left-hand side.

This tool is therefore a tabulation of group supervisory roles vs supervisory functions, highlighting the strength-based and supportive aspects as they may be blended with each other type of function and role.

I don't believe following it with exactness will be of any real benefit. It is an analytical tool for studying types of responses. The supervision session needs to be flexible, warm and responsive at every turn to be considered trauma-informed.

	Support	Teacher	Consultant	Evaluator
Alliance (Function: Mainly "Supportive")	Building psychological safety.	Referring to group contract/ agreed standards.	Involving co-supervisors. Participation.	Being appreciative of supervisee's openness, courage.
Engagement (Mainly "Supportive")	Showing empathy, respect.	Facilitating	Managing the pace of the session: Eliciting the story (7 Eyed model: mode 1, "the situation")	Identifying the issues. (7 Eyed model: mode 2, "learning more about the intervention")
("Normative")	Similar dilemmas in other contexts	Exploring how the story interacts with the person's role / context.	Does the group have insight to relate to the context?	Evaluating how organisational, professional, and cultural, ethical contextual structures constrained/allowed/ facilitated client focus. (7 Eyed., mode 7)
Reflection (Mainly "Formative")	Expressions of faith in supervisee. Acknowledge the difficulty. Curiosity.	Paraphrasing, linking themes, checking in with the supervisee if they feel these are 'on track'. Psychological safety for client	Inviting supportive group reflection and questions early. Invite self-reflection/ self-rating. Responses to ideas	The counsellor's perspective on the client's experience. How might the client describe the interaction/ relationship? (7 Eyed., mode 3)
Feedback (Mainly "Formative")	Empathy for Counsellor's experience of the issue and life experience (7 Eyed., mode 4)	Theoretical and models perspective. Identifying the issue from various points of view.	(7 Eyed model, mode 5 Parallel processes, observing emotional reactions - co-supervisor /supervisee)	Identify if any risks, harm, blindsiding, problems are involved. Ideas for addressing.
Restorative ("Supportive")	Identification of strengths. Reflections of worth of the supervisee. Mindfulness. Reflective listening. Empathy.	Recap "What worked for you?" Ideas about addressing the issue/ fallout.	Awareness of own feelings in the session. My own feelings - mindfulness (7 Eyed, mode 6) The other's feelings. Supervisee feelings.	Expressions of hope within the individual, professional, cultural and systemic views. Commitments to action. Thankfulness. Close / Refreshment

Figure 17: Expanded Group Supervision roles by Stages and Functions of Supervision

APPENDIX 3: SOME SUGGESTED READING

Title	Author / Publisher	Central Themes	Source Information
Working Together Aboriginal and Torres Strait Islander Mental Health and Wellbeing: Principles and Practice. (2nd ed.).	Dudgeon, P., Milroy, H., & Walker R., (2014). Canberra, Pub. Commonwealth of Australia	Culturally sensitive practice. Narrative assessment.	Available online eg Amazon
The Mental Health Handbook A Cognitive Behavioural Approach	Trevor Powell 2009 UK: Speechmark	CBT tools with printable resources disk. Includes bereavement and mindfulness, carer support principles	
Your Brain in Sickness and in Health	Dr Sid Williams, Pub. Lulu Australian book.	The experience of dementia and other brain disorders	
Further Along The Road Less Travelled	Dr M. Scott Peck	Insights into the issues that confront and challenge all of us today: spirituality, forgiveness, relationships, and growing up	From the Wangaratta OPMH Reading list.
Identity and the Life Cycle	Erik H. Erikson	Life stage development	
Sky Above Clouds	Wendy L. Miller, Gene D. Cohen, and Teresa H. Barker	Finding Our Way through Creativity, Aging, and Illness	
Staring at the Sun (1 and 2)	Irvin David Yalom	Being at peace with your own mortality	
The Brain in Human Aging Vol 23	Gene D. Cohen, Springer		
The Brain that Changes Itself	Norman Doidge	Stories of Personal Triumph from the Frontiers of Brain Science	
The Creative Age:	Dr Gene D. Cohen	Debunks harmful myths about	

Awakening Human Potential in the Second Half of Life		aging and illuminates the biological and emotional foundations of creativity	
The Mature Mind: The Positive Power of the Aging Brain	Gene D. Cohen	Extraordinary accounts of cutting-edge neuroscience, groundbreaking psychology, and practical advice for personal growth strategies.	
Vital Involvement in Old Age	Erik H. Erikson, Joan M. Erikson, Helen Q. Kivnick	Erikson's now-famous concept of the life cycle delineates eight stages of psychological development through which each of us progresses.	
Oxford textbook of Old Age Psychiatry	Edited by Tom Dening and Alan Thomas Pub. Oxford University Press	Core Old Age Psychiatry text	RANZCP list, Psychiatry of the Older Person.
Community Mental Health for Older People	Gerard Byrne and Christine C Neville, Pub Elsevier	Alternate POA text, Australian author, and community based focus.	Web address is listed in References section
Geriatric Consultation Liaison Psychiatry	P S Melding & B Draper [Oxford Univ Press]	Useful POA and C–L text	There are many other topics on this list. Mostly Psychiatry testbooks.

Figure 18: Reading List suggestions

APPENDIX 4: THE 4A DELIRIUM SCREENING TOOL

This tool was recommended by the Focus Group – the only tick-box tool that they strongly advocated for – and I have included it on that basis. Too often delirium is confused as something else, and it is hoped that greater clarity about delirium will help unnecessary Polypharmacy issues, quicker attention to underlying issues, and more understanding of the nature of true psychotic issues.

This tool is freely downloadable at https://www.the4at.com/

…wherein it is given as the

"4AT rapid clinical test for delirium - free to download and use"

The website also states the following:

"It is a short and practical tool designed for use in busy areas where assessment for delirium is needed."

"The 4AT is among the most widely-used clinical tests for delirium internationally."

"Disclaimer: responsibility for the interpretation of scores and any actions rests with the clinical team using the 4AT. As per accepted clinical practice, a diagnosis of delirium should always be made following clinical assessment by suitably qualified staff."

I have copied in the tool for learning purposes. Please refer to the above web page to print off copies to use. (It is wonderful to see these tools being made available free to use and I congratulate the authors on their commitment and foresight.)

4AT

Assessment test for delirium & cognitive impairment

Patient name:
Date of birth:
Patient number:
Date: Time:
Tester:

                                                                                  CIRCLE

[1] ALERTNESS
This includes patients who may be markedly drowsy (eg. difficult to rouse and/or obviously sleepy during assessment) or agitated/hyperactive. Observe the patient. If asleep, attempt to wake with speech or gentle touch on shoulder. Ask the patient to state their name and address to assist rating

Normal (fully alert, but not agitated, throughout assessment)	0
Mild sleepiness for <10 seconds after waking, then normal	0
Clearly abnormal	4

[2] AMT4
Age, date of birth, place (name of the hospital or building), current year

No mistakes	0
1 mistake	1
2 or more mistakes/untestable	2

[3] ATTENTION
Ask the patient: "Please tell me the months of the year in backwards order, starting at December." To assist initial understanding one prompt of "what is the month before December?" is permitted.

Months of the year backwards

Achieves 7 months or more correctly	0
Starts but scores <7 months / refuses to start	1
Untestable (cannot start because unwell, drowsy, inattentive)	2

[4] ACUTE CHANGE OR FLUCTUATING COURSE
Evidence of significant change or fluctuation in: alertness, cognition, other mental function (eg. paranoia, hallucinations) arising over the last 2 weeks and still evident in last 24hrs

No	0
Yes	4

4 or above: possible delirium +/- cognitive impairment
1-3: possible cognitive impairment
0: delirium or severe cognitive impairment unlikely (but delirium still possible if [4] information incomplete)

4AT SCORE [ ]

GUIDANCE NOTES   Version 1.2. Information and download: www.the4AT.com
The 4AT is a screening instrument designed for rapid initial assessment of delirium and cognitive impairment. A score of 4 or more suggests delirium but is not diagnostic: more detailed assessment of mental status may be required to reach a diagnosis. A score of 1-3 suggests cognitive impairment and more detailed cognitive testing and informant history-taking are required. A score of 0 does not definitively exclude delirium or cognitive impairment: more detailed testing may be required depending on the clinical context. Items 1-3 are rated solely on observation of the patient at the time of assessment. Item 4 requires information from one or more source(s), eg. your own knowledge of the patient, other staff who know the patient (eg. ward nurses), GP letter, case notes, carers. The tester should take account of communication difficulties (hearing impairment, dysphasia, lack of common language) when carrying out the test and interpreting the score.

Alertness: Altered level of alertness is very likely to be delirium in general hospital settings. If the patient shows significant altered alertness during the bedside assessment, score 4 for this item. **AMT4 (Abbreviated Mental Test - 4):** This score can be extracted from items in the AMT10 if the latter is done immediately before. **Acute Change or Fluctuating Course:** Fluctuation can occur without delirium in some cases of dementia, but marked fluctuation usually indicates delirium. To help elicit any hallucinations and/or paranoid thoughts ask the patient questions such as: "Are you concerned about anything going on here?", "Do you feel frightened by anything or anyone?", "Have you been seeing or hearing anything unusual?"

Figure 19: 4AT Delirium Screening Tool

APPENDIX 5: GLOSSARY & JARGON

As can be seen from the previous Appendix, Jargon is the enemy to Recovery informed care!

In the focus group, OPMH clinicians favoured avoiding specialised jargon in training new clinicians:
- It was viewed more useful, realistic and efficient to expect new clinicians to develop their observational skills than to focus on learning specialist jargon;
- Consumers and families may not understand what is being said about them, potentially causing undue stress;
- Jargon insidiously creeps into misuse of terms with "Huge risks of error."

However we work within the medical model and have to understand a lot of specialised terms, and as they say in Reader's Digest "It pays to enrich your word power". This glossary is therefore not given to make your communications jargon rich, but to aid your understanding of illnesses.

Abreaction

Abreaction is a process of vividly reliving repressed memories and emotions related to a past event.

Abulia (or Aboulia)

A lack of will or initiative to act or make decisions independently.

Accusatory Hallucination

Hearing voices that characterise the person as morally evil, guilty, shameful, inadequate, or inappropriately responsible for adverse events.

Affect illusion

Misperceptions linked to the person's mood; for example, a person may see litter all over a town they hate living in, when in fact the street is clean.

Agnosia

Agnosia is a failure to recognize objects or associate an object with its meaning, use, or to recognise people or themself.

Akathisia

An inability to sit still or restlessness in the lower limbs, related to problems in the extrapyramidal system in the brain, sometimes caused by antipsychotic medication.

Akinesia

Muscle rigidity, or an impairment of voluntary movement, common in severe Parkinson's. It often begins with stiffness in the legs and neck. When it occurs in the face it results in a mask-like stare

Alexithymia

Alexithymia refers to an inability to identify and describe emotions in the self.

Alogia

"Not having words" either as "poverty of speech" or "poverty of thought". In poverty of speech the person may rely on habitual phrases. In poverty of thought there is an impoverishment of the entire thinking of the person. It is a negative symptom of advanced dementia, and is also seen in schizophrenia.

Amok

The phrase "running amok" describes the behavior of an individual, who is very agitated and can become a danger to others and himself. The syndrome of "Amok" is found in DSM-IV.

Anhedonia

Anhedonia refers to an inability to experience pleasure, and may be described as a feeling of emotional emptiness. It can be a negative symptom of schizophrenia. It also may be seen in severe depressive states and schizoid personality disorder.

Aphasia

An impaired ability to speak or understand speech. Includes difficulty in using written words.

Apraxia

A person may lack ability in motor planning movement when directed, despite component abilities remaining intact.

Asterixis

Also called the flapping tremor, is a tremor of the hand when the wrist is extended. It may occur with several conditions including structural brain diseases, kidney failure, or as a side effect of some drugs.

Ataxia
A loss of control in bodily movements. Ataxic Gait is where walking is uncoordinated. Ataxia can be limited to one side of the body, referred to as hemiataxia.

Automatic obedience
Automatic obedience is an exaggerated co-operation with an examiner's request, as if the patient were an 'automaton' robotically obeying a command. It is usually a sign of catatonia.

Avolition
Avolition is an inability to initiate and complete goal-directed behaviour. It can sometimes be misinterpreted as laziness, but it is actually a negative symptom of schizophrenia

Bradykinesia
The individual's movements become increasingly slow and over time muscles may randomly "freeze". Often found in Parkinson's.

Brain Fog
Brain fog is another term for Clouding of consciousness.

Catalepsy
Catalepsy is the term for catatonic rigidity of the limbs which often results in abnormal posturing for long intervals.

Catatonia
Catatonia involves a significant psychomotor disturbance, which can occur as catalepsy, stupor, exces-

sive purposeless motor activity, extreme negativism (seemingly motiveless resistance to movement), mutism, echolalia (imitating speech), or echopraxia (imitating movements). There is a catatonic subtype of schizophrenia.

Charles Bonnet Syndrome

After eye surgery some people experience recurrent visual hallucinations. They may see animals, "Lilliputian" or cartoon-like figures, faces or patterns on the walls. The person often has insight that they are seeing a hallucination.

Chorea

Chorea is manifest by abnormal involuntary movements. The term comes from Greek word "choreia" as meaning dance, since large groups of muscles are usually involved, which leads to writhing dance-like movements.

Circumstantial speech

Circumstantial thinking, or circumstantial speech, refers to a person being unable to answer a question without giving excessive, unnecessary detail. This differs from tangential thinking, in that the person does eventually return to the original point, circling back on-topic.

Clang association

Clang associations are ideas that are related only by similar or rhyming sounds rather than actual meaning. Example: "He ate the skate, inflated yesterdays gate toward the cheese grater."

Clouding of consciousness

Clouding of consciousness, also known as brain fog or mental fog, is a global impairment in higher central nervous functioning. All aspects of cognitive functioning are affected. On mental status examination it is manifest by disorientation in time, place and person, memory difficulties caused by failure to register and recall, aphasia, and agnosia. Impaired perception functioning can lead illusions and hallucinations which can precipitate agitation and distress and secondary delusions.

Confabulation
Confabulation is the confusion of imagination with memory, and/or the confusion of true memories with false memories.

Conversion disorder
Conversion disorder involves the unintentional production of symptoms or deficits affecting motor or sensory function that are not fully explained by a neurological or medical condition. This can manifest as paralysis, for example. It generally involves psychological factors, and symptoms may worsen in the context of situational conflict.

Cotard delusion
Cotard delusion involves the belief that one of the person's own bodily organs has changed in a bizarre way, has ceased functioning, or has disappeared. It is a type of delusion that can be experienced in schizophrenia.

Delusion
A persistent, false belief. Sometimes related to a faulty memory. Types include delusional mood, persecutory delusion, apophanous perception, Wahneinfall and de-

lusional memories.

Delusion Perceptions

A correctly sensed and interpreted perception that is given some additional (and possibly absurd) significance. These are different to Hallucinations.

Delusional Parasitosis

A delusion that the person's skin or body has been infested by parasites or insects. If a person is under the influence of a drug, or withdrawing from a drug, this condition is called formication.

Diurnal Variation

Diurnal variation of mood: Where depressive symptoms are worse in the early-morning part of the day – or sometimes the mood being regularly worse in the afternoon or evening. Diurnal Variation is a core feature of melancholia in major depressive disorder.

Dementia pugilistica

Dementia pugilistica, also called "chronic traumatic encephalopathy", "boxer's syndrome", and "punch-drunk syndrome", is a neurological disorder which affects career boxers and others who receive multiple dazing blows to the head.

Derailment

Derailment, also known as loosening of associations, refers to disorganized thinking that jumps between ideas that seem entirely unrelated. It can be seen in patients with schizophrenia, as well as those experiencing mania. This is in contrast with flight of ideas where connection is present between one topic and another.

Dyskinesia

Dyskinesia can range from a slight tremor in the hands to uncontrollable movement of the upper body or lower extremities, and can also occur internally especially with the respiratory muscles. It is a category of movement disorders, a symptom of several disorders distinguished by their underlying cause. It is characterized by involuntary muscle movements, including tics or chorea and diminished voluntary movements.

Dystonia

Dystonia is where sustained or repetitive muscle contractions cause twisting and repetitive movements or fixed postures. May resemble a tremor. Any muscle in the body may be affected, including arms or legs, the jaw, tongue and throat (which can impair breathing - a medical emergency), and the person may be in constant pain. Acute dystonia is a sustained muscle contraction that can appear soon after administration of antipsychotic medications (E.g. Haloperidol).

Echolalia

Meaningless vocal imitation of another person – as a psychiatric symptom.

Echopraxia

Imitation of actions. Echomimia is imitation of facial expressions

Euthymic Mood

Euthymia is a normal non-depressed, reasonably positive mood. In Bipolar illness, it refers to the neutral mood phase. Hyperthymia refers to an extremely happy mood while dysthymia, refers to a saddened or a depressed mood.

Extrapyramidal Symptoms

The term Extrapyramidal refers to the system that regulates muscle tone and posture. Symptoms such as akathysia, bradykinesia, dyskinesia, dystonia, parkinsonism, tardive Dyskinesia and tremor may be linked to the use of antipsychotics and other drugs and seen as triggering these side effects, particularly in the elderly.

Flight of ideas

Flight of ideas describes excessive speech at a rapid rate that involves causal association between ideas. Links between ideas may involve usage of puns or rhymes. It is typical of mania, classically seen in bipolar disorder.

Folie à deux

Also called induced psychosis, folie à deux is a delusional disorder shared by two or more people who are closely related emotionally. One has real psychosis while the symptoms of psychosis are induced in the other or others due to close attachment to the one with psychosis.

Formal Thought Disorder

Formal thought disorder is revealed by disorganized speech. Some types include tangentiality, thought derailment, poverty of speech, illogicality, perseveration, neologism, and thought blocking.

Hallucination

A sensory experience that is a false perception of something the person hears, sees or feels, that is perceived as real and can't be readily rationalised away. They can be vivid perceptions of something external to the person. They can be more mild experiences, at the periphery of the senses, called a disturbance. Hallucinations can occur in all sensory areas. In older persons in particular, they can often occur at the borders between waking and sleeping. Although there is overlap, in psychiatric illness there is a stronger likelihood of auditory hallucinatory experiences, while organic disorders (including dementias, delirium etc) tend to produce the more visual hallucinations.

Ideas of influence
Thoughts that one's own action is caused by someone else's will or some other external cause.

Ideas of reference
Ideas of reference are a delusional belief that general events are personally directed at oneself. For example, someone might believe that he or she is receiving messages from the TV that are directed especially at him or her.

ISBAR
(Identify, Situation, Background, Assessment and Recommendation) is a mnemonic created to improve safety in the transfer of critical information. Although developed for nuclear submarine warfare, it has been adopted widely in large health services as a way of helping the speaker give a concise and accurate summary during handover to other professionals in time-pressured situations.

Illusion
An illusion is a false perception of an actual stimulus.

LID

In Parkinson's, LID (Levodopa-induced dyskinesia) can first appear in the foot, on the most affected side of the body in people who have been treated using levodopa (LDOPA) for an extended period.

Lilliputian hallucinations

Lilliputian hallucinations are characterized by abnormal perception of objects as being shrunken in size. It can be hallucinations of tiny people or children. Usually seen in delirium tremens, and in Lewy Body dementia.

Mutism

Mutism is absence of speech with apparently normal level of consciousness. Mutism can be dissociative in which an individual stops speaking at once; or it can be elective (selective) such as when a child does not speak in certain situations but speaks well in other conditions (like at home or at play).

Myoclonus

Twitches, jerks, muscular seizures and also hiccups. They often occur in people when they are falling asleep, but when widespread or pervasive these can be indicated in diseases such as MS, Parkinson's, Alzheimers, Dystonia etc.

Negative Symptoms

In Mental Health, this term covers signs and symptoms of illnesses that involve a loss or absence of normal function. These may include blunted affect, alogia, anhedonia, avolition, thought disorder, social isolation and stress. These may have a higher functional impact and care burden, and be harder to treat than positive symptoms.

Neologism
A new word invented within speech

Neuroleptic Malignant Syndrome
A life-threatening disorder with an adverse, sometimes rapid reaction to drugs, including Antipsychotics and/or Neuroleptic medications. Can be indicated by an onset of muscle rigidity, fever, autonomic instability (such as varying blood pressure) and delirium. Often unrecognised, it is a medical emergency and requires expert psychiatric assessment and treatment.

Omega sign
The omega sign is the occurrence of a fold (like the Greek letter omega, Ω) in the forehead, above the nose, produced by the excessive action of the corrugator muscle. It is sometimes seen in depression.

Overvalued Idea
(Idée fixe) In this condition, a belief that might seem reasonable both to the patient and to other people comes to dominate completely the patient's thinking and life.

Palilalia
Palilalia is characterized by the repetition of a word or phrase; i.e., the subject continues to repeat a word or phrase after once having said. It is a perseveratory phenomenon.

Partition Delusion
Characterised by a sense of other entities that may pass through walls, or exist in a space adjacent to the room the person occupies. The person may believe there are people in a room upstairs, when there is no upstairs.

People may have a sense that they are being contaminated, victimised, or infected by these others across physical barriers. For example, one patient spoke of a river of foul water flowing under their floor.

Persecutory Delusion

A false belief or perception that the person is being maliciously hunted, followed, and victimised by someone who wishes to hurt, harm your reputation, sabotage or kill them.

Perseveration

Repetition of a response, such as a word, gesture, or phrase, or written pattern after it would have otherwise usually discontinued naturally. Seen in organic disorders of brain, head injury, delirium or dementia, however can be seen in punding and schizophrenia as well.

Pill rolling

A tremor seen in Parkinson's disease. The thumb touches the pad of the index finger and moves around in a circular motion when the hand is apparently at rest.

Poverty of Speech

Speech, though adequate in verbiage, conveys very little information and may consist of stock phrases or vague references.

Poverty of thought

Impoverishment of the entire thinking of the person, who, as a result, says very little. A negative symptom of schizophrenia. It may also be seen in advanced dementia.

Pseudologia fantastica

Pseudologia fantastica is a condition in which a person grossly exaggerates his symptoms or even tells a lie about his symptoms in order to get medical attention.

Psychological pillow

Where the individual holds his/her head a few centimetres above the bed. No explanation is offered for this. It is a symptom of catatonia and can last for hours.

Psychological safety

Psychological safety is all about creating environments in which people feel accepted and respected. Reflection on engagement, and how the relationship with the consumer progresses can help identify the consumer's sense of psychological safety. In Trauma-Informed care, the empowerment, equality and ownership that the consumer feels affects psychological safety.

Psychomotor agitation

A series of unintentional and purposeless motions that are related to mental tension and anxiety. It may consist of actions such as repetitive pacing, hand wringing, tongue movements, and behaviours such as dressing and undressing. Although usually linked to mental wellness, it can be linked to physical conditions such as hyponatremia.

Psychomotor retardation

A slowing of thought and physical movement. For example, in depression. it can cause a visible slowing of physical and emotional reactions including in speech and affect.

Punding

Punding is a term for complex prolonged, purposeless, and stereotyped behaviour. Originally observed in Sweden in chronic amphetamine and other drug users, it was later described in Parkinson's disease, where it has been recognised as a side-effect of Dopamine replacement therapy medications. Punding activity is characterized by compulsive fascination with and performance of collecting and sorting behaviours, fidgeting, grooming, walking and other normal behaviours done far in excess, and has also been linked to gambling and sex addiction.

Rabbit syndrome

This syndrome is characterized by rapid rhythmic movements of lips so that it resembles a rabbit chewing. It is a type of dystonic reaction.

Responding

Audio hallucinations can occur during psychiatric assessment. While voices and what they say (eg command hallucinations) can be disturbing to the hearer, the stress of being assessed can mean the person tries to avoid having the hallucination detected by the clinician. At times, a person may, for example, suddenly look around as if having heard their name called, then refocus attention back to the clinician. This, if detected, can be seen as responding to unseen stimuli.

Restless Legs Syndrome

RLS is a neurological sleep disorder characterised by a compelling urge to move the legs, with throbbing, pulling, creeping, or other unpleasant sensations. Particularly occurs when in bed, and can contribute to sleep deprivation and fatigue. Although the cause is unknown, it is thought to be related to the neurotransmitter dopamine.

Stereotypies

A repetitive or ritualistic movement, posture, or utterance.

Includes body rocking, self-caressing, crossing and uncrossing of legs, and marching in place. It is common in frontotemporal dementia, intellectual disabilities, autism spectrum disorders, tardive dyskinesia, and some types of schizophrenia, but may also be encountered in normal individuals as well. Related terms include punding and tweaking to describe repetitive side effects of some drugs.

Stupor

A state of near-unconsciousness or insensibility, a low level of consciousness wherein a sufferer only responds to base stimuli such as pain.

Sundowning

Some elements of function can fluctuate in delirium and dementia, according to the time of day. This is thought to be related to the brains circadian rhythms interacting with functional areas and processes that may have differing degrees of impact of dementia. Sundowning is important to the assessment process as it may account for differences between reports and presentation at MSE, depending on the time of day the assessment is conducted.

Tangential Thinking

Tangential thinking or tangential speech is where the person moves quickly from topic to topic or wanders in their conversation without ever resolving back to the original topic or direction of speech.

Tardive Dyskinesia

Tardive dyskinesia (TD) is a difficult-to-treat and often incurable form of dyskinesia having a slow or belated onset – often occurring 3 months after commencement or from high-dose use of antipsychotic drugs, or with a month of withdrawal from medications. Tardive Dyskinesia results in involuntary, repetitive body movements. It can be incurable, and effects women and also, to a lesser degree, men. Older consumers can be very vulnerable to this.

It causes repetitive, involuntary movements including tremors and writhing movements of the body and limbs, and abnormal movements in the face, mouth, and tongue:

- Grimacing
- Tongue protrusions and movements in the mouth
- Lip smacking and puckering
- Pursing of the lips or pouting
- Excessive eye blinking

Telegrammatic or telegraphic speech

In telegraphic speech conjunctions and articles are missed out; meaning is retained and few words are used.

Thought blocking

Thought blocking, also referred to as thought withdrawal, refers to an abrupt stop in the middle of a train of thought; the individual might or might not be unable to continue the idea. This is type of formal thought disorder that can be seen in schizophrenia.

Tic

A sudden, nonrhythmic but repetitive movement of muscles. It can cause a vocalisation as the movement occurs, including throat clearing.

Traumatic bonding

Traumatic bonding occurs as the result of ongoing cycles of abuse in which the intermittent reinforcement of reward and punishment creates powerful emotional bonds that are resistant to change.

Tremor

Tremors often happen with the limb is at rest. Can be seen when the arm is held in a stiff, unsupported position, but can be present in the lips, feet or tongue. In Parkinson's tremors are the most noticeable early symptom. It often begins very localised, such as in a finger of one hand, and gradually spreads throughout the whole arm.

Volubility

Also known as "Logorrhoea". A patient's fluent and rambling speech using numerous words.

Waxy flexibility

Waxy flexibility is characterized by a patient's movements having the feeling of a plastic resistance, as if the person were made of wax. This occurs in catatonic schizophrenia, and a person suffering from this condition can have his limbs placed in fixed positions as if the person were in fact made from wax. (Also, Waxy rigidity.)

Word-salad

Confused, and often repetitious, language with no apparent meaning or relationship attached to them. It is often symptomatic of various mental illnesses, such as psychoses, including schizophrenia.

APPENDIX 6: MY RECOVERY/ SATISFACTION SURVEYS

In my private counselling practice I see people from a wide range of age groups. I have developed a consumer satisfaction questionnaire based upon CHIME and Daley's work, for a threefold purpose.

1. I utilize the questionnaire mid-way through the counselling sessions to educate and trigger people into thinking about their recovery, as part of the therapeutic process.
2. Sometimes, as an exit survey, I use it for feedback on my counselling practice.
3. I tell my clients that it may influence my studies in Recovery in older people, and ask for their permission to record their age to cross-check against their circled answers.

It is done face to face with me (which of course would have bearing on the outcome). It is done very informally and often results in discussion that influences therapy. I have not asked every client to participate, due to a range of factors. Although the results can only be regarded as anecdotal evidence, so far the results are very interesting, and I wonder about future research along these lines.

Where exploring themes of Recovery, if the person responds a value strongly, I encourage them to circle the short heading (left hand column). Where there is discussion about specific aspects I ask them simply to circle the relevant aspects on the right, or to write something different if they see fit. My plan is to learn more about the age division in the CHIME and Daley models, and where counselling fits with Recovery.

A (shrunk down) view of the anonymous survey is as follows:

• •

Age ___Gender _____ Ethnicity
_____

Living Situation (tick any that apply)
At home, With Partner, With Family, Alone, Shared arrangement, In supported accommodation

What does recovery mean to me?
_____
__
_____
__
_____
__
_____
__
_____
__
_____

Here are some themes of Recovery that others have identified, with details.
Feel free to underline/ comment on/ circle any of them.

Connectedness
Peer support and support groups, relationships, support from others, being part of the community

Hope and optimism about the future
Belief in possibility of recovery, motivation to change, hope inspiring relationships

Identity
Dimensions of identity, Rebuilding/redefining positive sense of identity.
Overcoming stigma. Regaining sense of self

Meaning in life
Meaning of mental illness experiences, spirituality, quality of life, meaningful life and social roles, rebuilding life

Empowerment
Personal responsibility, control over life, focussing on strengths

Impact of Illness
Loss of established role, social networks and occupation.

Impact of co-existing physical illness.
Impact of dementia

Making Sense of the Experience
Medication. Diagnosis. Responsibility and control over recovery. Self-drive in recovery

Dealing with Illness
Coping mechanisms

Recovery of self
Getting back to me

More on Coping mechanisms.
Feel free to underline/ comment on/ circle any of them that are important to you.

Living Support and Compensatory techniques
Use of diaries, lists and home re-organisation, practical help such as a cleaner

Continuation of social, networks, roles and meaningful activities
Continuation of existing, rather than new, social networks, roles and established activities.

Illness information
Finding out more about illness, fully understanding diagnosis and ways of coping.
Includes information from professionals, either individually or in groups

Self-help activities
Undertaking activities which are perceived to be helpful to overall health and well-being such as diet, or taking a daily walk

Being part of the world
Includes engaging with others and knowing what is going on in the world.

Counselling
Professionally led debriefing, reflection, therapy

Any feedback on this counselling service?
_____
_____
_____
_____
_____

People seemed to like this process. I feel it's empowering. It's why consumer consultation is so important. It's also respectful.

Only a minority of the respondents have experience of Community Mental Health or Inpatient care. That's not data I was looking for, because that runs the risk of defining people by illness. The survey simply asks how important medication or diagnostic treatment is to their recovery, rather than classifying the respondents by illness. I want them to tell me what is important to their Recovery.

Looking at the survey data, it appears the CHIME values of Connectedness and Hope and Optimism are rated as important over all age groups, Identity and Meaning slightly less so for those over 65. However, the value of Recovery of Self (getting back to me) seems to be an expression of the Identity value, and was very strongly nominated as a Recovery value in the older age group. It seems to me to suggest that the difference is that the older age group tends to have a more settled concept of identity. Empowerment also appeared less important to the older people in the surveys.

Dealing with Illness was a Recovery value that was extremely important in the older group, but also to younger consumers who suffer from chronic illnesses. From this I wondered if those with complex health co-morbidity have been under-represented in Recovery literature.

The following values were a little more important to older people than the general group: "Making Sense of the Experience", "Living Support and Compensatory techniques", "Continuation of social, networks, roles and meaningful activities", "Illness information", "Counselling". However these were meaningful to all age bands. On the other hand, "Self-help activities" and "Being part of the world" were slightly less meaningful in the older clients than in the general group of responses.

New workers need to be able to learn what consumers need and understand that failure to try to relate to consumers on the basis of these values will likely become, at times, very visible and painful failures of systemic care. They need to be prepared to re-visit values again and again from client to client.

Whatever could be said about the qualities of this as a survey (!) consumer consultation is a vital aspect in Recovery. If done in a narrative format, it actually creates hope that someone is really interested in the consumer's point of view, forms part of the connection and empowerment principles, and supports identity and choice. I have uniformly found that the process of discussing themes of Recovery energises the client and invigorates the therapeutic process. It helps them see their strengths, their responsibility toward themselves, and the responsibility of services to engage positively with them.

REFERENCES

ANMC. (2006). National competency standards for the registered nurse, Nursing and Midwifery Board of Australia, Retrieved 31 May, 2017, from https://www.nursingmidwiferyboard.gov.au

Australian Health Ministers Advisory Council, 2013, A National Framework For Recovery-Oriented Mental Health Services: Guide For Practitioners and Providers, Commonwealth of Australia, Canberra

Beddoe, L., (2010), Surveillance or Reflection: Professional Supervision in 'the Risk Society', *The British Journal of Social Work, 40(4), 1279-1296,* https://www.researchgate.net/publication/235947581_Surveillance_or_Reflection_Professional_Supervision_in_'the_Risk_Society'

Bell, H., & Kulkarni, S., & Dalton, L., (2003), Organizational Prevention of Vicarious Trauma, Families in Society, *The Journal of Contemporary Social Services,* 84, 463-470. 10.1606/1044-3894.131.

Beyond Blue Professional Education to Aged Care (PEAC) program. (2016) Retrieved from https://www.beyondblue.org.au/about-us/about-our-work/older-adults-program/professional-education-in-to-aged-care-peac-program

Brijnath, B., (2015), Applying the CHIME recovery framework in two culturally diverse Australian communities: Qualitative results, International Journal of Social Psychiatry, 1(8)

Clement, J. P., Bazzoli, G. J., & Zhao, M. (2012). Nursing Home Price and Quality Responses to Publicly Reported Quality Information. Health Services Research, 47(1 Pt 1), 86–105. http://doi.org/10.1111/j.1475-6773.2011.01306.x

Daley S, Newton D, Slade M et al. (2013), Development of a framework for recovery in older people with mental disorder. International Journal of Geriatric Psychiatry ;28: pp 522-9.

Department of Health and Ageing. (2010). Technical Paper on cost, revenue and productivity trends in residential care (for the Productivity Commission Inquiry, Caring for Older Australians). Retrieved from http://www.pc.gov.au/inquiries/completed/aged-care/residential-care-trends

Department of Health and Aging. (2013). A national framework for recovery-oriented mental health services – Guide for Practitioners and Providers. Retrieved from http://www.health.gov.au/internet/main/publishing.nsf/content/67D17065514CF8E8CA257C1D00017A90/$File/recovgde.pdf

Ducat, W., Martin, P., Kumar, S., Burge, V., & Abernathy, L., (2015), Oceans apart, yet connected: Findings from a qualitative study on professional supervision in rural and remote allied health services: Professional Supervision in Health Services, *Australian Journal of Rural Health*, 24, 10.1111/ajr.12192.

Dummer T (2008). Health geography: Supporting public health policy and planning. Canadian Medical Association Journal, 178(9): 1177–1180

Dudgeon, P., Milroy, H., & Walker R., (2014). Working Together Aboriginal and Torres Strait Islander Mental Health and Wellbeing: Principles and Practice. (2nd ed.). Canberra, Australia: Commonwealth of Australia https://www.telethonkids.org.au/globalassets/media/documents/aboriginal-health/working-together-second-edition/working-together-aboriginal-and-wellbeing-2014.pdf

Eagar K, Westera A, Snoek M, Kobel C, Loggie C and Gordon R (2019) How Australian residential aged care staffing levels compare with international and national benchmarks. Centre for Health Service Development, Australian Health Services Research Institute, University of Wollongong

https://agedcare.royalcommission.gov.au/publications/Documents/research-paper-1.pdf

Erikson, E. & Erikson, J., (1998), The Life Cycle Completed: Extended Version, New York, USA: W. W. Norton

Falender, C. A., & Shafranske, E. P. (2008). Casebook for clinical supervision a competency-based approach. Washington, D.C: American Psychological Association

Fallot, R., & Harris, M., (2006), Trauma-Informed Services: A Self-Assessment and Planning Protocol Community Connection Retrieved at https://www.theannainstitute.org/TISA+PPROTOCOL.pdf

Foster, A. D., & Lee, Y. S. (2015). Staffing Subsidies and the Quality of Care in Nursing Homes. Journal of Health Economics, 41, 133–147. http://doi.org/10.1016/j.jhealeco.2015.02.002

Geraedts, M., Harrington, C., Schumacher, D., & Kraska, R. (2016). Trade-off Between Quality, Price, and Profit Orientation in Germany's Nursing Homes. Ageing International, 41, 89–98. http://doi.org/10.1007/s12126-015-9227-1

Goldstein, E. (2013-06-11). Psychosocial Framework. Encyclopedia of Social Work.Retrieved 8 Dec. 2017, from http://socialwork.oxfordre.com/view/10.1093/acrefore/9780199975839.001.0001/acrefore-9780199975839-e-320.

Hagel. J., Seely Brown, J., Ranjan, A., Byler, D., (2014) Passion at work: Cultivating worker passion as a cornerstone of talent development, Deloitte Insights, 7 Oct 2017. Retrieved from https://dupress.deloitte.com/dup-us-en/topics/talent/worker-passion-employee-behavior.html

Hall, J., and Powell, J. (2011), Review Article: Understanding the Person through Narrative, Nursing Research and Practice, Volume 2011 Article ID 293837, 10 pages. http://dx.doi.org/10.1155/2011/293837 BeardenPsych ,

Knoxville, USA

Hawkins, P., & Shohet, R. (2012). *Supervision in the Helping Professions (4th Ed)*. Berkshire, UK: Open University Press.

Hilts, P. J. (1999, June 1, p. D7). Life at age 100 is surprisingly healthy, *The New York Times*. As quoted at http://open.lib.umn.edu/sociology/chapter/12-3-sociological-perspectives-on-aging/. This is a derivative of SOCIOLOGY: UNDERSTANDING AND CHANGING THE SOCIAL WORLD by a publisher who has requested that they and the original author not receive attribution, which was originally released and is used under CC BY-NC-SA. This work, unless otherwise expressly stated, is licensed under a Creative Commons Attribution-NonCommercial-ShareAlike 4.0 International License.

Holloway, E. L., & Johnston, R., (1985), Group Supervision: Widely Practiced But Poorly Understood. *Counselor Education and Supervision*, 24, 332–340. doi:10.1002/j.1556-6978.1985.tb00494.x

Hooyman, N. R., & Kiyak, H. A. (2011). *Social gerontology: A multidisciplinary perspective* (9th ed.). Upper Saddle River, NJ: Pearson

Jesse S, Bråthen G, Ferrara M, Keindl M, Ben-Menachem E, Tanasescu R, Brodtkorb E, Hillbom M, Leone MA, Ludolph AC (2017) Alcohol withdrawal syndrome: mechanisms, manifestations, and management. *Acta Neurologica Scandinavica* 135:4–16

Keast, J. (2015, November 25) *Mental health remains a*

'critical concern' for aged care: expert. Retrieved from http://www.australianageinga-genda.com.au/2015/11/25/mental-health-remains-a-critical-concern-for-aged-care-expert/

Kenna, H. A., Poon, A. W., de los Angeles, C. P. and Koran, L. M. (2011), Psychiatric complications of treatment with corticosteroids: Review with case report. *Psychiatry and Clinical Neurosciences,* 65: 549–560. doi:10.1111/j.1440-1819.2011.02260.x

Lindsey, P.L. (2009). Psychotropic Medication Use among Older Adults: What All Nurses Need to Know. *Journal of Gerontological Nursing,* 35(9), 28-38.

Mckay, R., & McDonald, R., & Lie, D., & McGowan, H, (2012). Reclaiming the best of the biopsychosocial model of mental health care and 'recovery' for older people through a 'person-centred' approach. Australasian psychiatry: bulletin of Royal Australian and New Zealand College of Psychiatrists. 20. 10.1177/1039856212460286. https://www.researchgate.net/publication/232705131_Reclaiming_the_best_of_the_biopsychosocial_model_of_mental_health_care_and_'recovery'_for_older_people_through_a_'person-centred'_approach

Magarey, J. (2017, January 15). Government under pressure to remove 'discriminatory' rule on elderly mental health care. Sydney Morning Herald. Retrieved from
http://www.smh.com.au/national/health/

nursing-homes-follow-head-20170111-gtpis6.html

Magarey, J. (2017, January 7). Nursing home residents denied GP mental health treatment plans and psychological therapy. Sydney Morning Herald. Retrieved from
http://www.smh.com.au/national/health/nursing-homes-story-headline-20161228-gtiqc6.html

Mental Health Commission of New South Wales. (2017). Older people: Everyone in the community benefits when we have the right kind of supports to let people age well: 2017. Retrieved from https://nswmentalhealthcommission.com.au/mental-health-and/older-people

Mental Health Commission of NSW (2017). Living Well in Later Life: The Case for Change. Sydney, Mental Health Commission of NSW https://nswmentalhealthcommission.com.au/sites/default/files/documents/living_well_in_later_life_-_the_case_for_change.pdf

Nickson, A., Gair, S., & Miles, D., (2016), Supporting Isolated Workers in their Work with Families in Rural and Remote Australia: Exploring Peer Group Supervision, *Children Australia*, 41(4), pp. 265-274.

Northern Territory Aged Care Services (webpage). Viewed in November 2017 at https://nt.gov.au/wellbeing/health-subsidies-support-and-home-visits/aged-care-services

NSW Department of Health (2006). Specialist Mental Health Services for Older People (SMHSOP) - NSW Service Plan - 2005-2015. North Sydney: NSW Department of Health

NSW Department of Health (2011). Specialist Mental Health Services for Older People (SMHSOP) Core Competencies for Beginning Community Clinicians, North Sydney: NSW Department of Health, Retrieved 21 Sept, 2017 from http://www.health.nsw.gov.au/mentalhealth/programs/mh/Documents/core-comp-measurecrit-comclinbklet.pdf

NSW Ministry of Health (2017) Specialist Mental Health Services for Older People (SMHSOP) Community Model of Care Guideline,

Olsberg Prof. D, (Date not supplied, Last Accessed 3/4/2017) Ageing in Place: Feeling Safe and Secure at home to age in place. Ageing Disability and Home Care, Retrieved from https://www.adhc.nsw.gov.au/__data/assets/file/0012/251130/Ageing_in_Place.pdf

Phan, T. T., & Fitzgerald M. H., (1996) Guide of the Use of Focus Groups in Health Research, Culture & Mental Health, 1:1 Retrieved 31 May, 2017 from http://www.dhi.health.nsw.gov.au/Transcultural-Mental-Health-Centre/Resources/Publications-and-Reports/Guide-for-the-Use-of-Focus-Groups-in-Health-Research/default.aspx

Pietkiewicz, I. & Smith, J.A. (2012) Praktyczny przewodnik interpretacyjnej analizy fenomenologicznej w badaniach jakościowych w psychologii, Czasopismo Psychologiczne, 18(2), 361-369. (In English, the title is "A practical guide to using Interpretative Phenomenological Analysis in qualitative research psychology")

Powell, T., (2009), *The Mental Health Handbook A Cognitive Behavioural Approach (3rd ed)*, UK: Speechmark Publishing.

(RANZCP) The Royal Australian and New Zealand College of Psychiatrists (2017). Recommended Texts / Useful Resources for Psychiatry Trainees. https://www.ranzcp.org/Files/PreFellowship/2012-Fellowship-Program/Recommended-Texts-and-Useful-Resources-for-Psychia.aspx

Rickard, L., (2019). The Assisted Living Golden Ratio: How Many Residents Can One Caregiver Serve? MyHealthSpin https://myhealthspin.com/the-assisted-living-golden-ratio-how-many-residents-can-one-caregiver-serve/

Royal Commission into Aged Care Quality and Safety, Media Release, (2019), https://agedcare.royalcommission.gov.au/publications/Documents/interim-report/interim-report-media-release-31-october-2019.pdf.

Russell, S. (2016, May 28). Aged care providers seeking profit instead of residents' wellbeing, Sydney Morning Herald. Retrieved from http://www.smh.com.au/comment/aged-care-providers-seeking-profit-instead-of-residents-wellbeing-20160527-gp5pg2.html

Russo, J. & Wallcraft, J., (2011) Resisting variables–service user/survivor perspectives on researching coercion, In Thomas W. Kallert, Juan E. Mezzich & John Monahan (eds.), Coercive Treatment in Psychiatry: Clinical, Legal and Ethical Aspects. Wiley-Blackwell. pp. 213 (2011)

SAMHSA (Substance Abuse and Mental Health Services Administration), (2014) *Trauma-Informed Care in Behavioral Health Services. Treatment Improvement Protocol (TIP) Series 57.* HHS Publication No. (SMA) 13-4801. Rockville, MD: Substance Abuse and Mental Health Services Administration,

Sanders RD, Gillig PM. Gait and its assessment in psychiatry. Gillig PM, ed.Psychiatry (Edgmont). 2010;7(7):38-43.

Schwendimann, R., Dhaini, S., Ausserhofer, D., Engberg, S., & Zúñiga, F. (2016). Factors associated with high job satisfaction among care workers in Swiss nursing homes – a cross sectional survey study. BMC Nursing, 15, 37. http://doi.org/10.1186/s12912-016-0160-8

Scottish Recovery Network
　https://www.scottishrecovery.net/chime-diagram/. This is a derivative of the webpage of the Scottish Recovery Network. The information and work on this website is licensed under a Creative Commons Attribution-NonCommercial-ShareAlike 4.0 International License. Last accessed 19/02/2018

Trenoweth, Steve. (2016). Promoting Recovery in Mental Health Nursing. London, UK: Sage

Vogel-Scibilia, S. E., McNulty, K. C., Baxter, B., Miller, S., Dine, M., & Frese, F. J. (2009). The Recovery Process Utilizing Erikson's Stages of Human Development. Community Mental Health Journal, 45(6), 405–414. http://doi.org/10.1007/s10597-009-9189-4 Accessed at https://www.ncbi.nlm.nih.gov/pmc/articles/PMC2791471/

Williams, S. (2017) Your Brain in Sickness and in Health: The experience of dementia and other brain disorders, USA, Lulu Publishing Services

Van Hoof, J., Verbeek, H., Janssen, B. M., Eijkelenboom, A., Molony, S. L., Felix, E., Wouters, E. J. M. (2016). A three perspective study of the sense of home of nursing home residents: the views of residents, care professionals and relatives. BMC Geriatrics, 16, 169. http://doi.org/10.1186/s12877-016-0344-9

Zaman H, Sampson SJ, Beck ALS, Sharma T, Clay FJ, Spyridi S, Zhao S, Gillies D. (2017) Benzodiazepines for psychosis-induced aggression or agitation. *Cochrane Database of Systematic Reviews* 2017, Issue 12. Art. No.: CD003079. DOI: 10.1002/14651858.CD003079.pub4.

Zimmerman, S., Bowers, B., Cohen, L., Grabowski, D., Horn, S., & Kemper, P., (THRIVE Research Collaborativea) (2016). New Evidence on the GreenHouse Model of NursingHome Care: Synthesis of Findings and Implications for Policy, Practice, and Research. HSR: Health Services Research 51:1, Part II (February)

ABOUT THE AUTHOR

Michael McSweeney is an Australian Social Worker who worked in Older Persons Mental Health in southern New South Wales for 6+ years. This period of his life was characterised by steep learning curves as a sole OPMH clinician and thousands of hours driving around rural and remote areas to see clients. During these years, he gained accreditation as a Mental Health Accredited Social Worker with the Australian Association of Social Workers and a Masters Degree in Applied Mental Health with an emphasis on Older Persons Mental Health. Following that, he has worked as a counsellor for the last 5 years.

While travelling overseas he has worked in a variety of nursing and care settings which, added to his OPMH experience, provided him with a critical awareness of the issues that people face entering care in a variety of contexts.

Recently he was awarded a Winston Churchill Memorial Fellowship. The theme was to study "Connecting isolated people through Community Theatre in rural and remote towns.', which reflects his passion for community theatre. This includes the study of programs around engagement of older isolated people within the community through the performing arts.

For more information visit www.swshhh.com